Culture Bound

CAMBRIDGE LANGUAGE TEACHING LIBRARY

A series covering central issues in language teaching and learning, by authors who have expert knowledge in their field.

Culture Bound

Bridging the cultural gap in language teaching

Edited by

Joyce Merrill Valdes

CAMBRIDGE
UNIVERSITY PRESS

For Renny and Zorn
who have obliged me by turning out
just the way I always hoped they would

PUBLISHED BY THE PRESS SYNDICATE OF THE UNIVERSITY OF CAMBRIDGE
The Pitt Building, Trumpington Street, Cambridge, United Kingdom

CAMBRIDGE UNIVERSITY PRESS
The Edinburgh Building, Cambridge CB2 2RU, UK
40 West 20th Street, New York, NY 10011–4211, USA
10 Stamford Road, Oakleigh, VIC 3166, Australia
Ruiz de Alarcón 13, 28014 Madrid, Spain
Dock House, The Waterfront, Cape Town 8001, South Africa

http://www.cambridge.org

First published 1986
11th printing 2001

Typeset in Sabon

Library of Congress Cataloging-in-Publication Data

Main entry under title:
Culture bound.
(Cambridge language teaching library)
Bibliogrpahy: p.
Includes index
1. Language and languages – Study and teaching.
2. Language and culture. 3. Intercultural communication.
I. Valdes, Joyce Merrill. II. Series.
P53.C76   1986   418¢.007   85-29970

ISBN 0 521 31045 8 paperback

Transferred to digital printing 2002

Contents

Contents

Preface

When a baby is born it is slapped on the back and made to cry – this much is virtually universal; but from that point on each person's life, attitudes, creeds, religion, politics (in a broad sense) – indeed, most of his world view – are shaped largely by his environment. Each person, wherever he dwells, is an individual, but an individual influenced by family, community, country, and even language. Certainly no culture is composed of herds of clones who have been defined by their environment; nevertheless, each culture is fashioned by pervading and prevailing tenets – whether they are conscious or subconscious, spoken or tacit. When a person who has been nurtured by one culture is placed in juxtaposition with another, his reaction may be anger, frustration, fright, curiosity, entrancement, repulsion, confusion. If the encounter is occasioned by study of another language, the reaction may be all the stronger because he is faced with two unknowns simultaneously. Such a predicament may be very threatening, and until the threat is removed, language learning may be blocked.

How such blocks can be removed is problematical. What does seem clear, however, is that the language learner must first be made aware of himself as a cultural being. Paradoxically, most people, of whatever nation, see themselves and their compatriots not as a culture but as "standard," or "right," and the rest of the world as made up of cultures, which are conglomerates of strange behavior. Once people are disabused of this notion and recognize that they are, truly, products of their own cultures, they are better prepared and more willing to look at the behavior of persons from other cultures and accept them nonjudgmentally, if not favorably. Along with this acceptance of a people comes acceptance of their language and a greater willingness to let go of the binding ties of the native language and culture – a willingness to enter, at least to a degree, into what can be the exciting adventure of another language and culture.

It is the responsibility of foreign and second language teachers to recognize the trauma their students experience and to assist in bringing them through it to the point that culture becomes an aid to language learning rather than a hindrance. What teachers need in order to achieve this result is a perspective of how language and culture affect one another in the human mind, considerable knowledge of cultural differences per se, specific traits of several different cultures, and some background and insight on how to use all of this in the classroom and in the teacher–student relationship. The greatest challenge no doubt exists in classes of mixed language backgrounds in which the target language is the language of the community. The variety of cultures represented in this classroom results in a miscellany of values, attitudes, and reactions in contrast to the more nearly solid cultural block of the class of students of a single background studying a foreign language in their own linguistic environment. For the former group, much more cultural detail is essential to their well-being for survival in the community and in the classroom than for the latter group, who are comfortably ensconced in their own environment. I recall, not without nostalgia, the days when I taught English to classes of freshman foreign students who were just off the plane from home – not fresh from an intensive English program in which they had been taught the ways of the world to which they had been transplanted. On the first day of classes, according to the customs of their own schoolroom experience, they would rise when I entered the classroom. I confess that it was always with a pang that I told my students that in future they need not stand when I entered. Seeing all those students rise to attention invariably made me feel that I was dressed in full academic regalia, and I allowed myself a mental toss of the tassel on my mortar board before I made the announcement. The sophomore foreign students that I now teach have reached an almost lamentable stage of cultural sophistication (particularly in such matters as how to beat the computer in registering for closed sections), yet they still have much to learn in this course in American life through literature. While cultural instruction may be less important to the survival of the foreign language student in his own environment, it is still essential to any depth of understanding of the language, to the motivation and attitude of the student, and to the interest of the course.

Most teacher-training programs for foreign and second language teachers recognize the need for supplying their prospective language teachers with a background in culture and provide courses, under a variety of titles, on culture as it affects the language learner, the language teacher, and therefore the language curriculum; those that do not offer specific courses devote a significant amount of consideration to the subject in courses with more general content, such as methodology or second language acquisition.

It goes without saying that the present enlightenment did not spring fully formed from the conglomerate head of applied linguistics; it has evolved from the work of many anthropological and sociological linguists to bring first awareness and then perception to that area of applied linguistics centered on second language study. Even a fifty-year-old French grammar on my shelf (Barton and Sirich 1933) contains in each lesson a reading that has a French setting and is designed to reveal some facet of French life – "Arrivée à Paris," "Dîner à l'hôtel," "A la terrasse d'un café" – and this book was certainly not an innovator in this regard. However, it should be recognized that the text was written for Americans who were studying French because a foreign language was required for graduation or because of a desire to make some claim to that other kind of Culture, the kind with the upper-case "C," and that the author's insertion of French scenes and situations was prompted by an inclination to motivate students who would be difficult to entice solely with such lesson titles as "The Partitive Construction" and "*Avoir* and *Etre* as Auxiliary Verbs."

While encompassing the motive of the venerable French grammar, the current view of the place of culture in language learning is far more sophisticated and is both deeper and broader in scope, including theories of language acquisition in both the affective and cognitive domains; the selection of culture concepts and practices to be presented to language learners in general; specific areas of cultural importance to learners from specific cultural backgrounds; and a multiplicity of ideas, convictions, notions, and fancies as to how culture should be presented.

The complexity of this current view of culture in language learning necessitates some sorting out to facilitate the work of the teacher. There are already numerous articles on one facet or another of this massive canvas; sections of books (e.g., "Language and Culture" in Brooks 1964); and whole books, such as Dell Hymes's impressive tome *Language in Culture and Society* (1964), which covers almost all theory up to the time of publication, but does not address the subject from the point of view of the language teacher who needs to know what to incorporate into the curriculum and how to treat it once it is incorporated, H. Ned Seelye's work *Teaching Culture: Strategies for Intercultural Communication* (1984), and Gail Robinson's presentation of the current trends in *Issues in Second Language and Cross-cultural Education: The Forest Through the Trees* (1981).

This book attempts to bring together representative theoretical and practical material of the last ten to fifteen years by a variety of scholars and teachers in the field, to serve as a guide to the teaching of culture in the foreign and second language classroom. Among the things it does not purport to do is to lay out a curriculum for the teacher, as there are many variations of viable content according to the levels of proficiency, backgrounds, attitudes, situations, purposes, aims, ages, and locales of each class, to name a few of the factors to be considered. Patently, the material presented to an intensive English class at a college or university in the United States will differ greatly from that presented to a class of elementary school children in Greece, or to a class of engineering students in Algeria studying English for the purpose of reading American textbooks. Some of the material in this book is derived from experience in a particular pedagogical setting; the conceptual bases, however, are universal and may be applied to any number of other settings. In this regard culture does not differ from the more traditional components of the curriculum – listening, speaking, reading, and writing – all of which must be tailored by the teacher to fit the specific individuals who make up each class.

There is a burgeoning number of classroom texts designed to teach culture to the nonnative speaker of English, with diversity of approach, content, technique, and, alas, quality (see Morain 1971a). Nearly all of these have been properly designated as appropriate to a particular age group, level of proficiency, and type of student, ranging from children in bilingual education programs to adult immigrants with varying amounts of education. The teacher who selects or is assigned a cultural text for a class, however, does not have the whole problem of the culture component solved; the teacher at this point more than ever needs the background from which to draw to determine methods and techniques of presentation, concepts and values to be stressed, areas requiring tact or extensive explication for certain ethnic groups, what to expand from the printed material and what to omit or compress, and, most vital of all, how to make it interesting and nonjudgmental: For while it is essential to include culture in the teaching of a language, it is equally essential to avoid chauvinism in teaching it, or, at the other end of the spectrum, negativism. Indeed, as Bochner has pointed out, what the sojourner or student must accomplish is a knowledge of the culture – to understand behavior, not necessarily to become a part of it:

"Adjusting" a person to a culture has connotations of cultural chauvinism, implying that the newcomer should abandon the culture of origin in favor of embracing the values and customs of the host society. On the other hand, learning a second culture has no such ethnocentric overtones. There are many examples in life when it becomes necessary to learn a practice even if one does not approve of it, and then abandon the custom when circumstances have changed. Americans will find that they have to stand much closer to an Arab during interactions in the Middle East than they would with fellow-Americans at home. Japanese must learn to have more eye-contact with westerners during conversation than is customary in their own culture. Australians in Great Britain of necessity have to learn to drink warm beer, a habit they discard as soon as they depart. An English gentleman in Japan will learn to push and shove his way onto the Tokyo subway, but resume his normal queuing practice after returning home. The possession of a particular skill by itself carries no value judgement – the act attracts notice only when the appropriate skill is not available, or the skill is used in inappropriate circumstances. (Bochner 1982: 164)

At the same time, recent research (see Tuttle, Guitart, Papalia, and Zampogna 1979) has indicated the salutary effect of teaching to foreign language classes in the United States more of the similarities between the two cultures rather than concentrating solely on the contrasts. In either case, the overriding point of view should always be that objectivity is the *sine qua non* for effectiveness in the teaching of culture to students from different backgrounds.

Part I of this book contains articles ranging across the broad spectrum of language, thought, and culture, and these serve as a foundation for all that follows. The theory regarding the relationship of language and mind is essential to an understanding of culture as it affects language learning.

Part II aims to present some cultural phases of particular groups in order to assist teachers to a better understanding of some of their students. We all too often become impatient with students because we fail to understand the cultural values that underlie their behavior. Perhaps the most widespread occasion for our impatience is the high frequency of plagiarism, despite all of our protests. We could learn something from Agatha Christie in *Hickory Dickory Death*, in which she presents an African student in London:

'All this morning,' said Akibombo mournfully, 'I have been much disturbed. I cannot answer my professor's questions good at all. He is not pleased at me. He says to me that I copy large bits out of books and do not think for myself. But I am here to acquire wisdom from much books and it seems to me that they say better in the books than the way I put it, because I have not good command of the English.' (1955: 149–50)

Mrs. Christie may have missed her calling.

Part III brings into focus a number of approaches to presenting culture to students in the classroom, from practical suggestions regarding useful materials to theory underlying the teaching, understanding, and grading of compositions by nonnative speakers of a language.

It is to be hoped that this collection will provide teachers with the required basis for making the most of the culture component of the language course, as well as for bringing about a clearer understanding of the students and of themselves.

Joyce Merrill Valdes

Part I Language, thought, and culture

In 1911 when Franz Boas published his *Handbook of American Indian Languages*, he could not possibly have imagined that one day an excerpt from it would serve as an introductory article in a book that might be used in a course on teaching culture in foreign- and second-language classes; in fact, the teaching of foreign languages at that time was far removed from his sphere. Yet his work inspired a generation of anthropologists and sociologists before the applied linguists took up the subject of the effect of culture on languages and vice versa, and shaped it to their own use. The process of learning more about the interrelationship between culture and language within the native environment led the way to consideration of the effect of a second culture on second language learning.

The extent to which language, culture, and thought have influenced one another, and which is the dominant aspect of communication, have been matters of controversy for three quarters of a century; the influence of the work of Boas, Sapir, Whorf, Hoijer, et al. is seen in the amount of both speculation and careful research that has ensued. Stated perhaps simplistically, the current consensus is that the three aspects are three parts of a whole, and cannot operate independently, regardless of which one most influences the other two. To see them as three points in a constantly flowing circular continuum is surely more accurate than, say, to see them as an isosceles triangle, with one dominant over the other two. It is conceivable that the lack of acceptance of artificial languages such as Esperanto may be explained by their isolation of language from culture. Thought, in any real sense, is very difficult to express without an underlying value system understood tacitly by both the sender and the receiver in a communication, whether both, one, or neither speaks the language natively, no matter how scientifically successful the language may be. While it is true that an artificial language may be a politically wise choice for intercultural communication because it is offensive to none, on the other hand it is a poor choice for a more basic reason: No one can *feel*, or therefore think deeply, in an artificial language.

The research that has been produced in this century has evolved the

1

theory that a native culture is as much of an interference for second language learners as is native language. Likewise, just as similarities and contrasts in the native and target languages have been found to be useful tools in language study, so cultural similarities and contrasts, once identified and understood, can be used to advantage. Devotion to a language other than one's own is quite common among those who venture into other languages, most often with the connection in mind between the language and the people who speak it. One says, "I love French – it's so musical and expressive," and produces a mental image of a Frenchman or woman speaking in pleasing notes with sparkling eyes and communicative gestures. Another says, "I love German – it's so precise, regular, and dependable," and the stereotype that peeks out from the mind of the speakers is of a sturdy blond plodding down a straight path, keeping a wary eye out for accusatives and datives. Such reactions to both languages and people are subjective, impressionistic, and, fortunately, variable. Yet it is very natural to associate a people – in appearance, manners, and possibly thought patterns – with the language they speak. The most successful language learners are able to take on the "mindset" of the speakers of the second language, assuming the culture along with the language (though not, of course, without reservations that are consistent with their own mindsets). Yet most people are not aware of themselves as cultural beings, products of their own environments, whether or not they are aware of the cultural base for the behavior of persons from other environments. After the learners are guided to a recognition of the cultural base of their own attitudes and behavior, they are ready to consider others in a more favorable light. Through this process, what has seemed quaint, peculiar, or downright reprehensible becomes more reasonable and acceptable. Once the second language learner comes to understand the behavior of the speakers of the target language, regardless of the original motivation for study, the task of adding the language becomes far simpler, both through acceptance of the speakers of the language and through increased knowledge of what the language means, as well as what it says.

The research of Gardner and Lambert (e.g., 1972) and of Acton and Walker de Felix (in this volume) determined that integrative motivation (the intention of becoming a part of the target culture as well as speaking the target language) resulted in more effective language learning than did instrumental motivation (the intention of learning the language to serve a purpose, such as getting a job, with no wish to mix socially with speakers of the language). While subsequent research (e.g., Brown 1980) casts some doubt on this theory, no one has hypothesized that motivation per se is a negative attribute for second language learning. A positive attitude is seen as a boon to any learning situation, and comprehension of a people's behavior patterns and their underlying values clearly gives a more positive attitude to the person who is trying to learn that language, as will be seen in the article by Acton and Walker de Felix. Furthermore, language meaning is obscured without some recognition of cultural values. Even the learner whose motivation is so instrumental as to cover only the intention to read technical texts in English, for example, is likely to fail to grasp the significance of some explanations and directions if unaware of the American/British value regarding time, especially in the technical field: Things must be done in the least possible time, and ways to do them must be set forth in the least possible space, in order to reduce the reading time. Brevity + directness = efficiency. A learner from another culture may be put off by the lack of eloquence and feel that some important information has been omitted.

The most obvious influence of language and culture on thought is that of vocabulary. As Boas points out, words are suited to the environment in which they are used. Linguistics students are always amazed at the often-cited vast number of words for snow in Eskimo languages (see Brown, in this volume), yet they fail to consider all the words used for rain in warmer climates. In a glossary of Old English the number of warlike words is conspicuous, but the tribes of Ancient Britain were a warlike people, a fact that is naturally reflected in their language and, hence, in their literature, which reflects their thought.

Many influences of the structure of language have been noted (see Henle 1958, ch. 1). Translations, particularly of literary works, point up the differences. Literal translations are seen to be true to the form of the original, while free translations depart from the text to find expression that fits the tone and meaning in essence but not exactly in language. A truly literal translation is virtually impossible from any one language to any other, primarily because of vocabulary and structures. For example, the degree of formality in which a work is written can be translated into another language, but the cultural and linguistic influence that resulted in that formality in the original work is lost in the translation. The degree of formality of a language surely affects thought, just as surely as it is affected by culture, and just as surely as it affects culture.

The influence of language on thought and behavior can perhaps best be seen in the world of advertising. The culture – beliefs, attitudes, overt and covert aspirations, pragmatic designs and fantasies, actions and reactions – is studied by advertisers around the world to find the basis for the concepts and language that will inspire the people of any given locale to buy a product of one manufacturer rather than that of another. What sells in Chicago may also sell in Kyoto, but not through the same advertising. The influences of the language of advertising are revealed in Nilsen and Nilsen, *Language Play* (1978), in Bolinger, *Language – The Loaded Weapon* (1980), in Brown (this volume), and in many articles in the popular press. Again, however, the influences are reciprocal. Although the linguistic influence of advertising on the people is undeniable, the culture and thought of the people influence advertising.

Whether one begins or ends with language, thought, or culture, the other two are woven in; the circular pattern holds, with each influencing and being influenced by each of the others. They are not all the same thing, but none can survive without the others. Second language learners must not only be aware of this interdependence but must be taught its nature, in order to convince them of the essentiality of including culture in the study of a language which is not their own. The articles offered in Part I provide the theory that underlies the practice, each in its own way. Boas looks to primitive cultures to illustrate his views on the mutual influences of language, thought, and culture, Kaplan traces the history and development of writing and indicates the cultural aspect of this component of language, Acton and Walker de Felix consider acculturation from the point of view of various researchers, and Brown gives an overview of the topic and clarifies its significance.

1 Language and thought

Franz Boas

First of all, it may be well to discuss the relation between language and thought. It has been claimed that the conciseness and clearness of thought of a people depend to a great extent upon their language. The ease with which in our modern European languages we express wide abstract ideas by a single term, and the facility with which wide generalizations are cast into the frame of a simple sentence, have been claimed to be one of the fundamental conditions of the clearness of our concepts, the logical force of our thought, and the precision with which we eliminate in our thoughts irrelevant details. Apparently this view has much in its favor. When we compare modern English with some of those Indian languages which are most concrete in their formative expression, the contrast is striking. When we say *The eye is the organ of sight*, the Indian may not be able to form the expression *the eye*, but may have to define that the eye of a person or of an animal is meant. Neither may the Indian be able to generalize readily the abstract idea of an eye as the representative of the whole class of objects, but may have to specialize by an expression like *this eye here*. Neither may he be able to express by a single term the idea of *organ*, but may have to specify it by an expression like *instrument of seeing*, so that the whole sentence might assume a form like *An indefinite person's eye is his means of seeing*. Still, it will be recognized that in this more specific form the general idea may be well expressed. It seems very questionable in how far the restriction of the use of certain grammatical forms can really be conceived as a hindrance in the formulation of generalized ideas. It seems much more likely that the lack of these forms is due to the lack of their need. Primitive man, when conversing with his fellowman, is not in the habit of discussing abstract ideas. His interests center around the occupations of his daily life; and where philosophic problems are touched upon, they appear either in relation to definite individuals or in the more or less anthropomorphic forms of religious beliefs. Discourses on qualities without

Reprinted by permission of Smithsonian Institution Press from Bulletin of the Bureau of American Ethnology Number 40, Part 1, *Handbook of American Indian Languages* by Franz Boas. Smithsonian Institution, Washington, D.C. 1911.

connection with the objects to which the qualities belong, or of activities or states disconnected from the idea of the actor or the subject being in a certain state, will hardly occur in primitive speech. Thus the Indian will not speak of goodness as such, although he may very well speak of the goodness of a person. He will not speak of a state of bliss apart from the person who is in such a state. He will not refer to the power of seeing without designating an individual who has such power. Thus it happens that in languages in which the idea of possession is expressed by elements subordinated to nouns, all abstract terms appear always with possessive elements. It is, however, perfectly conceivable that an Indian trained in philosophic thought would proceed to free the underlying nominal forms from the possessive elements, and thus reach abstract forms strictly corresponding to the abstract forms of our modern languages. I have made this experiment, for instance, with the Kwakiutl language of Vancouver Island, in which no abstract term ever occurs without its possessive elements. After some discussion, I found it perfectly easy to develop the idea of the abstract term in the mind of the Indian, who will state that the word without a possessive pronoun gives a sense, although it is not used idiomatically. I succeeded, for instance, in this manner, in isolating the terms for *love* and *pity*, which ordinarily occur only in possessive forms, like *his love for him* or *my pity for you*. That this view is correct may also be observed in languages in which possessive elements appear as independent forms, as, for instance, in the Siouan languages. In these, pure abstract terms are quite common.

There is also evidence that other specializing elements, which are so characteristic of many Indian languages, may be dispensed with when, for one reason or another, it seems desirable to generalize a term. To use the example of the Kwakiutl language, the idea of *to be seated* is almost always expressed with an inseparable suffix expressing the place in which a person is seated, as *seated on the floor of the house, on the ground, on the beach, on a pile of things,* or *on a round thing,* etc. When, however, for some reason, the idea of the state of sitting is to be emphasized, a form may be used which expresses simply *being in a sitting posture*. In this case, also, the device for generalized expression is present, but the opportunity for its application arises seldom, or perhaps never. I think what is true in these cases is true of the structure of every single language. The fact that generalized forms of expression are not used does not prove inability to form them, but it merely proves that the mode of life of the people is such that they are not required; that they would, however, develop just as soon as needed....

If we want to form a correct judgment of the influence that language exerts over thought, we ought to bear in mind that our European languages as found at the present time have been moulded to a great extent by the abstract thought of philosophers. Terms like *essence* and *exist-*

ence, many of which are now commonly used, are by origin artificial devices for expressing the results of abstract thought. In this they would resemble the artificial, unidiomatic abstract terms that may be formed in primitive languages.

Thus it would seem that the obstacles to generalized thought inherent in the form of a language are of minor importance only, and that presumably the language alone would not prevent a people from advancing to more generalized forms of thinking if the general state of their culture should require expression of such thought; that under these conditions the language would be moulded rather by the cultural state. It does not seem likely, therefore, that there is any direct relation between the culture of a tribe and the language they speak, except in so far as the form of the language will be moulded by the state of the culture, but not in so far as a certain state of culture is conditioned by morphological traits of the language.

Questions for consideration

1. How does Boas refute the notion that the form of a language may constitute an obstacle to thought?
2. How would you expect the Kwakiutl to express the term *friendship*?
3. From the characteristics supplied by Boas, how do you believe the Kwakiutls' language might affect their thought? Their thought pattern?
4. How might a language express a new concept, such as a Kwakiutl's explanation of his first encounter with television?

2 Culture and the written language

Robert B. Kaplan
University of Southern California

The relationship between culture and language is well established; it is probably not as dramatic as the strong version of the Sapir-Whorf hypothesis (see p. 46) would maintain, but it is perhaps more salient than the weak version. It is certainly possible to claim that the phenomenology of a community of speakers is reflected in the language spoken, and the language spoken helps in some way to shape the phenomenology.

The situation with respect to written language is somewhat more complex. First, it is clear that historically, over the existence of the human species, oral language preceded written language by hundreds of thousands of years. Our ancestors, the australopithecines, were group hunters, were nomadic, were territorial, and these features increased the evolutionary pressure for the development of language. It is highly probable that the australopithecines had an elaborated call system; the argument for that probability rests with the established group hunting behavior, because group hunting demands some sort of communication system. The combination of nomadism and territoriality argues for an ability to abstract; if one moves one's territory about nomadically, it is essential to be able to abstract a map of the territory to carry about in the head as well. The species is, in addition, blessed with one of the most slowly developing young in the animal kingdom; while the young of other mammals are normally able to move with the group and to contribute to its survival within a year or two of birth, human children are essentially useless for six or seven years after birth. (The more sophisticated human societies have become, the longer the period of uselessness has been interpreted, so that in the present time the young are pretty much excluded from significant contribution to the survival of the group until they are between 18 and 21 years of age; indeed, the development of complex schooling patterns serves to impede their entry into useful activity for a considerable time while it also serves to inhibit their competition with adults for increasingly scarce labor opportunities. But the biology of the species points to an earlier entry into the arena of useful contribution; puberty still seems to occur in the earliest teen years.) The fact remains that our earliest ancestors probably had a sophisticated call system – the kind of system essential to group hunting and to the care of a painfully slowly developing offspring.

Incomplete archaeological evidence seems to suggest that the organs necessary to language as we know it probably did not develop until about 100,000 years ago. The changing of the shape of the buccal cavity, the development of the brain, and the necessary changes in the structure of the aural mechanism appear to have coincided and become available at the same time. The speech mechanism is overlaid on other structures (the mouth and the ears) – structures which have older and more basic functions. In short, spoken language of the sort that we take for granted probably appeared in the species on the order of 100,000 years ago. Furthermore, this capability seems to have appeared widely in the species without regard to geographical separation. Indeed, the basic ability to use spoken language is so widely distributed and so universal that it has become the criterion for defining the species norm. We regard as "abnormal" those individuals who cannot speak either because of some impediment in the brain or some aberration of the mouth or ears. The ability to speak and to understand speech defines the normative ranges. In earlier stages of social development, individuals so marked were not permitted to survive, and thus were unlikely to participate in the breeding population.

Written language is, however, a much later phenomenon. It appeared about 10,000 years ago, and it appeared in selective populations; even in the present day, not all human populations have written language, but all human populations within the normative range have spoken language. When written language first appeared in human populations, it was regarded as magical; the earliest forms of writing contained spells, curses, and other magical elements. It was considered dangerous to allow others to have possession of one's real name because the inclusion of one's real name, particularly in written spells, could produce serious harm. Only very gradually did the ability to read and write spread beyond the clergy. The earliest manuscripts were attempts to codify religious information – to "freeze" the myths and legends of a culture.

The wide distribution of writing in the population is a very recent phenomenon indeed. Before literacy could become widespread it was necessary for written language to become more widely available. There were two post-biological evolutionary events that had to occur: the invention of printing (the use of movable type) and the automated word-processing revolution, which is presently going on about us.

The invention of writing made possible a dramatic change in the relation between human beings and information. In orate societies – those that depend exclusively upon spoken language – information is of necessity stored in memory. That fact has two important implications: First, there must be a group of individuals who specialize in becoming information carriers, and second, the nature of information is very flexible. Individuals who are repositories of information necessarily achieve special status in a society; they are important to the survival of culture. Information itself is variable because retrieval is variable; it depends upon the condition of the information repository (whether the person is fatigued or fresh, drunk or sober, cooperative or recalcitrant, respectful or disrespectful of the audience), and it depends upon the circumstances of retrieval (whether the audience is one or many, whether the setting is work-related or leisure). Under these conditions, not only is information variable, but there is necessarily a different attitude toward *fact* and *truth* such that fact is also variable and truth mutable. Once information can be written down, however, it can be retrieved invariably over time and space. It is possible for a twentieth-century English speaker in the United States to read the actual words of the Greek philosopher Plato, though they are separated by 2,000 years and 10,000 miles. If the twentieth-century reader knows classical Greek, he can read the actual original words; but even if he does not know classical Greek, he can still have access to accurate written translation.

The ability to retrieve information across time and space in invariant form creates a new environment. It changes attitudes toward *fact* and *truth*; it makes fact invariable and truth immutable. More than that, it makes possible the whole structure of what we have come to call *science* – an activity that is absolutely dependent on large quantities of invariable information and upon a kind of thinking that knows how to deal with cumulative invariant fact. Our whole notion of noetic control over nature is an algorithm derived from the availability of written information. Furthermore, the ability to store information in written form results in actual changes in the structure of language. Language which is to be stored in living memory requires various kinds of rhetorical devices which make information easier to remember, such as rhythm, rhyme, mnemonics, and the like. Once information can be written down, these aids are no longer necessary. Furthermore, once information exists in written form, it becomes possible to comment on the structure as well as the content of a written text. As long as information remains a function of memory, and is variably retrieved, it is possible to comment on the structure of only a given act of retrieval. Thus, as written language has accumulated, the quantity of commentary has come to exceed the quantity of original information. The twentieth-century reader has not only the words of Plato, but 2,000 years of commentary on the words of Plato, which help the reader to interpret what they mean.

The electronic revolution has contributed a number of important new phenomena. Most obviously, the electronic revolution makes possible the preservation of oral text in the form of disks, tapes, and the like. In a curious somewhat circular process, we have come to view preserved oral material as so important that we would only rarely permit it to contain unrehearsed information; we have invented a "script," which permits us to write out what we want to "say." But beyond the enhanced capacity to preserve oral texts in ways never accessible to mere human memory, we have, through the electronic revolution, greatly speeded the process of text creation and dissemination. In earlier times, for example, an author – one who wished to create a written text – wrote it out longhand with a pen, then gave it to a publisher, who converted it into a collection of movable type and eventually printed and bound the pages. Only then did the text become available to a public. This process of moving from a handwritten text to a "book" took many months or even years. But thanks to the electronic revolution, an author can produce a text directly on a typewriter, and the typescript can be photocopied, bound, and printed. That "shortcut" reduces the time from conception to dissemination significantly. Still more expedient processes are already available; an author can now produce text on a word processor, which can send the electronically stored words over telephone wires directly to a printer somewhere else in the world, and thus the words can be widely disseminated almost at the instant that they are created.

These changes in mechanism inevitably will have an effect upon the structure and content of language. It is already observable that texts composed directly on a word processor are more redundant than texts more conventionally produced; the reasons at this point can only be guessed at, but it seems likely that the sheer speed of dissemination encourages less editing, and the constraints of viewing the text on a screen, as opposed to viewing a printed version, are such that the author does not see the text as a whole. But it is not the purpose of this discussion to look into the future; rather it is to discuss the kinds of changes that writing and printing and automated word processing have evoked. There is no question that "literate" societies – those having the capacity to store and retrieve written information – are categorically different from orate societies – those which store and retrieve information only in relation to living memory. These differences have to do with attitudes toward fact and truth, with the existence of science and coincidentally of scientific method. These differences also have to do with the existence of commentary on form as well as content, with the bridging of time and space, with the ease of dissemination, and with actual changes in the structure of language resulting from these capabilities. Last, these differences have to do with the influence of written forms on oral language. Not only do we "script" oral material that is to be stored in some sort of recorded form (records, films, videotapes, etc.), but we have come to the "written speech" – a carefully crafted written text that is delivered as though it were being spoken. Perhaps the most important manifestation occurs in the political arena, where the President of the United States reads a carefully scripted text from a screen that is out of range of the video camera. In this way he appears to "speak" what he is actually "reading," and thus appears to "speak" with greater wisdom and with more coherence than the message may actually bear.

Written languages did not come into existence simultaneously in all cultures; on the contrary, a relatively small number of written languages emerged initially. In this century, there has been a great effort to reduce many still orate languages to written form. As new nations have emerged out of the breakdown of European colonial empires, for example, they have been faced with the problem of selecting national languages in order to facilitate their development. In most cases, new nations have been forced to choose a language which already has a written form; but even the choice of a language which can be written has not always resulted in immediate solution of the nation's problems. Since many languages have acquired written capacity only relatively recently, some of these written languages have not yet achieved a standard form. Even a written language as old as Mandarin achieved standardization only quite recently. Arguments over the "standard" form of a written language have inhibited development rather than enhanced it.

Indeed, the whole notion of development has in itself tended to create a series of very complex problems. Development is commonly seen as a method for more efficient use of human and natural resources in order to create a better standard of living; in other words, development almost invariably involves the exploitation of scientific information. The implicit need for access to scientific information creates two very difficult problems. The first of these problems involves the notion of *access*. It is a phenomenon of the contemporary world that scientific information tends to exist largely in English. In the period since World War II, English has come to dominate scientific information in important ways. In science, there is a somewhat circular truism; the greatest producers of information are also the greatest users of information. Since the industrial revolution, the place of the English-speaking nations has been growing in relation to the creation and the use of scientific information; since World War II and the decline of Germany as a state importantly involved in research, and because the victorious allies agreed at the end of World War II that their languages would become the languages of international information transfer, Chinese, English, French, and Russian have become the key languages. Chinese fell behind because of the sheer complexity of the system of characters in which it is written; that left English, French, and Russian. By international agreement, during the time when the great international information storage and retrieval networks came into being, information to be entered in the networks had to be either written or abstracted in one of these languages. This convention, together with the industrial and research leadership of the English-speaking nations, has conspired to create a situation in which, according to FID (the Fédération Internationale de Documentation), something on the order of 80% of technical information currently available is in English. There is also a second truism in information science; those who contribute most to a system and who also draw most from a system – those who use the system most – tend to acquire control of the system. In the same way that information in English has come to dominate the international storage and retrieval systems, English has also come to dominate the systems themselves; that is, the descriptors which are used to organize information in the system tend to be based on a sociology of knowledge which is both English in the words entered into the dictionary and English in its semantic structure. In sum, nations which wish to access technical information will in all probability have to do so through English. This fact has done much to facilitate the international spread of English, but the English which has spread is to some degree free of cultural (though not linguistic) bias, since it is not specifically the English of the United States or the English of Australia, but rather the English of science and technology.

The second difficult problem has come through the impact of English on other writing systems. That impact has been an outcome of the need for all developing nations to have access to science and technology. Let us look at a concrete example. Before the fifteenth century, all written communication in Korea occurred in the form of Chinese characters. In the period between 1420 and 1430 a group of Korean scholars, recognizing the difficulty of fitting Chinese characters to the structure of Korean, created a unique phonically based system under the sponsorship of King Se-Jong; this system was known as *Hangul* (People's Writing). Modern Hangul (having only four minor changes from its fifteenth-century variety) is the primary writing system in Korea; however, over all these centuries it has essentially coexisted with Chinese characters, and even at present some Chinese characters are used in written Hangul in newspapers, magazines, and some academic journals. These conditions have created a peculiar situation in which there are really three written varieties of Korean:

1. Hangul only;
2. Hangul + (Chinese), in which certain key words are written in Hangul but have Chinese character equivalents following in parentheses;
3. Hangul and Chinese, in which certain key words are written only in Chinese characters.

More recently, as Korea has attempted (quite successfully) to modernize in the period following World War II and more specifically in the period following the Korean War, scientific and technological information has become an important commodity and has brought English into direct contact with Hangul + (Chinese characters). As a consequence, the writing of Korean has elaborated into a larger set of varieties:

1. Hangul, English, and Chinese characters;
2. Hangul, English, Chinese characters, and transliteration;
3. Hangul and transliteration;
4. Hangul and Chinese characters + (English), with certain English words in parentheses;
5. Hangul + (English), with certain English words in parentheses;
6. Hangul only.

Variety 1 uses English script for foreign words; variety 2 uses English for unfamiliar forms and transliterates familiar foreign terms into Hangul; variety 3 transliterates all foreign nouns; variety 4 translates technical terms into Hangul but uses Chinese characters with English equivalents in parentheses for unfamiliar terms; variety 5 provides everything in Hangul but inserts English equivalents for certain words in parentheses; and variety 6 translates all foreign terms into Hangul. There is evidence that the use of English is increasing, particularly in technical and scholarly publications, while the use of Chinese characters is remaining constant. In sum, then, there are eight written varieties currently in use in Korea, and, although Hangul clearly dominates all varieties, the amount of English being used is on the increase.

The number of varieties in use constitutes only part of the problem. Given that there is a relationship between culture and rhetorical style, it is reasonable to assume that Korean culture has developed a unique rhetorical style. Below is a complete text written by a Korean scholar and taken from the English language newspaper, the *Korean Times*:

It has been reported that the Ministry of Home Affairs is planning to lengthen the period of training for public officials from the present 3 days to 6 days per annum in order to solidify their spiritual stance and probably at the [Spiritual Cultural Institute] which is normally and aptly translated as the Institute for Korean Studies. Here the term [spiritual] has the additional meaning "national" in addition to its conventional meanings as incorporeal, moral, intellectual, etc.

Though I doubt that this new meaning will take root in the English language the semantic distortion of the original Korean word [...] may establish itself in the Korean language some day as we see in the widely accepted tautological compound [spiritual culture.] I would accept this term if there were such a thing as material culture. I suspect that the term was coined originally by pedantic nationalists.

Some years ago I heard a member of the Korean Alphabet Society complain that the architectural design and the internal decoration of the Institute for Korean Studies made it resemble a Buddhist temple, which he did not regard as traditionally Korean. His question was: "Are all these Chinese characters spiritually tenable?" The questioner apparently regarded the Institute as a place for enhancing the Korean spirit as it was intended to be. However, many Korean people would no doubt regard Buddhism as a traditionally Korean religion though it was imported from India. How should we interpret the historically attested strong national movements on the part of Korean Christians? Is Christianity less Korean than Buddhism because of its short history in this nation? Note also that all those Sino-Korean words which comprise more than 50 per cent of the total lexical entries in Korean language dictionaries are no longer regarded as foreign words.

It is then not difficult to see that any attempt to demarcate what is national and what is foreign is doomed to fail in most instances, and that such an attempt is often unworthy and unnecessary, if not trivial.

I do not, however, advocate anarchism or antinationalism. I am well aware that the geopolitical characteristics of this country requires some nationalist stance for security reasons. All I want to point out is that too much emphasis on nationalism may do more harm than good to the nation.

Therefore, instead of inspiring nationalism we should appeal to universal reason and proper moral conduct which clearly take precedence over parochial nationalism. The erection of the Independence Memorial Hall will hopefully enhance the patriotic spirit, but in case the patriotic spirit can not trigger the civil spirit, love of one's immediate neighbor, it will mean very little, for the civil spirit must take precedence over the national spirit, though the relationship between the two is certainly reciprocal.

I am constantly reminded of this simple truth whenever I change my subway at Sinsoldong interchange. Despite the loudspeaker's warning against passengers' trespassing on the security line, many of them rush into the cars en masse to occupy seats for themselves for the less than 15-minute ride to the Chamil sports complex terminal, where the 1988 Olympics are to be held. I wonder how we enhance the nation's prestige through a sports event. To make the funny sight funnier, this often happens even when there are not enough passengers to fill the seats available! I don't want to blame anybody but myself because as a career teacher I am partly responsible for this deplorable situation. What a moral degeneration! As a middle-school boy I never dreamed of taking a seat in a long distance bus which carried me for two days from one end of Hwanghae Province to the other.

Spiritual poverty or the lack of civil spirit may best be observed in a metropolitan area like Seoul. I really do not understand why our public transit system is so multi-layered. At the bottom there are cheap buses which are sophistically called "standing seats" [...] buses which provide very few seats. The regular buses with seats, charging three times the fare for a standing seat bus. Finally taxis which move about constantly to catch more passengers.

Once you get on one of these you have to listen to whatever pops out of the radio at the mercy of the fingertip of the driver who seems to be deaf to any big noise.

Dear administrators, please do not talk about spiritual things unless you are interested in implementing concrete ethical conduct.[1]

It should be clear that the rhetorical structure of this piece is rather unlike what one expects to find in English. This sort of rhetorical structure may provide some insight into what happens in Korean. The problem at the present time is that there appear to be two different rhetorical styles in Korean (just as there are a number of different written varieties). One of the rhetorical styles common in Korean resembles the one illustrated here; a second style has developed among younger Koreans who have been educated in the United States or elsewhere in the industrialized world. This second style is much closer to the rhetorical style employed in scientific and technical writing in English. Korean scholars writing in the more traditional Korean rhetorical style have some difficulty in understanding the newer style and have a tendency to reject it; Korean scholars employing the newer style are impatient with the older style and have a tendency to reject it. In sociological terms, the existence of these two rhetorical traditions has tended to drive a wedge between two important segments of the academic community in Korea. Because the newer style is not accepted by more traditionally trained scholars, younger scholars have a harder time getting their ideas accepted and have a harder time receiving the recognition to which their work entitles them. The existence of these two styles tends to work against the notion of development rather than to enhance it.

Thus, the introduction of science and technology into traditional societies – even ones which have had literate cultures over a long period of time – and the introduction of English into these cultures through the mechanism of scientific information create two kinds of problems: on the one hand, the incorporation of English technical words into the lexicon and written text (either as English words, as transliterations, or as equivalent terms from the language itself or from another language available in the environment), and on the other hand, the incorporation into the rhetorical structure of a new rhetorical style which is based in English but is more directly a function of scientific information. Both of these changes tend to destabilize even a standardized writing system.

As noted earlier, in orate societies those individuals who are designated the repositories and transmitters of information hold a special place in the social structure of the community. But the introduction of writing tends to destabilize the social structure, because it changes the social value of this group of individuals. Writing tends to make information available to anyone who can read the language in which material is

1 Y.S. Pae, "Thoughts of our times: What is spiritual?" The *Korean Times* (Seoul: The Korean Times Press, 1982). The material enclosed in square brackets is in the original text in Hangul symbols.

stored; thus, the book repository (the "library") takes the place of the individual who has traditionally been the repository of information and takes the control of information out of the hands of that set of individuals. It "democratizes" information in the sense that it makes the quest for information a matter of personal choice rather than a situation under the control of an elite within the population. In some traditional societies, the individuals who have been the repositories of information actively oppose the spread of literacy. Not only does that spread undermine their social status, but the spread of literacy also changes the character of information; it focuses the attention on a whole new range of information over which the old repository individual has no control, and it downgrades the value of the sort of information available from that individual.

In a sense, much of what has been said may be construed as an argument against the spread of literacy. On the contrary, it does not speak against the spread of literacy, but it does call attention to the fact that there are some problems associated with the spread of literacy. The introduction of literacy into a previously oral culture needs to be done under controlled conditions such that the changeover from an orate to a literate information system does not destabilize the society. Furthermore, what has been said argues that there is a need to understand the linguistic base of the information structure that is being introduced into a developing society. The linguistic base itself may be sufficiently at variance with the existing social-cultural structure to make its rapid introduction counterproductive.

More than either of these points, however, the argument presented here is that there is a close connection between the culture of a society and the written language system it chooses to employ. In fact, scientific and technical written text has developed a separate culture of its own. Although this scientific culture tends to be expressed through English at the present time, it is in no way inextricably bound to English; and the English that is in use is, at least to some extent, free of the culture of a particular society, such as the United States, Britain, Canada, Australia, New Zealand. In other words, the English of science and technology is more closely affiliated with science and technology than it is with the culture of any national society.

In another way, this discussion argues that written language has had an effect on the spoken language, or rather, the two varieties have had an effect on each other. There is no question that at one point in the development of the written variety, written language represented nothing more than transcribed speech, but that relationship is no longer sufficient. The written variety has developed a life of its own. It has had an effect on the spoken language in that we now pretend to deliver written language orally and to make it appear like spoken language. But beyond that, it has an independent existence; when we begin to examine written legal statutes, for example, we quickly recognize that the language recorded there is in no way like spoken language, was never intended to be spoken, is difficult to speak, and serves quite different sociolinguistic purpose. In literate societies, however, we have come to rely more and more on this special sociolinguistic function of written language. We have come to believe that the written form is inherently (or can be made to be) more accurate than the spoken variety, and as a consequence we *write* our contracts and treaties (despite the difficulty of providing versions that are genuinely equivalent in two different languages). When we disagree about the interpretation of written documents and bring each other into a court of law where we can adjudicate our differences, we give oral testimony, but we employ a court reporter to transcribe what we say into written language, and when we wish to check the accuracy of what was said we refer only to the written version. The cycle is complicated by virtue of the fact that witnesses may write out ("script") what they wish to "say," may "say" it orally so that a court reporter may retranscribe it into written text, and ultimately may check one written version against another to confirm the accuracy of either or both.

In the end, there are several issues that relate to the question of the relationship between language and culture. Although there is no doubt that anything may be said in any language, the relationship between language and cultures makes it easier to say certain things in some languages than in others. The introduction of writing has profoundly modified the relationship between language and culture in ways that we do not yet fully understand. Written language has taken on a life of its own in some cultures (like our own) and has, in turn, had a profound impact on the spoken language. Being a person who spends a substantial part of his life producing written texts for other people to read (and not only articles on more-or-less scholarly subjects like the one you are reading now, but also letters, memoranda, and a range of other rather specialized varieties), I am convinced that my experience with writing has changed the way I speak. I do not believe that I write as I speak or speak as I write; rather, I believe that for me each form has moved closer to the other and I speak more like I write and write more like I speak.

Let me not pretend that much of what I have to say here is based on careful empirical scholarship. On the contrary, much of it is based on conceptualizations dealing with language which arise simply from thinking long about the issues. Much of what I have said is subject to empirical verification; I invite those who wish to investigate that verification to do so. Some of what I say probably cannot be verified and at least in our current state of knowledge about language must remain speculative. But it seems to me that we must move to a broader base for our theoretical models for language. In order to have orderly paradigms, we have tended to constrict the boundaries of language too much. The relationship between spoken and written language needs intensive investigation; we need to determine much more precisely what the relationship between language and culture, between written and spoken language really is, and we cannot do so by positing that written language is merely transcribed speech. The problem is that we do not have good definitions for either language or culture; because we are totally enmired in both, it is hard to get outside them enough to try to define them. Hard as it may be, it is once more time to try.

Questions for consideration

1. How does this historical perspective of spoken and written language assist in the study of contemporary language?
2. What has been the effect of technology on the production of speech?
3. To what degree might the difference in one's spoken and written language be affected by one's occupation?
4. What does the Korean article tell the linguistics student about cultural aspects of style?
5. What conclusions do you draw from this article on how cultural biases affect the rhetorical style of those who write English nonnatively for specific purposes, such as science and technology?

3 Acculturation and mind

William R. Acton and Judith Walker de Felix
University of Houston – University Park

"I may speak many languages, but there remains one in which I live."
M. Merleau-Ponty, *The Phenomenology of Perception*

The process of "acquiring" a second culture has been studied from a number of perspectives. *Acculturation*, the gradual adaptation to the target culture without necessarily forsaking one's native language identity, has been proposed as a model for both the adult entering a new culture and the child in the bilingual program in a public school. A problem with many models having to do with acculturation, however, is the often unexamined assumption that the essential or most important factor affecting acculturation is the "difference" or "social distance" between the two cultures (e.g., Schumann 1976a).

Researchers in various fields have developed frameworks for investigating the psychological processes that underlie acculturation. In this article we show how the phenomenon of acculturation may, in many cases, be better understood through such investigations of "mind," specifically cognitive and affective development, than through studies of differences between the native and target cultures. The first section deals with some current conceptualizations of acculturation in the field of second language acquisition; the second, with parallel models from cognitive psychology and linguistics; the third, with related research in the affective domain; and the fourth, with models of personality and role development that likewise illustrate the contribution of "mind" to the process of acculturation.

Acculturation

The characterization of acculturation that we will develop here is drawn from several sources, among them Schumann (1976a, 1978), Brown (1980), M. Clarke (1976), and Selinker (1972). John Schumann has written extensively on the intriguing similarity between second language acquisition and the process of pidginization. Pidginization can be best thought of as the result of language contact where the "communicants"

20

end up speaking a hybrid language that is functional only for day-to-day interaction, for business "on the street." The grammar and vocabulary are always highly restricted. Of particular importance here is that the person who speaks a pidgin language – if that is the only language he or she speaks in that culture – is stigmatized. The language itself is "frozen"; it does not develop into a fully communicative, elaborated code (Schumann 1978). In like manner, the speakers of the pidgin are, by definition, "fossilized" (i.e., fixed in one place, highly resistant to change) both linguistically and socially.

H. Douglas Brown (1980) has characterized that phase in learning a second language when the learner tends to speak an "interlanguage" (Selinker 1972) similar to a pidgin as the "sociocultural critical period." Brown maintains that there is an important initial phase in one's encounter with a new culture when motivation is especially strong, when culture shock is often experienced, when a great deal of language learning must be accomplished. If this period passes without learners having reached or surpassed a certain threshold of communicative competence, what we term the *acculturation threshold*, they may well become "stuck" at a level of "functional competence," something analogous to the pidginization phenomenon described by Schumann.

Mark Clarke (1976) has characterized certain aspects of the acculturation experience beyond Brown's sociocultural critical period. Beginning at the level of communicative competence, Clarke discusses what he terms the "clash of consciousness" problem. It is, in some sense, the "second wave" of culture shock, when the learner is reasonably capable of communicating with natives on matters requiring sophisticated use of the language but begins to run up against subtle dimensions of the culture that most second language learners never truly come to grips with. It takes on the form of the "permanent immigrant" state, where one is always able to understand the words but is never completely capable of comprehending all of their connotations. To pass beyond that final threshold is to become virtually a "native" – a state few ever reach.

Larry Selinker (e.g., 1972) was among the first to pay attention systematically to "fossilization" in second language learning. Simply put, fossilization occurs when learners incorporate incorrect forms or grammatical structures into their relatively fixed, or completed, version of the target language. Although Selinker has not focused on the place of fossilization within the general process of acculturation, its impact and presence are undoubtedly most evident beyond the acculturation threshold.

Our model of acculturation entails four stages:

1. *Tourist*. The early phase, in which the new culture is almost totally inaccessible; the phase often referred to as entailing some degree of culture shock. The language spoken might be termed "phrase-bookese." Learners draw extensively on first language strategies and resources.
2. *Survivor*. The stage of functional language and functional understanding of the culture. One must pass through this stage to be considered an educated, competent speaker of the language. Many do not. For example, manual labor jobs often require little more than "survivor" competence in language and culture. To remain at this stage is to speak something akin to a "pidgin."

[The Acculturation Threshold]

3. *Immigrant*. The degree of acculturation we expect of an educated learner, one who is literate in his or her own language. It is the stage reached by most literate people who spend an extended period of time working and living in a foreign culture. Most, however, do not progress beyond this stage.
4. *Citizen*. The stage that is almost at the level of the native speaker, in which one has acculturated to the degree that one is only rarely tripped up by the subtleties of the language and culture. We would expect this person to have both pronunciation and gestures very similar to those of natives.

Cognitive development

The work of British cognitive psychologist Vernon Hamilton (1983) has provided us with a useful theoretical framework for clarifying further the contribution of general cognitive abilities to the phenomenon of acculturation, albeit implicitly. Hamilton's basic position is that models of personality must be cognition-centered. He has impressively brought together research demonstrating how verbal, spatial, and visual processes, though coded differently, require a single data-encoding system, one that can interpret the specialized codes of the different systems for associative links to become meaningful. This data-encoding system is, of course, language.

Hamilton's argument is essentially that knowledge resides in concepts – concepts that are, in turn, abstractions from facts and states. Those facts and states are, according to Hamilton, best represented formally as being in memory in the form of what he calls "semantic labels," a notion not unlike our everyday understanding of the "meaning" of a word. The acquisition of these semantic labels of the culture, for Hamilton, is the essence of socialization and the crux of cognitive development. Assuming that theory to be the case, we will interpret it to mean that acculturation in the second language is in important ways analogous to socialization in the first language. (See Hamilton 1983 for a full exposition of this issue.) In other words, from an epistemological perspective, acculturation is first a reflection of universal cognitive processes or faculties; the remaining variance in "successful" acculturation may be accounted for by looking in other related areas, such as cross-cultural psychology and anthropology. Here we will look briefly at the work of three theorists who have had significant impact on the field in the area of cognitive considerations in second language acquisition: James Cummins, Lily Wong-Fillmore, and David Ausubel, interpreting them in light of Hamilton's model.

Cummins (1981) was the first to propose the distinction between what he called basic interpersonal communication skills (BICS) and cognitive-academic language proficiency (CALP). CALP is, in very general terms, that language valued in the school setting and measured on achievement tests. Cummins claims that BICS can be developed in two or three years by children, whereas CALP probably requires over five years to evolve to a satisfactory level. Although BICS are fundamentally different in any two languages, to a great extent a function of the sociocultural milieu and conversational conventions, CALP will always overlap to some degree because of the more universal strategies of academic thinking and prose.

Wong-Fillmore (1983), in characterizing the important stages in second language acquisition, came to somewhat similar conclusions, but with a finer set of distinctions (adapted from the role of rules in the skill levels of chess). Focusing on relatively specific language skills, she noted five qualitatively different stages in second language acquisition. Novice speakers (her stage 1 and ours) depend almost exclusively on situational clues and first language strategies and vocabulary (see Hatch 1978, for example). Advanced beginners (her stage 2 and ours) understand most face-to-face conversations and can use rules to produce language but are generally limited to functional kinds of tasks and interactions. "Competent speakers" (her stage 3 and ours) know most basic rules of grammar and conversation, think in the language, and make relatively few serious mistakes. "Proficient speakers" (her stage 4 and ours) can select language effectively to meet specific goals, even if they have to bend the rules to do so; they have developed reliable intuitions as to which word form is most appropriate. Her fifth level, which we have not incorporated here, she exemplifies as entailing the ability to write professional-quality poetry in the second language.

By applying Hamilton's model to Cummins's and Wong-Fillmore's models, we see that in stages 1 and 2, the semantic networks that underlie the cognitive schemata (representations of cognitive and language systems in memory) are almost exclusively first-language based. For learners

23

in stages 1 and 2 to acquire BICS is relatively easy. New second language lexical items, for example, are processed through existing first language schemata (many of which are eminently transferable and productive – although often not even close to being appropriate!). With experience, more and more of the central cognitive processing shifts to schemata and structures of the second language. Wong-Fillmore noted that the biggest "leap" is from advanced beginner to "competent," between stages 2 and 3 (what we term the *acculturation threshold*). Developing the adequate CALP in the second language requires a great deal of socialization and acculturation to create the cognitive/semantic networks similar to those a native speaker would construct. Cummins argues persuasively that for academic purposes cognitive processing must take place almost exclusively through second language CALP. The relevance of that claim for us is that it also suggests a cognitive threshold that correlates with a recognized linguistic-skill and acculturation barrier.

Another well-known model of cognitive development that lends support to the overall argument is that of Ausubel (1968). He delineated four stages of cognitive development: exploration, manipulation, knowledge acquisition, and ego enhancement. He described in general terms the types of cognitive processing and learning that seem to predominate at various points in one's intellectual development. Juxtaposing Ausubel's model with those of Cummins and Wong-Fillmore further illustrates the cognitive underpinning of acculturation (Table 3.1).

Affect and acculturation

The current view of the affective domain in second language research has been greatly influenced by the work of Robert Gardner and Wallace Lambert (e.g., 1972). They have argued that students learning a second language benefit from a positive "orientation" toward learning the language. In addition to intelligence and aptitude, a desire to identify with or closely associate with members of the target culture, termed *integrative orientation*, was shown to promote acquisition of a second language. (Schumann [1978] went even further in suggesting that unless second language learners are "driven" to internalize the culture as well, they will not go far in learning the language.) Gardner and Lambert found that integrative orientation was particularly advantageous when members of the dominant group in a society actively attempted to integrate into the target culture. Integrative orientation has also been shown to have potentially serious negative consequences, however, for language minority students learning the dominant language (Lambert and Freed 1982).

Studying Mexican-Americans acquiring English in the Southwest,

TABLE 3.1. THREE KEY MODELS OF COGNITIVE DEVELOPMENT

Model	Tourist (1)	Survivor (2)	Immigrant (3)	Citizen (4)
Cummins	BICS	BICS	CALPS	CALPS
Wong-Fillmore	Novice	Advanced beginner	Competent	Proficient
Ausubel	Exploration	Manipulation	Acquisition of knowledge	Ego enhancement

Perez (1984) and others have documented a strong instrumental orientation (a desire to learn a language for more utilitarian purposes, such
as getting a job) and even a strong anti-integrative orientation associated
with successful second language learning. Similar studies overseas of
students studying a prestige language show that the more competent
tend to have instrumental orientation (Lukmani 1972).

The integrative/instrumental studies suggest that either orientation
may support one past the acculturation threshold, into stage 3, but
apparently only strong integrative orientation may be sufficient to get
one through 3 and into 4. In contexts where social integration was truly
possible, integrative orientation seems the preferable attitude; in cases
such as Lukmani (1972), where young professional women in India fared
far better with instrumental orientation, it may well be that "integration"
was not even a realistic option.

Two other much cited, affect-based models fit in well here, Maslow
(1954) and Bloom (Krathwohl, Bloom, and Masia 1974). Abraham
Maslow identified what he termed a hierarchy of "human needs," beginning with the need for food and security (our stage 1) to develop a
clear sense of identity (our stage 2), self-esteem (our stage 3), and self-
actualization (our stage 4). Benjamin Bloom's taxonomy of the affective
domain (Krathwohl, Bloom, and Masia 1974) provides an interesting
parallel to that of Maslow and Ausubel (discussed previously). It ranges
from receiving (our stage 1) to responding and valuing (our stage 2),
organizing a value system (our stage 3), and acting in accordance with
a value system (our stage 4).

The affect-related studies add considerably to our characterization of
acculturation and are summarized in Table 3.2.

Personality and role development

Further parallels to the research on acculturation exist in the psychological literature on personality and role development. We will limit our
discussion here to four representative models particularly germane to
second language acquisition, those of Guiora (1972), Cope (1980), Lozanov (1979), and Curran (1976). Each adds a somewhat different and
unique dimension to our picture of acculturation.

Alexander Guiora's model for second language personality development (e.g., Guiora 1972, Guiora and Acton 1979), and especially his
conceptualization of a "language ego," is relevant here. Guiora has
described the process of developing a second language identity as that
of essentially adding on another personality. The experience of anyone
who has come close to mastering a second language surely supports that
notion. There inevitably comes a time when learners become aware of

TABLE 3.2. THREE KEY MODELS OF AFFECT AND ACCULTURATION

Model	Tourist (1)	Survivor (2)	Immigrant (3)	Citizen (4)
Gardner and Lambert	⟶ Instrumental and/or integrative ⟶			Integrative only
Maslow (needs)	Physical security	Identity development	Self-esteem	Self-actualization
Bloom (affect)	Receiving	Responding	Organizing a value system	Acting within a value system

their new personas in the new language, when instead of just "acting French," for example, they start to "be French" unconsciously, at least occasionally, perhaps doing things they would never think of doing in their native auras.

One's experience of acculturation, from Guiora's perspective, very much depends on the psychological health of the first language ego. If learners have strong self-esteem in their own culture, their chances of becoming true "citizens" of another culture are enhanced significantly. In a sense, although we can never "go home again," we cannot truly "leave" either. What that means, then, is that the variability we see in acculturation, especially at the more advanced stages, must be to a large extent a function of personality. From our four-stage perspective, Guiora's model would suggest that in the first two stages the learner is psychologically still anchored to the first-language identity. The third and fourth stages require the learner to possess a new, relatively autonomous second-language identity. The transition from stage 2 to stage 3 is crucial in that regard.

Corinne Cope (1980) identified four stages in the development of the skillful psychotherapist or counselor. The first she called "anxiety management," that period when the trainee enters the program and begins learning the vocabulary and theories of the trade while at the same time being required to start counseling, meeting with clients almost from the first day. If a trainee can just deal with the emotional stress of the new "culture," he or she will probably succeed. The second stage, interaction, characterizes that phase when the trainee has come to a reasonable control of the catchwords and strategies to keep the client talking but can do little more than that. The counselor can deal with day-to-day matters but can rarely reflect on his or her own behavior or adequately evaluate the effectiveness of an interaction. The move to the third stage, that of "self-monitoring," represents the critical step in the process. The counselor-trainee is now capable of more and more ongoing, real-time assessment of the session, being able to manipulate the interaction for appropriate therapeutic ends. The last stage of "acculturation" into the role of counselor, achieved by relatively few, is that of counselor-trainer, in which one has that rare, abstract, philosophical understanding of the process and "culture" of counseling sufficient to teach it to others.

In the last decade or so in the field of second language teaching there have been a number of theorists who have proposed approaches and methods that include implicit or explicit models of personality development. Two of the most influential have been Georgi Lozanov (e.g., 1978) and Charles Curran (e.g., 1976). In his various discussions of Suggestopedia as applied to second language teaching, Lozanov speaks of the "infantilization" of the adult, the process of allowing (or requiring) the adult learner to develop childlike attitudes, and the lack of inhibitions, as essential to his approach. He further specifies that learners must assume new second language names and identities to be used throughout the program. Although his rationale for that practice is somewhat ad hoc, the principle underlying the assumption of the necessity of developing a second language persona is sound.

Counseling-Learning/Community Language Learning, as originally developed by Curran (1976), is based on a model that emphasizes the evolution of the new self in the new language. The stages are somewhat different from what we have suggested here, however, in that in Curran the learner is depicted within the teacher–student relationship, gradually becoming more independent as he or she learns the language. Roughly speaking, the developmental view of Curran goes as far as the third stage of our model.

To summarize, the theories and models discussed in this section fit within our model as shown in Table 3.3. The overall picture is striking. The acculturation threshold as the critical juncture in the process, when seen from this perspective, seems intuitively to be very much in accord with our observations as researchers and teachers. Furthermore, it is at first surprising how the various models all fit together (Table 3.4).

It is obvious that acculturation is to a significant degree but one manifestation of a general human response to new learning situations and growth, a reflection of mind as well as culture. It is not so obvious, however, exactly what this means for second language pedagogy. It certainly does reaffirm the importance of sociocultural factors or variables, but it also highlights the interrelationships involved as well. It may be possible, for instance, for pedagogy to lead learners into stage 3, beyond the acculturation threshold, but it appears to require extensive socialization or acculturation beyond the classroom to proceed much further than that.

TABLE 3.3. FOUR PERSONALITY MODELS

Model	Tourist (1)	Survivor (2)	Immigrant (3)	Citizen (4)
Guiora	L1 ego only	L1 ego as L2 develops	L2 ego distinct	L2 ego is as integrated as L1
Cope	Anxiety management	Interaction management	Competence in self-monitoring	Teacher
Lozanov	Infantilization	New identity		
Curran	Dependence on teacher/group	Nurturing by teacher/group	Independence from teacher/group	

TABLE 3.4. THE FOUR-STAGE ACCULTURATION MODEL

Theorist	Tourist (1)	Survivor (2)	Immigrant (3)	Citizen (4)
Schumann	Pidginization	Pidginization		
Brown			←———— Clash of consciousness ————→	
Clarke	——— Sociocultural critical period ——→			
Cummins	Basic interpersonal communication skills (BICS)			Cognitive-academic language proficiency (CALP)
Wong-Fillmore	Novice	Advanced beginner	Competent	Proficient
Ausubel	Exploration	Manipulation	Acquisition of knowledge	Ego enhancement
Gardner & Lambert	——— Instrumental and/or integrative ——→		Instrumental and/or integrative	Integrative only
Maslow	Physical security	Identity development	Self-esteem	Self-actualization
Bloom	Receiving	Responding	Organizing a value system	Acting within a value system
Guiora	L1 ego only	L1 ego as L2 develops	L2 distinct	L2 ego is as integrated as L1
Cope	Anxiety management	Interaction management	Competence in self-monitoring	Teacher
Lozanov	Infantilization	New identity		
Curran	Dependence on teacher/group	Nurturing by teacher/group	Independence from teacher-group	

(Vertical text between Survivor and Immigrant columns: ACCULTURATION THRESHOLD)

William R. Acton and Judith Walker de Felix

Questions for consideration

1. The authors focus on only one side of the acculturation experience. How would one characterize the role of "culture" in acculturation?
2. What claim is made here as to the universal cognitive constraints on acculturation? Does the article have a "Western Weltanschauung" about it regarding the psychological constraints discussed?
3. What arguments can be made against the notion of the acculturation threshold?
4. Of what use is the concept of L2 identity to the second language teacher? At which stage of the language learning process does it have the greatest relevance?
5. Where does the notion of "communicative competence" fit into the schemata presented in this article?

4 Learning a second culture

H. Douglas Brown
San Francisco State University

...Second language learning in some respects involves the acquisition of a second identity. Guiora introduced the concept of language ego to capture the deeply seated affective nature of second language learning, stressing the necessity for permeable ego boundaries in order to successfully overcome the trauma of second language learning. Guiora and others have placed strong emphasis on affective characteristics of second language learning because of the highly *social* context of language. Second language learning is often second culture learning. In order to understand just what second culture learning is, one needs to understand the nature of acculturation, culture shock, and social distance.

Acculturation

If a French person is primarily cognitive-oriented and an American is psychomotor-oriented and a Spanish speaker is affective-oriented, as claimed by E. C. Condon (1973b: 22), it is not difficult on this plane alone to understand the complexity of *acculturation*, the process of becoming adapted to a new culture. A reorientation of thinking and feeling, not to mention communication, is necessary.

For instance, to a European or a South American, the overall impression created by American culture is that of a frantic, perpetual round of actions which leave practically no time for personal feeling and reflection. But, to an American, the reasonable and orderly tempo of French life conveys a sense of hopeless backwardness and ineffectuality; and the leisurely timelessness of Spanish activities represents an appalling waste of time and human potential. And, to a Spanish speaker, the methodical essense of planned change in France may seem cold-blooded, just as much as his own proclivity toward spur-of-the moment decisions may strike his French counterpart as recklessly irresponsible. (E. C. Condon 1973b: 25)

H. Douglas Brown, *Principles of Language Learning and Teaching*, © 1980, pp. 129–144. Reprinted by permission of Prentice-Hall, Inc., Englewood Cliffs, New Jersey.

33

The process of acculturation runs even deeper when language is brought into the picture. To be sure, culture is a deeply ingrained part of the very fiber of our being, but language – the means for communication among members of a culture – is the most visible and available expression of that culture. And so a person's world view, self-identity, his systems of thinking, acting, feeling, and communicating, are disrupted by a change from one culture to another.

In considering the relationship between second language learning and second culture learning, it is very important to consider several different types of second language learning contexts. (1) One context is technically referred to as the learning of a *second* language, or learning another language either (a) within the culture of that second language (for example, an Arabic speaker learning English in the United States) or (b) within one's own native culture where the second language is an accepted *lingua franca* used for education, government, or business within the country (for example, learning English in the Philippines or India). (2) Another context for learning another language is technically called *foreign* language learning – that is, learning a non-native language in one's own culture with few immediate and widespread opportunities to use the language within the environment of one's own culture (for example, learning French or German in the United States). It should be pointed out that in this article no such restricted or technical connotations have been implied in the use of the term "second language learning." "Second" language learning and "foreign" language learning have been used interchangeably.

Each type of second language situation involves different degrees of acculturation. Second language learning in a foreign culture (type 1a) clearly involves the deepest form of acculturation. The learner must survive within a strange culture as well as learn a language on which he is totally dependent for communication. Second language learning in the native culture (1b) varies in the severity of acculturation experienced by the learner, depending upon the country, the cultural and sociopolitical status of the language, and the motivations or aspirations of the learner. Kachru (1976) noted that learning English in India really does not involve taking on a new culture, since one is acquiring *Indian* English in India. As was noted earlier, a child learning French in grammar school in French-speaking Africa may not be faced with a difficult cultural conflict; he is faced more with a cognitive or "educational" conflict caused by the necessity for the acquisition of new modes of communication within an educational setting. The foreignness of the educational context may cause extreme conflict, akin to cultural conflict, but not in itself cultural conflict.

The *foreign* language context (type 2) produces the most variable degrees of acculturation since people attempt to learn foreign languages for such a variety of reasons. A person may learn a foreign language in order to communicate someday with the people in another culture; others learn foreign languages for instrumental purposes – for example, fulfilling a foreign language requirement in a university or gaining a reading knowledge within a field of specialization. Still others learn a foreign language simply out of an interest in languages, ranging from passing curiosity to highly technical linguistic interest in the language. Generally, however, the foreign language situation is more culturally loaded than second language learning in the native culture (1b), since the language is almost always learned in a context of understanding the people of another culture. Foreign language curricula therefore commonly attempt to deal with the cultural connotations of the foreign language.

Culture shock

Culture shock is a common experience for a person learning a second language in a second culture. Culture shock refers to phenomena ranging from mild irritability to deep psychological panic and crisis. Generally culture shock will be experienced only in the first of the second language contexts above (1a), and in the foreign language situation only upon actually entering the second culture (which is tantamount, at that point, to a second language (1a) situation). Culture shock is associated with feelings in the learner of estrangement, anger, hostility, indecision, frustration, unhappiness, sadness, loneliness, homesickness, and even physical illness. The person undergoing culture shock views his new world out of resentment, and alternates between being angry at others for not understanding him and being filled with self-pity. Edward Hall (1959: 59) describes a hypothetical example of an American living abroad for the first time:

At first, things in the cities look pretty much alike. There are taxis, hotels with hot and cold running water, theatres, neon lights, even tall buildings with elevators and a few people who can speak English. But pretty soon the American discovers that underneath the familiar exterior there are vast differences. When someone says "yes" it often doesn't mean yes at all, and when people smile it doesn't always mean they are pleased. When the American visitor makes a helpful gesture he may be rebuffed; when he tries to be friendly nothing happens. People tell him that they will do things and don't. The longer he stays, the more enigmatic the new country looks.

This case of an American in Japan illustrates the point that initially the person in a foreign culture is comfortable and delighted with the "exotic" surroundings. As long as he can perceptually filter his surroundings and internalize the environment in his *own* world view, he feels at ease. As soon as this newness wears off, and the cognitive and affective contradictions of the foreign culture mount up, he becomes disoriented.

Peter Adler (1972: 8) describes culture shock in more technical psychological terms:

Culture shock, then, is thought to be a form of anxiety that results from the loss of commonly perceived and understood signs and symbols of social intercourse. The individual undergoing culture shock reflects his anxiety and nervousness with cultural differences through any number of defense mechanisms: repression, regression, isolation and rejection. These defensive attitudes speak, in behavioral terms, of a basic underlying insecurity which may encompass loneliness, anger, frustration and self-questioning of competence. With the familiar props, cues, and clues of cultural understanding removed, the individual becomes disoriented, afraid of, and alienated from the things that he knows and understands.

The anthropologist George M. Foster (1962: 87) described culture shock in extreme terms: "Culture shock is a mental illness, and as is true of much mental illness, the victim usually does not know he is afflicted. He finds that he is irritable, depressed, and probably annoyed by the lack of attention shown him."

It is feasible to think of culture shock as one of four successive stages of acculturation. The first stage is the period of excitement and euphoria over the newness of the surroundings. The second stage — culture shock — emerges as the individual feels the intrusion of more and more cultural differences into his own image of self and security. In this stage the individual relies on and seeks out the support of his fellow countrymen in the second culture, taking solace in complaining about local customs and conditions, seeking escape from his predicament. The third stage is one of gradual, and at first tentative and vacillating, recovery. This stage is typified by what Larson and Smalley (1972) call *culture stress*: some problems of acculturation are solved while other problems continue for some time. But general progress is made, slowly but surely, as the person begins to accept the differences in thinking and feeling that surround him, slowly becoming more empathic with the persons in the second culture. The fourth stage represents near or full recovery, either assimilation or adaptation, acceptance of the new culture and self-confidence in the "new" person that has developed in this culture.

Wallace Lambert's (1967) work on attitudes in second language learning referred often to Durkheim's (1897) concept of *anomie* — feelings of social uncertainty or dissatisfaction — as a significant aspect of the relationship between language learning and attitude toward the foreign culture. As an individual begins to lose some of the ties of his native culture and adapt to the second culture, he experiences feelings of chagrin or regret, mixed with the fearful anticipation of entering a new group.

Anomie might be described as the first symptom of the third stage of acculturation, a feeling of homelessness, where one feels neither bound firmly to his native culture nor fully adapted to the second culture. Lambert's research has supported the view that the strongest dose of anomie is experienced when linguistically a person begins to "master" the foreign language. In Lambert's (1967) study, for example, when English-speaking Canadians became so skilled in French that they began to "think" in French, and even dream in French, feelings of anomie were markedly high. For Lambert's subjects the interaction of anomie and increased skill in the language sometimes led persons to revert or to "regress" back to English – to seek out situations in which they could speak English. Such an urge corresponds to the tentativeness of the third stage of acculturation – periodic reversion to the escape mechanisms acquired in the stage of culture shock. Only until a person is well into the third stage do feelings of anomie decrease as the learner is "over the hump" in the transition from one culture to another.

In keeping with these bleak descriptions of culture shock, Mark Clarke (1976: 380) likened second language learning and second culture learning to *schizophrenia*, where "social encounters become inherently threatening, and defense mechanisms are employed to reduce the trauma." Clarke cited Gregory Bateson's (1972: 208) description of the "double bind" that foreigners in a new culture experience:

1. ...the individual is involved in an intense relationship; that is, a relationship in which he feels it is vitally important that he discriminate accurately what sort of message is being communicated so that he may respond appropriately.
2. ...the individual is caught in a situation in which the other person in the relationship is expressing two orders of message and one of these denies the other.
3. ...the individual is unable to comment on the messages being expressed to correct his discrimination of what order of message to respond to, i.e., he cannot make a metacommunicative statement.

Clarke then goes on to note that virtually every encounter with people in a foreign culture is an "intense relationship" in which tremendous effort is expended to keep communication from breaking down. For example, "Getting a taxi driver to understand where you want to go; attempting to discover if he has indeed understood you, given that he says he has, but continues to drive in the wrong direction; and searching frantically all the while for the proper phrases to express yourself so that you don't appear stupid or patronizing; all of this combines to give a simple ride across town Kafkaesque proportions which cannot be easily put in perspective by the person who has suffered through them"

(p. 380). That such behavior can be compared with schizophrenia is clear from Bateson's (1972: 211) description of alternatives commonly adopted by a schizophrenic to defend himself:

1. He might...assume that behind every statement there is a concealed meaning which is detrimental to his welfare....If he chooses this alternative, he will be continually searching for meanings behind what people say and behind chance occurrences in the environment, and he will be characteristically suspicious and defiant.
2. He might...tend to accept literally everything people say to him; when their tone or gesture or context contradicted what they said he might establish a pattern of laughing off these metacommunicative signals.
3. If he didn't become suspicious of metacommunicative messages or attempt to laugh them off, he might choose to ignore them. Then he would find it necessary to see and hear less and less of what went on around him, and do his utmost to avoid provoking a response in his environment.

The schizophrenic period of culture shock and of language learning is therefore indeed a crucial period during which time the learner will either "sink or swim."

The description I have given of culture shock paints a rather severe picture of an unwitting and helpless victim of an illness, and points out that culture shock, while surely possessing manifestations of crisis, can also be viewed more positively as a profound cross-cultural learning experience, one that leads to "a high degree of self-awareness and personal growth." A *cross-cultural learning experience* can be defined as

a set of situations or circumstances involving intercultural communication in which the individual, as a result of the experiences, becomes aware of his own growth, learning and change. As a result of the culture shock process, the individual has gained new perspective on himself, and has come to understand his own identity in terms significant to himself. The cross-cultural learning experience, additionally, takes place when the individual encounters a different culture and as a result (a) examines the degree to which he is influenced by his own culture, and (b) understands the culturally derived values, attitudes and outlooks of other people. (Bateson 1972: 211)

Teachers of foreign languages would do well to heed Adler's words. While certainly not every learner will find a cross-cultural experience to be totally positive, many do derive positive values from the experience, and for those for whom learning a second culture might otherwise become a negative experience, or an illness, teachers can help that experience to become one of increased cultural awareness and self-awareness for the learner. Howard Nostrand (1966) recommended administration of careful "doses" of culture shock in foreign language classrooms. Thus equipped with self-understanding and a balanced understanding of the differences between two cultures, the learner slowly but empathically steps into the shoes of members of the foreign culture. Nostrand's suggestion is simplistic and unrealistic. Culture shock cannot be prevented with affective vaccinations. But teachers can play a therapeutic role in helping learners to move through stages of acculturation. If the learner is aided in this process by sensitive and perceptive teachers, he can perhaps more smoothly pass through the second stage and into the third stage of culture learning, and thereby increase his chances for succeeding in both second language learning and second culture learning.

It is exceedingly important that teachers allow the learner to proceed into and through that second stage, through the anomie, and not to force a quick bypass of the second stage. We should not expect the learner to deny the anger, the frustration, the helplessness and home-lessness he feels. Those are real feelings and they need to be openly expressed. To smother those feelings may delay and actually prevent eventual movement into the third stage. A teacher can enable the learner to understand the source of his anger and frustration, to express those feelings, and then gradually to emerge from those depths to a very powerful and personal form of learning.

Social distance

The concept of *social distance* has emerged as an affective construct to give explanatory power to the place of culture learning in second language learning. Social distance refers to the cognitive and affective proximity of two cultures which come into contact within an individual. "Distance" is obviously used in an abstract sense, to denote dissimilarity between two cultures. On a very superficial level one might observe, for example, that Americans (people from the United States) are culturally similar to Canadians, while Americans and Chinese are, by comparison, relatively dissimilar. We could say that the social distance of the latter case exceeds the former.

John Schumann (1976c: 136) described social distance as consisting of the following parameters: "In relation to the TL (target language) group is the 2LL (second language learning) group politically, culturally, technically or economically dominant, non-dominant, or subordinate? Is the integration pattern of the 2LL group assimilation, acculturation, or preservation? What is the 2LL group's degree of enclosure? Is the 2LL group cohesive? What is the size of the 2LL group? Are the cultures of the two groups congruent? What are the attitudes of the two groups toward each other? What is the 2LL group's intended length of residence in the target language area?" Schumann used the above factors (dominance, integration pattern, cohesiveness, congruence, attitude, and length of residence) to describe hypothetically "good" and "bad" language learning situations, and illustrated each situation with two actual cross-cultural contexts. Two hypothetical "bad" language learning situations were described (p. 139):

1. One of the bad situations would be where the TL group views the 2LL group as dominant and the 2LL group views itself in the same way, where both groups desire preservation and high enclosure for the 2LL group, where the 2LL group is both cohesive and large, where the two cultures are not congruent, where the two groups hold negative attitudes toward each other, and where the 2LL group intends to remain in the TL area only for a short time.
2. The second bad situation has all the characteristics of the first except that in this case, the 2LL group would consider itself subordinate and would also be considered subordinate by the TL group.

The first situation is typical, according to Schumann, of Americans living in Riyadh, Saudi Arabia. The second situation is descriptive of Navajo Indians living in the southwestern part of the United States.

A "good" language learning situation, according to Schumann's model (p. 141),

would be one where the 2LL group is non-dominant in relation to the TL group, where both groups desire assimilation (or at least acculturation) for the 2LL group, where low enclosure is the goal of both groups, where the two cultures are congruent, where the 2LL group is small and non-cohesive, where both groups have positive attitudes towards each other, and where the 2LL group intends to remain in the target language area for a long time. Under such conditions social distance would be minimal and acquisition of the target language would be enhanced.

Schumann cites as a specific example of a "good" language learning situation the case of American Jewish immigrants living in Israel.

Schumann's hypothesis is that the greater the social distance between two cultures, the greater the difficulty the learner will have in learning the second language, and conversely, the smaller the social distance (the greater the social solidarity between two cultures), the better will be the language learning situation.

In later research Schumann (1976a) and colleagues carried out research linking the construct of social distance to the *pidginization* of the interlanguage of a learner. A pidgin is a simplified and reduced form of language used for communication between people with different languages, and is characterized by a lack of inflectional morphology and a tendency to eliminate grammatical transformations. Pidginization was seen to occur as a result of social distance between cultures in the case of the language development of a learner of English as a second language in the United States, a contention supported later by Stauble (1978) in a study of a Spanish learner of English.

Perceived social distance

One of the difficulties in Schumann's hypothesis of social distance is the measurement of actual social distance. How can one determine *degrees* of social distance? By what means? And how would those means be quantifiable for comparison of relative distances? So far the construct has remained a rather subjectively defined phenomenon which like empathy, self-esteem, and so many other psychological constructs, defies definition even though one can intuitively grasp the sense of what is meant.

William Acton (1979) proposed a solution to the dilemma. Instead of trying to measure *actual* social distance, he devised a measure of *perceived* social distance. His contention was that it is not particularly relevant what the actual distance is between cultures, since it is what the learner perceives that forms his own reality. We have already noted that human beings perceive the cultural environment through the filters and screens of their own world view and then act upon that perception, however "biased" it may be. According to Acton, when a learner encounters a new culture, his acculturation process will be a factor of how he perceives his own culture in relation to the culture of the target language, and vice versa. For example, objectively there may be a relatively large distance between Americans and Saudi Arabians, but an American learning Arabic in Saudi Arabia might for a number of reasons perceive little distance, and in turn act on that perception.

By asking learners to respond to three dimensions of distance, Acton devised a measure of perceived social distance – the Professed Difference in Attitude Questionnaire (PDAQ) – which characterized the "good" or successful language learner (as measured by standard proficiency tests) with remarkable accuracy. Basically the PDAQ asked the learner to quantify what he perceived to be the differences in attitude toward various concepts ("the automobile," "divorce," "socialism," "policemen," for example) on three dimensions: (1) distance (or difference) between himself and his countrymen in general; (2) distance between himself and members of the target culture in general; and (3) distance between his countrymen and members of the target culture. By using a semantic differential technique, three distance scores were computed for each dimension. Acton found that in the case of learners of English who had been in the United States for four months, there is an *optimal* perceived social distance ratio (among the three scores) that typifies the "good" language learner. If a learner perceived himself as either too *close* to or too *distant* from either the target culture or the native culture he fell into the category of "bad" language learners as measured by standard proficiency tests. The implication is that the successful language learner sees himself as maintaining some distance between himself and *both* cultures. Unfortunately, Acton's PDAQ did not *predict* success in language. However, this is no great surprise since we know of no adequate instrument to predict language success or to assess language aptitude. But what the PDAQ did was to describe empirically, in quantifiable terms, a relationship between social distance and second language acquisition.

A cultural "critical period"?

Acton's theory of optimal perceived social distance supports Lambert's (1967) contention that mastery of the foreign language takes place hand in hand with feelings of anomie or homelessness, where the learner has moved away from his native culture but is still not completely assimilated or adjusted in the target culture. More importantly, Acton's model leads us closer to an understanding of culture shock and the relationship of acculturation to language learning by supplying an important piece to a puzzle. If you combine Acton's research with Lambert's a rather interesting hypothesis emerges – namely, that mastery or skillful fluency in a second language (within the second culture) occurs somewhere at the beginning of the third stage of acculturation. The implication of such a hypothesis is that mastery might not effectively occur before that stage, or even more likely, that the learner might never be successful in his mastery of the language if he has proceeded beyond early Stage 3 without accomplishing that linguistic mastery. Stage 3 may provide not only the optimal *distance*, but the optimal cognitive and affective *tension* to produce the necessary *pressure* to acquire the language, yet pressure that is neither too overwhelming (such as that which may be typical of Stage 2 of culture shock) nor too weak (Stage 4). Language mastery at Stage 3, in turn, would appear to be an instrument for progressing psychologically through Stage 3 and finally into Stage 4.

According to my hypothesis, an adult who fails to master a second language in a second culture may for a host of reasons have failed to synchronize linguistic and cultural development. The adult who has achieved nonlinguistic means of coping in the foreign culture will pass through Stage 3 and into Stage 4 with an undue number of *fossilized* forms of language, never achieving mastery. He has no reason to achieve mastery since he has learned to cope without sophisticated knowledge of the language; he may have acquired a sufficient number of the functions of a second language without acquiring correct forms. On the other hand, the person who has achieved linguistic mastery too early (before Stage 3) may be less likely to achieve healthy acculturation and be unable to cope psychologically even though his linguistic skills are excellent.

What I have suggested here might well be termed a culturally based *critical period* that is independent of the age of the learner. A young child, because he has not built up years and years of a culture-bound world view and view of himself, has fewer perceptive filters to readjust, and therefore moves through stages of acculturation more quickly, and of course acquires the language more quickly. He nevertheless may move through the same four stages, just as an adult does. Cases of unsuccessful child second language learning might possibly be attributable to less than optimal synchronization of stages of acculturation and stages of language mastery.

I am suggesting a hypothesis which of course needs further research and refinement. But previous research on sociocultural variables in language learning seems to bear out the hypothesis. Teachers could benefit from a careful assessment of the current cultural stages of learners with due attention to possible optimal periods for language mastery.

Language, thought, and culture

No discussion about cultural variables in second language acquisition is complete without some treatment of the relationship between language and thought. We saw in the case of first language acquisition that cognitive development and linguistic development go hand in hand, each interacting with and shaping the other. It is commonly observed that the manner in which an idea or "fact" is stated affects the way we conceptualize the idea. Words shape our lives. The advertising world is a prime example of the use of language to shape, persuade, and dissuade. "Weasel words" tend to glorify very ordinary products into those that are "sparkling," "refreshing," or even "scrumpdeliyicious." In the case of food that has been sapped of most of its nutrients by the manufacturing process, we are told that these products are now "enriched" and "fortified." A foreigner in the United States once remarked that in the United States there are no "small" eggs, only "medium," "large," "extra-large," and "jumbo." Euphemisms – or "telling it like it isn't" – abound in American culture where certain thoughts are taboo or certain words connote something less than desirable. We are persuaded by industry, for example, that "receiving waters" are the lakes or rivers into which industrial wastes are dumped and that "assimilative capacity" refers to how much of the waste you can dump into the river before it starts to show. Garbage men are "sanitary engineers"; toilets are "rest rooms"; slums are "substandard dwellings." Even a common word like "family" has for some social scientists been replaced by "a microcluster of structured role expectations."

Verbal labels can shape the way we store events for later recall. In a

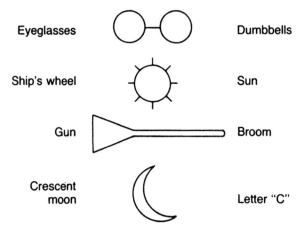

Figure 4.1 Sample stimulus figures used by Carmichael, Hogan, and Walter (1932)

classic study, Carmichael, Hogan, and Walter (1932) found that when subjects were briefly exposed to figures like those in Figure 4.1 and later asked to reproduce them, the reproductions were influenced by the labels assigned to the figures. For example, the first drawing tended to be reproduced as something like this:

if the subject had seen the "eyeglasses" label, and on the other hand like this:

if he had seen the "dumbbells" label.

Words are not the only linguistic category affecting thought. The way a sentence is structured will affect nuances of meaning. Elizabeth Loftus (1976) discovered that subtle differences in the structure of questions can affect the answer a person gives. For example, upon viewing a film of an automobile accident subjects were asked questions like "Did you see *the* broken headlight?" in some cases, and in other cases "Did you see *a* broken headlight?" Questions using *the* tended to produce more false recognition of events. That is, the presence of the definite article led subjects to believe that there *was* a broken headlight, whether they

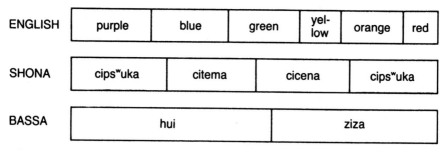

Figure 4.2 Color categories in three cultures

saw it or not. Similar results were found for questions like "Did you see some people watching the accident?" vs. "Did you see any people watching the accident?" or even for questions containing a presupposition: "How fast was the car going when it hit the stop sign?" (presupposing both the existence of a stop sign and that the car hit a stop sign, whether the subject actually saw it or not).

On the discourse level of language we are familiar with the persuasiveness of an emotional speech or a well-written novel. How often has a gifted orator swayed opinion and thought? or a powerful editorial moved one to action or change? These are common examples of the influence of language on our cognitive and affective organizations.

Culture is really an integral part of the interaction between language and thought. Cultural patterns, customs, and ways of life are expressed in language; culture-specific world views are reflected in language. Cultures have different ways of dividing the color spectrum, for example, illustrating differing world views on what color is and how to identify color. Gleason (1961: 4) notes that the Shona of Rhodesia and the Bassa of Liberia have fewer color categories than speakers of European languages and they break up the spectrum at different points, as Figure 4.2 shows. Of course, the Shona or Bassa are able to perceive and describe other colors, in the same way that an English speaker might describe a "dark bluish green," but the labels which the language provides tend to shape the person's overall cognitive organization of color and to cause varying degrees of color discrimination. Eskimo tribes commonly have as many as seven different words for *snow* to distinguish among different types of snow (falling snow, snow on the ground, fluffy snow, wet snow, etc.), while certain African cultures in the equatorial forests of Zaire have no word at all for snow.

But even more to the point than such geographically conditioned aspects of language are examples from the Hopi language (see Whorf 1956). Hopi does not use verbs in the same way that English does. For example, in English we might say "he is running," but in Hopi we would have to choose from a number of much more precise verbal ideas, depending upon the knowledge of the speaker and the validity of the statement. A different form of the verb expresses: "I know that he is running at this very moment," "I know that he is running at this moment even though I cannot see him," "I remember that I saw him running and I presume he is still running," or "I am told that he is running." Also, *duration* and *time* are expressed differently in Hopi. Time, for example, is not measured or wasted or saved in Hopi. Time is expressed in terms of events, sequences, and development. Plant a seed and it will grow; the span of time for growth is not important. It is the development of events – planting, germination, growth, blossoming, bearing fruit – that is important.

A tantalizing question emerges from such observations. Does language *reflect* a cultural world view or does language actually *shape* the world view? Drawing on the ideas of Wilhelm von Humboldt (1767–1835), who claimed that language shaped a person's *Weltanschauung*, Edward Sapir and Benjamin Whorf proposed a hypothesis that has now been given several alternative labels: the *Sapir-Whorf hypothesis*, the *Whorfian hypothesis*, *linguistic relativity*, or *linguistic determinism*. Whorf (1956: 212–14) sums up the hypothesis:

The background linguistic system (in other words, the grammar) of each language is not merely a reproducing instrument for voicing ideas but rather is itself the shaper of ideas, the program and guide for the individual's mental activity, for his analysis of impressions, for his synthesis of his mental stock in trade. Formulation of ideas is not an independent process, strictly rational in the old sense, but is part of a particular grammar and differs, from slightly to greatly, as between different grammars. We dissect nature along lines laid down by our native languages. The categories and types that we isolate from the world of phenomena we do not find there because they stare every observer in the face; on the contrary, the world is presented in a kaleidoscopic flux of impressions which has to be organized by our minds – and this means largely by the linguistic systems in our minds. We cut nature up, organize it into concepts, and ascribe significances as we do, largely because we are parties to an agreement to organize it in this way – an agreement that holds through our speech community and is codified in the patterns of our language. The agreement is, of course, an implicit and unstated one, but its terms are absolutely obligatory; we cannot talk at all except by subscribing to the organization and classification of data which the agreement decrees.

Today the Whorfian hypothesis has few zealous believers. Most linguists have little concern about a debate over whether language shapes thought or thought shapes language. They are more concerned, and rightly so, with the fact that language and culture interact, that world views among cultures differ, and that the language used to express that world view may be relative and specific to that view. Many linguists are more interested in the universality of language and consequently the universality of cognitive and affective experience: what is it that the human race shares in common? Guiora (1976) tested the Whorfian hypothesis for the effect of the gender of nouns between English and Hebrew, and found no support whatever for linguistic relativity. "The import of our findings seems to be that the pattern of our data may suggest the existence of the universality of symbols, at least across these two languages and these two cultures, thus adducing support to the notion of the universality of affective experience" (1976: 15).

Ronald Wardhaugh (1976: 74) expresses the antithesis of the Whorfian hypothesis even more strongly:

The most valid conclusion to all such studies is that it appears possible to talk about anything in any language provided the speaker is willing to use some degree of circumlocution. Some concepts are more "codable," that is, easier to express, in some languages than in others. The speaker, of course, will not be aware of the circumlocution in the absence of familiarity with another language that uses a more succinct means of expression. Every natural language provides both a language for talking about every other language, that is, a metalanguage, and an entirely adequate apparatus for making any kinds of observations that need to be made about the world. If such is the case, every natural language must be an extremely rich system which readily allows its speakers to overcome any predispositions that exist.

For second language teachers a knowledge of the commonalities between two languages or of the universal features of language appears to be fruitful for understanding the total language learning process. While we can recognize different world views and different ways of expressing reality depending upon one's world view, we can also recognize through both language and culture some universal properties that bind us all together in one world. The act of learning to *think* in another language may require a considerable degree of mastery of that language, but a second language learner does not have to learn to think, in general, all over again. As in every other human learning experience, the second language learner can make positive use of prior experiences to facilitate the process of learning by retaining that which is valid and valuable for second culture learning and second language learning. It is just the bathwater of interference that needs to be thrown out, not the baby of facilitation.

Questions for consideration

1. Have you ever experienced culture shock? Can you describe the experience? What did you learn from it?

2. Discuss your perception of the social distance between Germans and Vietnamese; between Japanese and Chinese.
3. What makes the "critical period" of language learning critical?
4. What are several examples of euphemisms that change our attitudes or cover our feelings?
5. What justification can you see for the strong version of the Sapir-Whorf hypothesis? for the view that culture shapes language? for the view that they shape each other?
6. Discuss the importance to the study of culture in second language learning of the Sapir-Whorf hypothesis and later research based on it.

Part II Cultural differences and similarities

At the base of intercultural understanding is a recognition of the ways in which two cultures resemble one another as well as the ways in which they differ. Resemblances usually surface through an examination of the differences. General discussions and theories regarding cultural differences are necessary for consideration of specific cultures in their relationship to the target culture, and the one without the other is like a river without a current.

The comparison of other cultures with the language being taught opens great vistas for the teacher and provides a basis for better understanding of persons from other backgrounds, as well as supplying new insights into approaches to teaching a second language. Obviously no one can learn everything about all cultures – no one knows everything about one's own culture – but even rather sweeping generalities, so long as they are not false, may be a help, if one avoids the pitfall of stereotyping and does not expect all members of a culture to fit the generality.

Any study of a culture must look to the behavior and values of the majority to form its observations and theories; it would be a rare culture indeed that had no exceptions. Entire subcultures, such as blacks in the United States, create exceptions – and subcultures of blacks create still greater diversity. Therefore making presumptions about a member of a particular group from a knowledge of his "culture" is a risky business, yet that knowledge can serve as a guide to better understanding in the effort to learn more about an individual. Stereotypical characteristics, such as the notion that Latin males are outgoing and effusive, are easy to refute by looking around at the Latin males who are quiet and shy. What should be postulated, perhaps, is that many Latin males – or a high percentage of Latin males, or a noticeable number of Latin males – are outgoing and effusive. More dependable observations are those based on behavior patterns, such as marriage rituals, and attitudes, such as a general acceptance in a society of male dominance.

Only after coming to know, understand, and appreciate something of other cultures can one realize the importance of providing cultural clues to assist the language learner in a new environment and to recognize what values and behavior patterns of the new culture the learner has most need to know. An example is the attitude toward older people in United States society. All experienced ESL teachers are acquainted with the revulsion expressed by students from almost any other culture toward the way in which Americans treat the elderly. They fail to understand what lies beneath this seeming indifference to the elderly. Particularly, they see the placement of elderly persons in nursing homes as a way of getting rid of them – never as a last resort, the only way to get proper care for someone who may be greatly loved and respected. Those who come from extended family dwellings cannot understand why so many elderly Americans live alone instead of with their children and grand-children. They see Americans as callous toward the elderly. A role play aimed at correcting this impression in a cross-culture class of advanced students at the Language and Culture Center of the University of Houston – University Park revealed the mistaken reactions of persons of one culture toward the behavior of those from another. The situation of an elderly woman walking along with a rather heavy burden was turned over first to a Malaysian male and then to an American male to act out as an encounter in pantomime. Predictably, when the Malaysian came upon the old woman and her burden, he turned to her immediately, relieved her of her load, and walked away with her. All of the foreign students in the class, from many different cultures, nodded their approval; they all respected and regarded highly the elderly people in society and felt protective toward them. The American, on the other hand, stopped when he saw the old woman, watched her for a few seconds, then shrugged his shoulders and went on. The foreign students frowned and almost clucked at precisely the behavior they would expect of Americans, those disrespectful louts who put their elderly parents in institutions instead of giving them loving care in their own homes. The American explained that his behavior was based on the fact that Americans place a high value on independence and being able to do things for themselves and he had decided, out of consideration for her feelings of self-worth, to leave her alone after he saw that the burden was not too much for her. He was afraid that if he offered to take her burden she would think he considered her old and feeble, and virtually no American woman ever gets old enough to want to be looked at in that way. He felt that by leaving her alone he allowed her to retain her pride, which was far more important to her than the discomfort of carrying a slightly heavy load. It was recognized by the class that both the Malaysian's behavior and that of the American were due to consideration for the old woman, though their reactions were different. The foreign students then considered the American's behavior acceptable, though not, actually, as proper as the Malaysian's had been. In intercultural communication, understanding and acceptance are enough to achieve; approval is not essential.

50

A knowledge of many cultures, superficial as it must be for the layman, is essential to the acceptance of those who have grown up in different environments. The transition from monoculturalism to bi- or even multiculturalism is a marvelous experience, and observing it is almost as marvelous. Nowhere is the transition more observable than in an intensive language program with students from many cultures. Recently a Hallowe'en party was held at the Language and Culture Center at which some students appeared in regular school clothes, some in native dress, some in spooky costumes, and some in indescribable combinations. A potential prizewinner was a young man in a beautiful, filmy Korean dress, his face done up in ghostlike white makeup. The teachers had prepared a lot of traditional Hallowe'en games for the students to play, but the games were rejected in favor of dancing. Disco dancing is clearly universal. A Lebanese in battle dress danced with a Chinese girl in blue jeans; a South American in drag danced with a teacher in a witch's costume; and a fanged Dracula from somewhere in the Orient danced with a girl of unknown national origin in a brown monk's robe and hood. Not all danced, to be sure; many observers sat around the room, but they, too, gained from the encounter. Perhaps the whole experience was epitomized by a pair of Spanish speakers who greeted each other at the door. One said, "*¿Que tal?*" ("How's it going?"), to which the other replied, "Hey, *bien*, man!"

Such acculturation to a world of differences enables language learner and language teacher alike to let go of the biases of their upbringing and enter with less fear the new world before them, making the learning and teaching experience both more pleasurable and more effective.

Since Hallowe'en parties are difficult to transfer to the pages of a book, a number of cultural studies are offered here to give a panoramic view of world cultures. Each of the articles in Part II supplies information about cultural mores of several groups, providing comparisons and contrasts. Robert Lado, in describing methods of comparing cultures, gives actual comparisons of many cultures. Genelle Morain presents a single aspect of cultural expression, kinesics, but her examples cover a number of cultures quite specifically. The same result is achieved in Nessa Wolfson's article on complimenting. Two perspectives of Middle Eastern culture are presented by Karl-Heinz Osterloh and Orin Parker, both accurate though not alike. John Condon's article brings Mexico, and with Mexico much of Latin America, into focus, and Alan Maley presents the chasms – and the bridges – between Chinese and Western educators. Various parts of the world are represented, but admittedly what is offered here is only a smattering of what is out there. Think of these offerings as hors d'oeuvres; there is sufficient meat in the entrée to last a lifetime.

5 How to compare two cultures

Robert Lado

"Culture," as we understand it here, is synonymous with the "ways of a people."... More often than not the ways of a people are praised by that same people while looked upon with suspicion or disapproval by the others, and often in both cases with surprisingly little understanding of what those ways really are and mean.

When a visitor is in the United States to study the American way of life or American culture, almost everyone is glad to show him that way and that culture, but what do we show him and what do we tell him? How do we know what to show and tell him?

If we are near an automobile plant, we will show him of course an assembly line and the tourist spots in the city. And perhaps we will show him a farm and a school. And we will tell him the favorable generalities that we have been taught about ourselves, which may happen to be the same favorable generalities he too has learned about himself and his culture. Occasionally someone among us wishing to pose as a detached intellectual may criticize a thing or two, or everything. But we are really rather helpless to interpret ourselves accurately and to describe what we do, because we have grown up doing it and we do much of what we do through habit, acquired almost unnoticed from our elders and our cultural environment.

Our inability to describe our cultural ways parallels our inability to describe our language, unless we have made a special study of it. The paradox is that we are able to use the complex structure that is our language with astonishing ease and flexibility, but when someone asks us when to use *between* and *among*, for example, we will tell him the most surprising fiction with the best intention of telling the truth. Similarly, we may be able to tie a bow tie with speed and ease, but the moment someone asks us to explain what we do, we become thoroughly confused and may give him completely false information. We describe ourselves as being free and at the same time may demand that our student

Reprinted from Robert Lado, *Linguistics Across Cultures*, pp. 110–123, © 1957. By permission of University of Michigan Press, Ann Arbor.

visitors attend class regularly, a restriction that is considered an invasion of personal freedom in some countries.

We cannot hope to compare two cultures unless we have more accurate understanding of each of the cultures being compared. We must be able to eliminate the things we claim to do but actually don't do. We must be able to describe the things we do without being conscious of doing them, and we must make sure we are able to describe practices accurately, not haphazardly or ideally. And we must be able to describe the situations in which we do what we do.

I assume with others that cultures are structured systems of patterned behavior. Following is a good definition given by anthropologists.

Cultural anthropologists, during the last twenty-five years, have gradually moved from an atomistic definition of culture, describing it as a more or less haphazard collection of traits, to one which emphasizes pattern and configuration. Kluckhohn and Kelly perhaps best express this modern concept of culture when they define it as 'all those historically created designs for living explicit and implicit, rational, irrational, and non-rational, which exist at any given time as potential guides for the behavior of men.' Traits, elements, or better, patterns of culture in this definition are organized or structured into a system or set of systems, which, because it is historically created, is therefore open and subject to constant change. (Hoijer 1953: 554)

Compare also the statement by Edward Sapir that "All cultural behavior is patterned" (Mandelbaum 1949: 546).

The individual acts of behavior through which a culture manifests itself are never exactly alike. Each act is unique, and the very same act never occurs again. Even in performing a play many times, each act performed by the player is unique, and it can be shown to be different from the "same" act in the very next performance. Yet in every culture certain acts which in physical terms are thus different are nevertheless accepted as same. Having orange juice, coffee, fried eggs, and white toast one morning and grapefruit juice, coffee, scrambled eggs, and whole wheat toast the next morning would usually be considered in the United States two occurrences of the same unit of behavior: eating breakfast. Yet they are different. The mold or design into which certain acts must fall to be considered breakfast in the United States constitutes a pattern of behavior, a functioning unit of behavior in that culture. These patterns are in turn made up of substitutible elements such as performer, act, objects, setting, time, manner, purpose, etc. These elements, though always unique and always different, are identified into "sames" and "differents" within certain molds which are cultural patterns also. These sames have characteristic features in each culture and they are usually of various classes. One such class in many cultures consists of items treated as static units, for example, men, women, children, doctor, nurse, teacher, barber, animals, horses, dogs, ghosts, witches, goblins, ideas, family, club, church, school, factory, store, farm, tree, building, museum, house, etc. Another class is constituted by items treated as processes, for example, to rest, to study, to fish, to run, to think, to sit, to die, etc. Still another includes items treated as qualities, as for example, fast, slow, good, bad, hot, cold, sleepy, sleepily, cruel, constructively, fishy, etc.

Such units of patterned behavior, which constitute the designs that are each culture, have form, meaning, and distribution....

The forms of these patterns of culture are identified functionally on inspection by the members of that culture, although the same individuals may not be able accurately to define the very forms that they can identify. Even such a clear unit of behavior as eating breakfast, immediately identified by the performer if we ask him what he is doing, may be described by him as the morning meal or the meal when you eat cereal, bacon, eggs, and coffee, yet a man who works during the night might be eating his breakfast in the evening, and a meal of cereal, bacon, eggs, and coffee might be lunch or even supper.

What is breakfast then? Can we define it? Yes, but the point being made is that the very same individuals who can tell us without hesitation and with accuracy "I am eating breakfast" may not be able to define breakfast for us and may do it erroneously. We can describe breakfast by observing a representative number of occurrences of breakfast and by noting the contrasts with those occurrences which seem to resemble breakfast but are identified as lunch, dinner, a snack, or supper by natives.

Meanings, like forms, are culturally determined or modified. They represent an analysis of the universe as grasped in a culture. Patterned forms have a complex of meanings, some representing features of a unit or process or quality, some grasped as primary, others as secondary, tertiary, etc. Eating breakfast, lunch, and dinner are engaged in usually to provide food and drink for the body. We say then that breakfast, lunch, and dinner usually have that primary meaning. In addition a particular form of breakfast at a particular time of day may have a meaning of good or bad on a moral or religious scale, on a health scale, on an economic scale, etc. A particular form of breakfast may carry as secondary meaning a social-class identification, a national origin identification, a religious identification. In short, any of the distinctions and groupings of a culture may be part of the meaning of a particular form unit.

All of these meaningful units of form are distributed in patterned ways. Their distribution patterns are complexes involving various time cycles, space locations, and positions in relation to other units. Breakfast, for example, shows time distribution on a daily cycle, a weekly cycle, and a yearly cycle. Breakfast shows a space or location distribution. It is also distributed after some units of behavior and preceding others.

Form, meaning, and distribution probably do not exist independent of each other in a culture, but they are spoken of operationally here as separate. Forms are relevant when they have meaning; meaning presupposes a form in order to be of relevance to us; and meaningful forms always occur in patterned distribution.

Within a culture we can assume that when an individual observes a significant patterned form in a patterned distribution spot, it will have a complex of culturally patterned meanings for him. Breakfast in the kitchen at 7 a.m., served by the same person who eats it, and including coffee, fruit juice, and cereal, will have a different complex of meanings than breakfast in bed at 11 a.m. served by a formally dressed waiter, and including caviar and other trimmings.

It may be worth pointing out at this time that the observation of a form may occur directly, indirectly through still photography, motion pictures, television, etc., or indirectly again by means of a language report.

The patternings that make it possible for unique occurrences to operate as sames among the members of a culture did not develop for operation across cultures. When they do occur in contact across cultures, many instances of predictable misinterpretation take place. We can assume that when the individual of culture A trying to learn culture B observes a form in Culture B in a particular distribution spot, he grasps the same complex of meaning as in his own culture. And when he in turn engages actively in a unit of behavior in culture B he chooses the form which he would choose in his own culture to achieve that complex of meaning.

Comparison of cultures

If the native culture habits are transferred when learning a foreign culture, it is obvious that, by comparing the two culture systems, we can predict what the trouble spots will be. Obviously, this is a huge undertaking, and we will present a few examples that may facilitate cultural analysis and comparison.

We will expect trouble when the same form has different classification or meaning in two cultures.

A very interesting kind of trouble spot is seen when any element of the form of a complex pattern has different classification or meaning across cultures. The foreign observer gives to the entire pattern the meaning of that different classification of one element.

Example. Bullfighting has always been in my observation a source of cross-cultural misinformation. It is a particularly difficult pattern of behavior to explain convincingly to an unsophisticated United States observer. I therefore choose it as a test case.

Form. A bullfight has a very precise, complex form. A man, armed with a sword and a red cape, challenges and kills a fighting bull. The form is prescribed in great detail. There are specific vocabulary terms for seemingly minute variations. The bullfighter, the bull, the picadors, the music, the dress, etc. are part of the form.

Meaning. The bullfight has a complex of meaning in Spanish culture. It is a sport. It symbolizes the triumph of art over the brute force of a bull. It is entertainment. It is a display of bravery.

Distribution. The bullfight shows a complex distribution pattern. There is a season for bullfights on a yearly cycle, there are favored days on a weekly cycle, and there is a favored time on a daily cycle. The bullfight occurs at a specific place, the bull ring, known to the least person in the culture.

Form, meaning, and distribution to an alien observer. An American observer seated next to a Spanish or Mexican spectator will see a good deal of the form, though not all of it. He will see a man in a special dress, armed with a sword and cape, challenging and killing the bull. He will see the bull charging at the man and will notice that the man deceives the bull with his cape. He will notice the music, the color, etc.

The meaning of the spectacle is quite different to him, however. It is the slaughter of a "defenseless" animal by an armed man. It is unfair because the bull always gets killed. It is unsportsmanlike – to the bull. It is cruel to animals. The fighter is therefore cruel. The public is cruel.

The distribution constitutes no particular problem to the American observer, since he has the experience of football, baseball, and other spectacles.

Misinformation. Is there an element of misinformation here, and if so, wherein is it? I believe there is misinformation. The secondary meaning "cruel" is found in Spanish culture, but it does not attach to the bullfight. The American observer ascribing the meaning cruel to the spectator and fighter is getting information that is not there. Why?

Since the cruelty is interpreted by the American observer as being perpetrated by the man on the bull, we can test to see if those parts of the complex form – the bull and the man – are the same in the two cultures.

Linguistic evidence. We find evidence in the language that seems interesting. . . . A number of vocabulary items that are applicable both to animals and to humans in English have separate words for animals and for humans in Spanish. In English both animals and persons have *legs.* In Spanish, animals have *patas* "animal legs" and humans have *piernas* "human legs." Similarly, in English, animals and humans have *backs* and *necks,* while in Spanish, animals have *lomo* and *pescuezo* "animal back" and "animal neck" and humans have *espalda* and *cuello* "human back" and "human neck." Furthermore, in English, both animals and humans *get nervous*, have *hospitals*, and have *cemeteries*, named by means of various metaphors. In Spanish, animals do not get nervous, or have hospitals or cemeteries. The linguistic evidence, though only suggestive, points to a difference in the classification of *animal* in the two cultures... In Hispanic culture the distinction between man and animal seems very great, certainly greater than that in American culture.

By further observation of what people say and do one finds additional features of difference. In Spanish culture, man is not physically strong but is skillful and intelligent. A bull is strong but not skillful and not intelligent. In American culture a man is physically strong, and so is a bull. A bull is intelligent. A bull has feelings of pain, sorrow, pity, tenderness – at least in animal stories such as that of *Ferdinand the Bull*. A bull deserves an even chance in a fight; he has that sportsman's right even against a man.

We can, then, hypothesize that the part of the complex form represented by the bull has a different classification, a different meaning, in American culture, and that herein lies the source of the misinformation.

We should test this hypothesis by minimal contrast if possible. We find something akin to a minimal contrast in American culture in tarpon fishing. In tarpon fishing we have a form: a fight to the exhaustion and death of the tarpon at the hands of a man with a line and camouflaged hooks. Much of the form is prescribed in detail. There is no large visible audience, but newspaper stories in a sense represent audience contact. In the complex of meaning, it is a sport, and it represents a triumph of skill over the brute fighting strength of the fish. The distribution seems somewhat different from that of a bullfight, but the difference does not seem relevant as an explanation of the difference we have hypothesized.

We now observe that the very same American who interpreted the bullfight as cruel, and applied that meaning to the spectator and the bullfighter, will sit next to the same spectator on a fishing boat and never think of the fishing game as cruel. I conclude that the part of the complex form represented by the fish is quite distinct from "human being" in both American and Spanish cultures, while the part identified as the bull is much more like "human being" in American culture than in Spanish culture.

Marginal supporting evidence is the fact that in American culture there is a Society for the Prevention of Cruelty to Animals which concerns itself with the feelings of dogs, cats, horses, and other domestic animals. Recently there was a front-page story in the local papers reporting that the Humane Society of New York City had sent a Santa Claus to distribute gifts among the dogs in the New York City pounds. We would not conceive of a society for the prevention of cruelty to fish.

A form in culture B, identified by an observer from culture A as the same form as one in his own culture, actually has a different meaning.

Example. A hiss, a sharp, voiceless sibilant sound, expresses disapproval in the United States. In Spanish-speaking countries it is the normal way to ask for silence in a group. Fries reports being taken aback the first time he faced a Spanish-speaking audience and heard the "hissing." He wondered if they were hissing at him. Later he learned that they were calling for silence (1955: 17).

Example. Drinking milk at meals is a standard practice in the United States. To us it has a primary meaning of food and drink, standard drink, at meal time. It does not have any special connotation of social class, national group, religious group, age group, or economic stratum. Wine, on the other hand, may be served on special occasions or by special groups of the population who have had special contacts with other cultures. Wine, thus, has the meanings special occasion, special group of people.

In France, milk at meals is not the standard drink. Some children may drink milk, some adults may drink milk for special reasons, some individuals or families or groups may drink milk because of special cultural contacts. Drinking milk at meals in France has the secondary meanings of special drink, special occasion, or special group of people. Its primary meaning would be food and drink for the body.

The reader may recall the sensation that former Premier Pierre Mendes-France caused in the United States when he began measures to extend the drinking of milk in France. Everybody recalls the favorable impression he made in the United States by drinking milk in public. Now, discounting those who may be familiar with scientific studies on the relative food value of milk as against wine, I take it that there was cross-cultural misinformation, and that there will be trouble in understanding another culture in similar cases. To the American public, Mendes-France was rescuing the French people from the special habit of drinking wine and teaching them the standard, wholesome practice of drinking milk.

We can expect another kind of trouble spot when the same meaning in two cultures is associated with different forms. The alien observer seeking to act in the culture being learned will select his own form to achieve the meaning, and he may miss altogether the fact that a different form is required.

Example. A young man from Izfahan, Iran, gets off the train in a small town of the United States. He claims his baggage and attempts to hail a taxi. A likely car with a white license plate and black letters goes by. The young man waves at it. The car does not stop. Another car appears with the same type of license plate. The young man waves again, without success. Frustrated because in the United States taxis will not stop for him, he picks up his suitcases and walks to his destination. He later finds out that taxis in the United States are distinguished not by a white license plate, but by bright flashing lights and loud colors. In Izfahan at that time the signal for a taxi was a white license plate. This was an intelligent university-level student stumbling over a predictable type of problem.

We can expect further trouble in the fact that the members of one culture usually assume that their way of doing things, of understanding the world around them, their forms and their meanings, are the correct ones. Hence, when another culture uses other forms or other meanings it is wrong. Hence, when another culture adopts a pattern of behavior from the first one, the imitated culture feels that something good and correct is taking place.

Example. When foreign visitors from areas where coffee is served very black and very strong taste American coffee, they do not say that it is different; they say that American coffee is bad. Likewise, when Americans go abroad to countries where coffee is black and strong, they taste the coffee and do not say that it is different; they, too, say that it is bad.

Example. When Americans go abroad during the cold season, they complain that houses are cold. We often think that such cold houses cannot be good for one's health. When foreign visitors spend a winter in the colder areas of the United States, on the other hand, they complain that our houses are kept too hot and that the changes in temperature when going in and out of houses must be bad for one's health.

There is trouble in learning a foreign culture when a pattern that has the same form and the same meaning shows different distribution. The observer of a foreign culture assumes that the distribution of a pattern in the observed culture is the same as in his native culture, and therefore on noticing more of, less of, or absence of a feature in a single variant he generalizes his observations as if it applied to all variants and therefore to the entire culture. Distribution is a source of a great many problems.

Example. For some time it was puzzling to me that on the one hand Latin American students complained that North American meals abused the use of sugar, while on the other hand the dietitians complained that Latin Americans used too much sugar at meals. How could these seemingly contradictory opinions be true at the same time? We can observe that the average Latin American student takes more sugar in his coffee than do North Americans. He is not used to drinking milk at meals, but when milk is served he sometimes likes to put sugar in it. The dietitian notices this use of sugar in situations in which North Americans would use less or none at all. The dietitian notices also that the sugar bowls at tables where Latin Americans sit have to be filled more often than at other tables. She therefore feels quite confident in making her generalization.

The Latin American student for his part finds a salad made of sweet gelatin, or half a canned pear on a lettuce leaf. Sweet salad? He may see beans for lunch – a treat! He sits at the table, all smiles (I have watched the process), he takes a good spoonful and, sweet beans! They are Boston baked beans. Turkey is served on Thanksgiving Day, but when the Latin American tastes the sauce, he finds that it is sweet – it is cranberry sauce. Sweet sauce for broiled turkey! That is the limit – these North Americans obviously use too much sugar in their food. And whatever secondary meanings are attached to too much sugar in a person's diet tend to be attached to the people of the country who prepare and eat such meals.

Another type of problem related to distribution differences, or rather to assumed distribution differences, occurs when members of one culture, who normally recognize many subgroups in the population of their own culture, assume that another culture with which they come in contact is uniform. Hence, observations made about one individual of that other culture tend to be generalized to the entire population.

Example. Folk opinions abroad about the morals of American women are partly connected with this assumed uniformity of population and partly, too, with the fact that the same form may have different meanings in the two cultures. Those who see American movies or come in contact with American tourists often misinterpret the forms of the behavior they observe, and often also they ascribe to the whole culture, the whole population, what may well be restricted to a special group on a special distribution spot. We in turn often ascribe to French and other Latin cultures moral behavior that may be restricted to special samples coming in contact with special visitors.

The notions filtered through the above types of misinformation and through others becomes part of the native culture as its "correct" view of the reality of the foreign one, and as young members grow up they receive these views as truth through verbal reports and all the other vehicles of enculturation. These preconceived notions constitute very serious obstacles to the understanding of another culture.

Gathering cultural data for a structural description

Since good structural descriptions of the cultures that may require our attention will usually not be found ready-made, we present below a checklist of possible patterns of behavior that in various cultures constitute functioning units. This checklist may be helpful in calling attention to areas that might otherwise go unnoticed.

To prepare for a comparison of another culture with the native one it may be valuable to use the informant approach coupled with systematic observation of the culture in its nòrmal undisturbed operation.

One can interview representative informants who are articulate enough to talk about what they do. We can ask them what they do each day of a typical week and on the various special days of the month and year. We can ask them what is done on the special days of the various turning points in the life cycle, that is, birth, growing up, courtship and marriage, raising their young, retiring, dying.

What the informant reports may be classified for easier grasp and later verification and comparison into things he does to meet the needs of his body: sleep and rest, food and drink, shelter, clothing, exercise, healing, cleanliness, etc.; things he does to meet the needs of his soul: religious activities. Other things may more conveniently be classified as tool activities: transportation, communication, work, training, organizations, government, etc. These groupings do not imply valid cultural categories or units. Quite often a pattern of behavior, a structural unit such as marriage, will involve the body, the personality, the soul, and tool activities.

One must not make the mistake of generalizing on inadequate sampling. The informants should represent at least the major significant groups of the population. In describing a culture as complex as that of the United States one should see that what a religious person does on Sunday is not generalized to all religious groups and much less to the nonreligious members of the culture.

Merely describing what any number of informants do in a culture does not constitute a structural description of the culture. Some of the things done will not be significant; that is, whether they are done or not or whether they are done one way or another will not change the unit of behavior. Other things, those we are interested in, will be significant: that is, doing something else will mean something else.

One must test variations to see if a change in meaning correlates with them. For example, we would observe that people sleep in a given culture and that they sleep in all cultures. We might observe that, say, in culture A most of our informants slept from between nine and eleven at night to between six and eight in the morning. We would check to see what would be thought of a person who habitually slept from one in the morning to eleven. We might find that the person would be considered lazy, or rich and lazy, or sick. The time of sleep would therefore be considered structurally significant. If the reaction were that sleeping those hours was all right because the person liked those hours, we would consider the time of sleeping not structurally significant.

Still checking on the pattern of sleep, one might observe in culture B that most of the informants slept or rested after the midday meal. One can check to see if not sleeping or resting at that time would have any particular meaning. If we found that people who did not rest at that time would be considered reckless with their health, overly ambitious, or foreigners or foreign-influenced, we would consider the afternoon nap a significant type of rest pattern.

Similarly, if the informants in culture A do not sleep or rest after the noon meal, we might check for the meaning to them of a member of their culture that sleeps afternoons. If he is considered lazy, or sick, or a weakling, we would take it that not sleeping after lunch was part of the rest structure in that culture.

In that same culture A if we found that one of the informants slept regularly during the day and worked during the night, would it have any special meaning? It probably would. The meaning might be that the informant was a night watchman or had to work on a night shift at the factory.

We can illustrate this search for structure with eating patterns or any other patterns in the culture we seek to understand. If an informant in culture A eats fish on Friday, would he also eat meat? If he would not eat meat, it might be for a religious reason.

Systematic observation of the culture in operation will do much to eliminate the errors that the interviews will inevitably introduce in our data. Testing in various ways for significance will also help us eliminate useless information as well as errors.

Even though a total analysis and comparison of any two highly complex cultures may not be readily available for some time to come, the kind of model and sample comparison discussed in this chapter will be helpful in interpreting observations made in the actual contact of persons of one culture with another culture.

Questions for consideration

1. What are four generalities that you believe could be applied to your native culture? What exceptions do you find to each?
2. Describe a sporting event in your culture in terms of *form, meaning,* and *distribution.* What do you believe would be the reactions to this event of a recently arrived person from another culture?
3. Has your own reaction to bullfighting or tarpon fishing been

altered by the reasoning in this article? Why or why not?
4. How might one compare two cultures in regard to courtship and marriage? Apply the system you devise to two cultures with which you are reasonably familiar.

6 Kinesics and cross-cultural understanding

Genelle G. Morain
University of Georgia

I grew up in Iowa and I knew what to do with butter: you put it on roastin'
ears, pancakes, and popcorn. Then I went to France and saw a Frenchman
put butter on radishes. I waited for the Cosmic Revenge – for the Eiffel
Tower to topple, the Seine to sizzle, or the grape to wither on the vine. But
that Frenchman put butter on his radishes, and the Gallic universe continued
unperturbed. I realized then something I hadn't learned in five years of language study: not only was *speaking* in French different from speaking in English, but *buttering* in French was different from buttering in English. And
that was the beginning of real cross-cultural understanding. (Morain 1977)

Those who interact with members of a different culture know that a
knowledge of the sounds, the grammar, and the vocabulary of the foreign
tongue is indispensable when it comes to sharing information. But being
able to read and speak another language does not guarantee that *understanding* will take place. Words in themselves are too limited a dimension. The critical factor in understanding has to do with cultural
aspects that exist beyond the lexical – aspects that include the many
dimensions of nonverbal communication.

   ... Americans are becoming increasingly interested in nonverbal communication. The current spurt of books on movement and gesture finds
an audience eager to speak "body language" and to "read a person like
a book." To the student of communication, however, there is something
disquieting about this popular approach to a sober subject. A book jacket
whispers, "Read BODY LANGUAGE so that you can penetrate the
personal secrets, both of intimates and total strangers" – and one imag-
ines a sort of kinesic peeping Tom, eyeball to the keyhole, able to use
his awful knowledge of blinks, crossed legs, and puckers to some sinister
end. In reality, the need for gestural understanding goes far beyond
power games or parlor games. There is a critical need on the part of
anyone who works with people to be sensitive to the nonverbal aspects
of human interaction.

Reprinted from Genelle G. Morain, *Kinesics and Cross-cultural Understanding*, No. 7
in the series *Language in Education: Theory and Practice*, © 1978, pp. 1–23. By permission of Center for Applied Linguistics, Washington, D.C.

Dean Barnlund has developed a formula for measuring communicative success in person-to-person interaction. His "interpersonal equation" holds that understanding between people is dependent upon the degree of similarity of their belief systems, their perceptual orientations, and their communicative styles (Barnlund 1975). With regard to belief systems, Barnlund contends that people are likely to understand and enjoy each other more when their beliefs coincide than when their beliefs clash. . . .

The second factor described by Barnlund – perceptual orientation – refers to the way people approach reality. There are those who look at the world through a wide-angle lens – savoring new experiences, new ideas, new friends. Because they have a high tolerance for ambiguity, they can suspend judgment when confronted with a new situation and postpone evaluation until further information is acquired. There are others who look at the world through a narrowed lens. They prefer familiar paths, predictable people, ideas arranged in comfortable designs. Because the unknown unnerves them, they do not go adventuring. They resolve ambiguities as quickly as possible, using categories ("hippies," "Orientals," "good old boys") to protect themselves from the pain of exploration. Those who perceive the world through the same lens – be it wide-angle or narrow – feel more comfortable with others who share the same perceptual orientation.

The third element of Barnlund's formula – similarity of communicative styles – presents the likelihood that congenial communicants enjoy talking about the same topics, tune easily into the same factual or emotional levels of meaning, share a preference for form (argument, banter, self-disclosure, exposition), operate intelligibly on the verbal band, and – most critical to the present discussion – understand each other on the nonverbal level. . . .

The nonverbal channel of expression

Teachers in our highly literate society are oriented toward the verbal channel of expression. They tend to see the word as the central carrier of meaning. At an intuitive level they recognize the importance of prosodic elements (pitch, loudness, rhythm, stress, resonance, and pauses), because these add emotional dimension to the spoken word. They are less inclined, however, to accord importance to what Edward Hall (1959) terms "the silent language." Enmeshed in the warp and woof of words, teachers find it hard to believe that the average American speaks for only ten to eleven minutes a day, and that more than 65 percent of the social meaning of a typical two-person exchange is carried by nonverbal cues (Birdwhistell 1974).

For simplicity, the nonverbal aspects of communication may be divided into three classes:

1. *Body language*, comprising movement, gesture, posture, facial expression, gaze, touch, and distancing;
2. *Object language*, including the use of signs, designs, realia, artifacts, clothing, and personal adornment to communicate with others;
3. *Environmental language*, made up of those aspects of color, lighting, architecture, space, direction, and natural surroundings which speak to man about his nature.

Although it is critical that students of other cultures be perceptive when it comes to understanding both object and environmental language (Morain 1976b), the focus of this article is on body language. Ray L. Birdwhistell (1974) gave the name "kinesics" to the discipline concerned with the study of all bodily motions that are communicative. An understanding of kinesics across cultures necessitates a close look at posture, movement, facial expression, eye management, gestures, and proxemics (distancing).

Posture and movement

Because human bodies are jointed and hinged in the same fashion, we tend to think of all people around the globe as sitting, standing, and lying in virtually identical postures. Actually, scholars have found at least 1,000 significantly different body attitudes capable of being maintained steadily. The popularity of one posture over another and the emotion conveyed by a given posture seem to be largely determined by culture (Hewes 1955). Among those postures used to signal humility, for example, Krout (1942) cites the following:

Sumatrans: Bowing while putting joined hands between those of other person and lifting them to one's forehead.

Chinese: Joining hands over head and bowing (signifying: "I submit with tired hands").

Turks and Persians: Bowing, extending right arm, moving arm down from horizontal position, raising it to the level of one's head, and lowering it again (meaning: "I lift the earth off the ground and place it on my head as a sign of submission to you").

Congo natives: Stretching hands toward person and striking them together.

New Caledonians: Crouching.

Dahomeans (now Benins): Crawling and shuffling forward; walking on all fours.

Batokas: Throwing oneself on the back, rolling from side to side, slapping outside of thighs (meaning: "You need not subdue me; I am subdued already").

No matter how poetic the meaning, this gymnastic parade of posture would either embarrass or disgust most Americans, who are not readily inclined to show humility in any guise. A slight downward tilt of the head and lowering of the eyes are as much kinesic signaling as they would be willing to accord that emotion. In fact, Americans are conditioned to accept a relatively narrow band of postures. A few parental admonitions continue to ring in the ear long after childhood and find their way to adult lips: "Stand tall!" "Sit up straight!" "Keep your hands in your lap!" But because the postural vocabulary of Americans is limited, they have difficulty accepting the wider range of postures found in other cultures. For example, the fact that one-fourth of the world's population prefers to squat rather than to sit in a chair leaves Americans uneasy. To most Americans, squatting is something savages do around campfires. They find it inconceivable that refined adults might sit on their heels in movie theater seats, as they sometimes do in Japan (Hewes 1957)....

Cross-cultural studies of posture and movement indicate that macro-kinesic systems may be determined by cultural norms. Sociologist Laurence Wylie, studying mime in Paris with students from twenty-five countries, found that national differences seemed to be accentuated by nonverbal techniques (Wylie and Stafford 1977). For example, when improvising trees, French students are "espaliered pear trees, and the Americans, unpruned apple trees." Differences in walking styles are so marked, Wylie maintains, that "in Paris one can recognize Americans two hundred yards away simply by the way they walk." To the French eye, the American walk is uncivilized. "You bounce when you walk" is their negative assessment. Wylie concludes that French child-rearing practices, which stress conformity to a disciplined social code, produce adults who reflect the tension and rigidity of French society. "They stand," he observes, "erect and square-shouldered, moving their arms when they walk as if the space around them were severely limited." Americans, on the other hand, seem to have a loose and easy gait. They walk with free-swinging arms, relaxed shoulders and pelvis, as though "moving through a broad space scarcely limited by human or physical obstacles" (Banks 1975). Interestingly, this perception of American gait conflicts with the findings of an unpublished study reported by Hall (1976), in which Spanish Americans perceive Anglo Americans as having an uptight, authoritarian walk whenever they aren't deliberately ambling; the Anglo, conversely, perceives the Spanish American male walk as more of a swagger than a purposeful walk.

The degree to which kinesic activity is culture-bound becomes obvious when one watches a foreign movie where English has been dubbed in by the process of "lip-synching." The audience watches the foreign actors but hears a specially taped version of the script read in English by native speakers. Although the English words are timed and even shaped to fit the lip movements, they do not accord with the total body gloss as represented by facial expression, gestures, and posture. French actors, for example, are seen gesturing in the tight, restricted French manner while seeming to say English words that require broad, loose gestures. Observers may feel amused or irritated, but the sense of imbalance is so subtle that they rarely pinpoint the source (Eisenberg and Smith 1971).

Speeches given by New York's colorful mayor, Fiorello LaGuardia, who spoke fluent Italian, Yiddish, and American English, illustrate how closely kinesic activity is linked to culture. An observer familiar with the three cultures could watch LaGuardia on a newsreel film without a sound track and tell readily which of the three languages he was speaking. There seems to be a subtle shift of kinesic gears when a fluent speaker slips from one language to another....

Facial expression

It takes a kinesicist like Birdwhistell... to analyze how man uses those few square inches of his face. According to his research (Birdwhistell 1970), middle class Americans display about thirty-three "kinemes" (single communicative movements) in the face area....

The implications of such complex kinesic behavior for language learners who would master the nonverbal system of another culture are staggering. Even Americans cannot *consciously* produce the thirty-three subtle variations... without some instruction. To further complicate matters, kinesicists believe that in addition to the facial displays that are readily visible, there are others that are "micromomentary" – occurring so rapidly that they are invisible to the conscious eye....

Gaze and eye management

Whether the eyes are "the windows of the soul" is debatable; that they are intensely important in interpersonal communication is a fact. During the first two months of a baby's life, the stimulus that produces a smile is a pair of eyes (Argyle and Cook 1976). The eyes need not be real: a mask with two dots will produce a smile. Significantly, a real human face with eyes covered will not motivate a smile, nor will the sight of only one eye when the face is presented in profile. This attraction to eyes as opposed to the nose or mouth continues as the baby matures. In one study, when American four-year-olds were asked to draw people, 75 percent of them drew people with mouths, but 99 percent of them drew people with eyes. In Japan, however, where babies are carried on their mother's back, infants do not acquire as much attachment to eyes as they do in other cultures. As a result, Japanese adults make little use of the face either to encode or decode meaning. In fact, Argyle reveals that the "proper place to focus one's gaze during a conversation in Japan is on the neck of one's conversation partner" (Argyle 1975).

The role of eye contact in a conversational exchange between two Americans is well defined: speakers make contact with the eyes of their listener for about one second, then glance away as they talk; in a few moments they re-establish eye contact with the listener to reassure themselves that their audience is still attentive, then shift their gaze away once more. Listeners, meanwhile, keep their eyes on the face of the speaker, allowing themselves to glance away only briefly. . . .

Erving Goffman (1966) discusses an American eye management technique that he calls "civil inattention." An interpersonal ritual used in public places, it involves looking at other persons just long enough to catch their eye in recognition of the fact that they are other human beings, then looking away as if to say, "I trust that you will not harm me, and I recognize your right to privacy." When two people perform this ritual on the street, they may eye each other up to approximately eight feet, then cast their eyes down or away as the other passes – a kind of "dimming of lights," as Goffman puts it. Actually, the timing of this act requires considerable subtlety; the individual's gaze cannot be absent, or averted, or prolonged, or hostile, or invitational; it has to be *civilly inattentive*, and one acquires a feel for it without formal instruction.

Two strategies in contrast to the civil inattention courtesy are the deliberate withholding of all eye contact – which has the effect of a dehumanizing, nonverbal snub – and the intense focusing of gaze known as "the hate stare." The author observed an example of the latter several years ago in a church. An obviously unhappy matron, perturbed to find a racially mixed couple seated in a pew near the front of "her" church, walked slowly down the aisle past the couple and fixed them with a baleful glare. So intent was she upon prolonging her hate stare that she maintained eye contact even after passing the couple, which necessitated considerable craning and twisting of her neck. Unable to watch where her steps were leading her, she smacked into a marble pillar with what was to most observers a satisfyingly painful thud.

In-depth studies of eye management in foreign cultures are not readily available. A skimming of differences across cultures reveals that there is great variation in this aspect of communication. British etiquette decrees that the speaker and listener focus attentively on each other. While an American listener nods and murmurs to signal that he is listening, the Englishman remains silent and merely blinks his eyes. Germans tend to maintain a steady gaze while talking. The American shift of gaze from eye to eye and away from the face entirely is not a pattern familiar to Germans. Peruvians, Bolivians, and Chileans consider insulting the absence of eye contact while talking. Arabs, too, share a great deal of eye contact and regard too little gaze as rude and disrespectful. In North Africa, the Tuaregs stare unwaveringly at the eyes during a conversation, perhaps because the eyes are the only part of the body not hidden beneath a swirl of veils and robes. On the streets, Israelis stare at others without self-consciousness. The French are also likely to stare at strangers, as anyone who has ever walked past a sidewalk café can attest....

Just why one culture should evolve an eye contact pattern diametrically opposed to that of another is not clear. Underlying some avoidance behaviors may be the primitive concept of "the evil eye." Believers feel that an actual substance – a malevolent ray – comes from the eye and influences the person or object it strikes. Witches endowed with the evil eye supposedly leave a thin film of poison on the surface of a mirror when their gaze strikes it. In Naples, even today, priests and monks are thought to possess the evil eye and passersby assiduously avoid their gaze (Argyle 1975)....

Gestures

Members of the same culture share a common body idiom – that is, they tend to read a given nonverbal signal in the same way. If two people read a signal in a different way, it is partial evidence that they belong to different cultures. In Colombia, an American Peace Corps worker relaxes with his feet up on the furniture; his shocked Colombian hostess perceives the gesture as disgusting. Back in the United States, a university president poses for a photograph with his feet up on the desk; newspaper readers react with affection for "good old President Jones." While Americans use the feet-on-the-furniture gesture to signal "I'm relaxed and at home here," or "See how casual and folksy I am," neither message is received by a Colombian, who reads the signal as "boor!" An understanding of the role gestures play within a culture is critical to sensitive communication.

Frances Hayes (1940) divides gestures into three categories that facilitate discussion: autistic gestures, technical gestures, and folk gestures. Autistic – or nervous – gestures are made by individuals in response to their own inner turmoil and are thus not strictly conditioned by culture. They may take the form of biting the lips or fingernails, cracking the knuckles, jiggling a leg, or twitching a facial muscle. Occasionally, however, they become stereotyped signs for certain attitudes – toe-tapping to indicate impatience, thumb-twiddling to show boredom – and thus pass into the realm of tradition.

Other movements fall under the heading of technical gestures and include such complex systems of communication as the sign language of the deaf, the gestures of umpires and referees, military salutes, and the signals of music conductors, traffic directors, and radio performers. Technical gestures carry uniform meaning for members of a specialized group and are usually taught formally.

Folk gestures, on the other hand, are the property of an entire culture and are passed on by imitation. Something as simple as the act of pointing is a folk gesture. Residents of Europe and North America point with the forefinger, the other fingers curled under the palm. American Indians, certain Mongoloid peoples, and sub-Saharan Africans point with their lips (Eisenberg and Smith 1971). Members of these cultures are not taught by their parents *how* to point (although they may be told when *not* to point). They learn by observation – the same way in which they acquire a complete repertoire of folk gestures.

Descriptive gestures include movements used to accompany such statements as "He wound up like this and threw that old ball"; "It swooped down and flew under the bridge"; "She was about this tall." It might seem that these gestures are culture-free, determined simply by the nature of the motion described. Analysis reveals, however, that many descriptive gestures are indeed culture-bound. Reid Scott discusses the gestural background in Mexico for the statement "She was about this tall."

In parts of Mexico the gesture for indicating how tall something is has three definite cultemes (aspects of culture essential to understanding). The arm held vertically with the index finger extended and the rest of the fingers folded indicates the height of a person. The arm and hand held horizontally, thumb up and little finger down, indicates the height of an animal. The same position, except with palm down, indicates the height of an inanimate object. In most countries, there is only one culteme; it includes measuring humans, sub-humans, and all other objects, and it has a single gesture, the last one described, to express it. We can imagine the laughter and even anger that one would cause if he were to measure your dear aunt with the gesture reserved for cows. (Scott 1969)...

Because folk gestures are in circulation, they tend to develop variations in meaning and execution. Nevertheless, they are the gestures that are most profitably learned by those who intend to interact with members of another culture. Whether "learned" means incorporated into students' active kinesic systems so that they can produce the gesture on demand, or merely learned in the sense that they can recognize the meaning of the gesture in its appropriate social context, is a matter of debate among language educators....

One solution would be for the teacher to draw up a list of gestures in order of their communicative value and teach them in descending order of importance. Gestures associated with greeting and leave-taking are critical, since it is difficult to function courteously within any culture without participating actively in these rituals. Gestures used for "yes" and "no," for showing approval and disapproval, and for making and refusing requests would also be useful. . . .

Gestures that would be wise to know but not emulate are those considered vulgar or obscene by the foreign culture. Equally important for cross-cultural understanding is a knowledge of those gestures that are repugnant to Americans but regarded as acceptable in other cultures. A quick survey reveals the complexity of emotional response to kinesic interaction. In New Zealand and Australia, the hitchhiking signal used by Americans is tabu. The "O.K." gesture so familiar to North Americans is considered obscene in several Latin American cultures. In Paraguay, signs made with crossed fingers are offensive, but crossing the legs is permissible as long as the ankle does not touch the knee (the leg-cross position preferred by many American men). In Germany, people who enter a row of seats in a theater should face those already seated in the row as they pass in front of them; to turn the back is considered insulting. Korean etiquette decrees that loud smacking and sucking sounds made while eating are a compliment to the host. And although one should never blow one's nose at a Korean table, sniffling throughout the repast is acceptable behavior. . . .

Proxemics

Edward T. Hall, whose book *The Hidden Dimension* (1966) deals with the perception and use of space (proxemics), demonstrates that individuals follow predictable patterns in establishing the distance between themselves and those with whom they interact. In each culture the amount of space varies depending upon the nature of the social interaction, but all cultures seem to distinguish the four basic categories delineated by Hall (Weitz 1974).

Middle class Americans, for example, have established the following interaction distances within the four categories (Hall 1966):

1. *Intimate distance.* From body contact to a separation space of eighteen inches. An emotionally charged zone used for love making, sharing, protecting, and comforting.
2. *Personal distance.* From one and one-half to four feet. Used for informal contact between friends. A "small protective sphere or bubble" that separates one person from another.
3. *Social distance.* From four to twelve feet. The casual interaction distance between acquaintances and strangers. Used in business meetings, classrooms, and impersonal social affairs.
4. *Public distance.* Between twelve and twenty-five feet. A cool interaction distance used for one-way communication from speaker to

audience. Necessitates a louder voice, stylized gestures, and more distinct enunciation.

Proxemic distances preferred by Americans do not correspond to those preferred by people of other cultures. Observance of interaction zones is critical to harmonious relations, but because these zones exist at a subconscious level, they are often violated by nonmembers of a culture. The amount and type of all physical contacts – including touching and the exchange of breath and body odors – vary among cultures. One study dealt with the number of times couples touched each other in cafés: in San Juan, Puerto Rico, they touched 180 times per hour; in Paris, 110; and in London, 0 (Argyle 1975). The London couples would be prime candidates for culture shock in an African culture where two people engaged in casual conversation intertwine their legs as they talk.

In general, high-contact cultures (Arabs, Latin Americans, Greeks, and Turks) usually stand close to each other. Low-contact cultures (northern Europeans, Americans) stand further apart. Barnlund's cross-cultural study of the public and private self in Japan and in the United States points out the dramatic contrasts in proxemic relationships between the two peoples. As a channel of communication, touch appears to be twice as important within the American culture as it is among the Japanese (Barnlund 1975). Although during infancy and early childhood the Japanese foster a closer tactile relationship than do Americans, the situation changes markedly as the child nears adolescence. In one study, a considerable number of Japanese teenagers reported no physical contact at all with either a parent or with a friend. The adult Japanese extends the pattern by restricting not only tactile communication but facial and gestural display as well.

The reasons why one culture will prefer a close interaction distance and another demand more space are not clear. Hall (1966) theorizes that cultures have different perceptions of where the boundaries of the self are located. Americans and northern Europeans think of themselves as being contained within their skin. The zone of privacy is extended to include the clothes that cover the skin and even a small space around the body. Any infringement of these areas is looked upon as an invasion of privacy. But in the Arab culture, the self is thought of as being located at a sort of central core. "Tucking the ego down within the body shell," as Hall puts it, results in a totally different proxemic patterning. Arabs tolerate crowding, noise levels, the touching of hands, the probing of eyes, the moisture of exhaled breath, and a miasma of body odors that would overwhelm a westerner. The ultimate invasion of privacy to the Western mind – rape – does not even have a lexical equivalent in Arabic (Hall 1966)....

Genelle G. Morain

Kinesic universals

In the midst of an overwhelming number of gestures whose meanings differ across cultures, scholars are searching for examples of kinesic behavior whose meaning is universal. The so-called nature/nurture controversy finds researchers divided as to whether some expressive behaviors might stem from phylogenetic origins (nature) and thus be common to all mankind, or whether kinesic behaviors are learned from social contacts (nurture) and thus differ from one culture to another.

Birdwhistell, a cultural relativist on the "nurture" side, wrote in *Kinesics and Context* (1970: 81):

Insofar as we know, there is no body motion or gesture that can be regarded as a universal symbol. That is, we have been unable to discover any single facial expression, stance, or body position which conveys an identical meaning in all societies....

Eibl-Eibesfeldt (1972) contends that kinesic similarities exist across cultures not only in basic expressions but in whole syndromes of behavior. Such patterns include greetings that involve embracing and kissing (Eibl-Eibesfeldt feels that these are apparently very old since they occur also in chimpanzees), the smiling response, and actions to indicate coyness, embarrassment, and flirting (hiding the entire face, or concealing the mouth behind one hand). Another example is the cluster of actions that express anger, including "opening the corners of the mouth in a particular way," scowling, stamping the foot, clenching the fist, and striking out to hit objects. The anger syndrome can be observed in the congenitally deaf-blind, who have had no opportunity to learn by watching others. In fact, Eibl-Eibesfeldt's studies of these children show that they portray the facial expressions regarded as "typical" when they laugh, smile, sulk, cry, and express fear or surprise, a fact that tends to support the "innate" viewpoint.

Researching facial expressions across cultures, Paul Ekman and associates (1974) concluded that "there are a set of facial components that are associated with emotional categories in the same way for all men, since the same faces were found to be judged as showing the same emotions in many cultures....

The role of kinesics

While it is clear that all cultures make use of kinesic behaviors in communication, scholars do not agree on the precise nature of the role they play. Scheflen and Scheflen (1972) point out that there are currently two schools of thought in the behavioral sciences. The "psychological school" follows the view set forth by Charles Darwin that nonverbal behavior expresses emotions. Most students of language and culture are aware of the emotive role of gesture, posture, and facial expression: drooping shoulder indicates depression; a scowl registers displeasure, etc. The more recent "communication school," including many ethnologists and anthropologists, holds that nonverbal behaviors are used to regulate human interaction. Scheflen and Scheflen insist that the two views are not incompatible – that the behaviors of human communication are both expressive and social.

To understand the idea of kinesic behavior as social control, however, one must become sensitive to the nonverbal behaviors that regulate – or monitor – social interactions. Ordinarily they are performed so automatically and at such an unconscious level that even those performing them are unaware of their own actions. Some have counterparts in the behavior of animals. Examples of this type of monitoring include:

1. Turning and looking at the source of a disruption (often quells the disturbance);
2. Looking "through" a person who is trying to join a gathering (a signal that he is not wanted);
3. Turning away from someone who is initiating an action (indicates that he will not receive support);
4. Recoiling or flinching from a sudden loud or aggressive display (warns the offender to step back or speak more softly).

(Scheflen and Scheflen 1972)

Kinesics and perceptual education

Sapir spoke of nonverbal behavior as "an elaborate and secret code that is written nowhere, known by none and understood by all." Unfortunately for cross-cultural understanding, the "all" refers only to members of the same culture. Bursack filmed Minneapolis men and women who deliberately tried to express "agreement" and "courtesy" nonverbally in an interview situation (Bursack 1970). The filmed sequences were studied by citizens of Beirut, Tokyo, and Bogotá. The foreigners were unable to "read" with accuracy the Americans' nonverbal attempts to communicate the two feelings critical to establishing a warm social climate.

We have seen how inextricably movement is linked to meaning. Those who have "learned" a language without including the nonverbal component are seriously handicapped if they intend to interact with living members of the culture instead of with paper and print. Insights into posture, movement, facial expression, eye management, gestures, and distancing as they affect communication not only increase sensitivity to other human beings but deepen inevitably students' understanding of their own kinesic systems.

Research on nonverbal communication is patiently unraveling Sapir's "elaborate and secret code." We know now that in order to really *understand*, we must be able to hear the silent message and read the invisible word. The study of kinesics across cultures must be a crucial part of our perceptual education.

Questions for consideration

1. Without being heard to speak, people may be classified as "foreigners" even though their clothes were bought in local stores. What are some of the ways "outsiders" are recognized as such?
2. Give an example of a kineme. How might this kineme vary from one culture to another in its expression or its interpretation?
3. An American businessman might lose a contract by innocently showing the soles of his feet, considered an insult to an Arab. Do you know of other examples of this nature?
4. Do you agree that there is no body motion or gesture that can be regarded as a universal symbol? Can you think of one that is? What does this mean to a teacher in a class of mixed cultural backgrounds?

7 Intercultural differences and communicative approaches to foreign-language teaching in the Third World

Karl-Heinz Osterloh
Goethe Institute

Language is not simply a formal system of sounds, words, and syntactical structures; language also reaches into the domain of human interaction, which for its own part follows certain rules. Every native speaker assimilates individual social experiences characteristic of his own culture. These experiences inhere in statements that obtain their communicative significance through interpretation: "Die Bedeutung eines sprachlichen Zeichens kennen heisst wissen, wie es verwendet werden kann, d.h. wie man mit ihm handeln kann, welche Regeln für seinen Gebrauch gelten" (Heringer et al. 1977: 7). Each society accumulates rules according to which concrete statements are interpreted abstractly and which are valid among communicating partners through common usage.

Between societies of greatly differing socioeconomic structures, however, intercultural differences play a significant role when members of the one culture learn the language of the other. A German, for example, does not need to acquire a new social experience when he has to learn how to welcome an acquaintance in French. Not so for a Senegalese. The Senegalese social experience of welcoming someone entails a litany of expressions which might easily demand a quarter of an hour's time. The welcoming process in French has shrunk to the short expression: "Bonjour, ça va?" which includes a greeting and a wish for the well-being of the person. The Senegalese, however, must develop a whole ritual in his mother tongue to communicate the same intentions. Thus a Senegalese will have to learn not only a short language formula, but even more important, that the initial greeting is of little consequence to a Frenchman: what is important is what is said next. The same is true of other everyday language actions such as congratulating someone, saying good-bye, excusing oneself, and expressing anger or happiness.

In comparison to societies in which social life centers around the family (i.e., a community of several generations of relatives often living under the same roof and often barely subsisting), the linguistic exponents of these actions that occur in industrialized countries are emotionally sub-

Reprinted by permission from *Studies in Second Language Acquisition* 3 (1): 64–70. © 1980 by Indiana University, Bloomington.

dued and functionalized. Students from preindustrial countries must acquire new ways of dealing with others socially and emotionally, if they want to communicate successfully in a European language. I would go so far as to claim that language has changed its social function since the emergence of industrialized society. It is evident not only that new kinds of texts have come into existence but that the rules of dealing with a text have changed considerably.

The sanctity of the text

One outstanding intercultural difference can be seen in the differing attitudes of readers to written texts. In developing societies the reader's attitude is strongly influenced by the fact that until a few decades ago only sacred topics were written down. In Islamic countries the Koran is in the back of the reader's mind when dealing with a text. Hence, what is written is necessarily associated with absolute truth (Osterloh 1977).

Since both content and form of texts are in principle solemn, holy, and incontestable, it follows that language learning becomes very difficult when it comes to analyzing a text and testing its validity. In order to do so successfully a student will have to go through a series of new social experiences. He has to learn that in Western civilization something written is something man-made, and that everything written is to be seen as an individual presentation or personal opinion which can be contested. By contrast, the text of the Koran is regarded as entirely mature, accomplished, and unalterable. Since the prophet delivered his messages by divine order, anyone questioning them would be condemned as a heretic.

As can be seen from the examples mentioned above, in Third World cultures the function of something written differs greatly from the function Westerners apply to it. Texts are of biased nature, contain magic knowledge, and are of heavenly origin. Since the reader is expected to impress upon his mind such records even if he does not understand what has been written, nearly the only way to handle such a text is to memorize and recite it. One can observe again and again how the learner does exactly that in the foreign language class. Because of his cultural experience, the reader regards the text as a fixed unit in which everything is of equal importance. Text is, so to speak, a plateau rather than a hierarchical structure of statements. Such a perception again becomes quite evident if one looks at the physical aspects of the Koran which, as is well known, does not have any paragraphs. Since the traditional development of reading skill stresses all verbal elements more or less equally, everything written is perceived primarily as a linear presentation rather than as a composition with a logical order. A student in the Third

World who wants to learn a modern European language has to learn that most texts (literary texts form a special category here) are of a profane and disenchanted nature and that they can be further utilized for communicative processes: i.e., in order to understand a text in the foreign language he has to learn at the same time how that written material is communicatively handled in the given culture. He must learn not only that in the foreign language a text is something made by an individual for other persons but he must also acquire new reading habits. He lacks a number of reading skills that seem obvious to us. For example, he will not look over a text to determine whether the text is worth reading. Neither does he possess the reading skills to distinguish between important and unimportant information – reading skills that enable *us* to determine the informative content of different kinds of texts. Our student can hardly make use of his mother tongue when dealing with certain types of texts, for example when asked to write another text based on an original: note taking, making a résumé, passing on particular passages of a text to others, and commenting on a text. Such language actions are not automatically mastered in countries of the Third World; they have to be acquired deliberately.

Identification of author and text

There is another difference between developing cultures and industrialized countries. To a person of a developing country it is of much greater importance *who* said something than is the case in the Western world. If one asks an African village principal about what he has heard in the news, he is likely to answer: "Oh, there was very important news today; first the prime minister spoke, then the minister of foreign affairs and last of all, the minister of education. These are all important personalities. ... " The next day's news, however, may be commented upon quite differently: "Today – nothing special. Just some unimportant people spoke. That was nothing... " (correspondence with Paul Parin, Goethe Institute, Zurich). We find that our student estimates the significance of the text by the status of the author: the higher the status, the more important the speech. (That the informative character of a text is often determined by the significance attributed to the writer's origin holds true for texts from our own history, such as a letter by a medieval prince or a document from some old chancellery. In those times an important part of the text was dedicated to the status and title of the writer, whereas today such verbal ceremony would not be possible.) In language teaching, one can make use of such a student's social experiences by personalizing discoursive texts. Such was our intention when we planned a new German textbook for Turkish high schools. We simplified a complicated reading text on politics and the developing countries by summarizing the most relevant points and attributing them to individual speakers in a purported discussion. Similarly, exercises can be personalized by attributing abstract phrases in a multiple-choice test to certain speakers. Of course the student must learn that in industrialized countries so-called impartial information is of utmost importance.

Concomitant with the progress of the industrial revolution was a disenchantment of language. New kinds of texts came into existence, in which the author and reader remain anonymous. Advertisements, signs and nameplates, bureaucratic forms, time tables, city maps, and statistics cannot be classified in terms of the writer's status. These texts contain an informational structure which is rationalized to the last detail. Graphically and linguistically, the student may have a lot of difficulty approaching such written material, primarily because he is unaware of how to interact beyond mere understanding. Therefore when introducing a time table, a city map or an advertisement in class it is highly recommended that the teacher also instruct his students on how to proceed to deal with such material in a real situation.

The task of producing such texts on their own is remarkably more difficult for our students. After all, the chaos in Third World bureaucracies often begins with chaotic language. I remember very well a sign on the gateway to Ankara, twenty lines long, beginning: "Dear driver," and ending "yours, sincerely, City Authorities." All that just to ask for slow and cautious driving in the city. Numerous drivers reading the sign caused terrible traffic jams, and the authorities had to remove the sign. It follows from this experience that in the language class we cannot avoid discussing the informational structure of such a text. For the student to master such texts and be able to change a given text into another form, we can help him use other steps such as changing a letter into an advertisement or vice versa or have him change a biography into a curriculum vitae.

Collective opinions and interpersonal conflict

In the domain of discursive language, intercultural differences play an important role and result in manifold problems. Argumentation in particular enjoys a completely different social place in preindustrialized societies. One of the reasons for this difference lies again in the close relation between the person and his statement. Opinions indicate the status and the origin of the person and are as representative as weapons or costumes are. Accordingly our student knows little about forming his own opinion; he is still used to the collective opinion that dominated his previous social experience. Students at Turkish universities, for example, who came from the same village often belong to the same political party. And since opinion serves only as an *element to be integrated* into a certain group, they are rather inflexible and can be influenced only with great difficulty. Dissenting opinions will call in question the right to be a member of the group. The way in which such collective opinions come into existence, of course, depends on the inner structure of the group. In Turkey and in the Arab World it is often the oldest or most respected member who forms the group's opinion. Normally, for example, no one may give any information to a visitor without the leader's consent. And no one will give his opinion about anything before he has spoken to the leader. Social experiences of that sort naturally influence classroom interaction: an individual is often not prepared to formulate opinion prior to the establishment of a class hierarchy, at which time the individual's opinion is dominated by that of the most respected person. New language interactions, such as those occurring in industrialized cultures, can only be achieved on a long-term basis and only if the group's composition does not change. Thus a major problem for our student is the acquisition of a social behavior that will enable him to deal with dissenting opinions – even those that represent deep underlying conflicts – by means of discourse.

The student's cultural background prompts him to perceive a difference of opinion as an attack on both himself and the group of which he is a part. It usually leads to a personally involved conversation, i.e. disagreements quickly lead to personal attacks. Thus language assumes the function of a conversational fight; the student breaks peace with his adversary, provokes him and calls him names. It is not for nothing that languages have developed ample means of insult. The presence of the group or of relatives or friends is indispensable to such a conversational fight; these individuals, too, take sides or try to act as mediators.

As a matter of principle conflicts are not settled verbally; they lead to a fight. Often the two parties concerned will only speak with one another again after the conflict has been resolved. Language then takes over the function of confirming the new peace agreement through rituals of friendship. The foreign language instructor is confronted here with a most difficult psychosocial problem. From the linguistic point of view the problem can be resolved relatively easily. All we need do is make a list of all means of communication necessary for a conversation: how to contradict someone politely, how to join in a conversation, how to draw attention to common points of view, how to come to conclusions. Through making such a list one quickly realizes that European languages in particular have created lots of such linguistic means that do not exist in Third World languages. What will be much more difficult for the individual from the Third World, however, will be to change his social behavior to fit the linguistic situations mentioned above.

We highly recommend developing such discoursive language behavior first through preplanned games. By working with discourse chains and charts, with which the student takes turns in playing various roles, the teacher can depersonalize opinions and arguments so that the student can understand them to be separate from their originator (Bundesarbeitsgemeinschaft Englisch 1978). It can also be helpful – in the last resort in the student's mother tongue – to explain the social role of language in industrialized countries and how it functions in resolving conflicts.

Abstraction in Western languages

Whenever the student tries to understand a text in a foreign language or to compose one himself, or to settle conflicting opinions through argumentation, he will experience the new social function that language – particularly written language – has acquired in industrialized cultures. Many texts are a draft of standards and rules according to which the industrialized world functions or is supposed to function. A timetable standardizes railway traffic, administration regulations standardize civil servants' activities, a scientific essay tries to standardize rules to which a certain domain of our environment is subject. Such manifestations of language represent some sort of *second reality*, which confronts the sphere of our concrete experiences. In acquiring a modern European language, the student from the Third World has to accept, in contrast to his own culture, the close bond between most of our interactions – above all, intellectual ones – and norms, rules, theories, ideas, and opinions. Tradition-oriented cultures have also created and handed down a conception of the world and rules of conduct for the individual. But they differ from ours in that these rules are of transcendental character and therefore are unchangeable and of eternal validity. Casuistry dominates such traditional texts. They originate from concrete details which are placed in a linear composition. What has happened in industrialized societies since the beginning of modern times can be summarized with the following schema: Our sphere of life has been linked more and more to language rules which resulted from a progressive functionalization of terms and discourse structures. Concrete elements in our languages are of diminishing relevance. It will suffice to look at an example of a medieval code, scientific text, or book title in order to understand to what degree Western languages have become abstract. The communicative structure of Third-World languages is determined to a high degree by religion, magic, and status; the traditional text does not expect the reader to object to what is being written. This attitude differs quite notably from Western language productions, that aim at the *individual* experience of the reader and expect him to relate to the text's manifestations and react accordingly. This use of the language is most difficult for the student from the Third World. Since interactions in preindustrialized cultures are not necessarily linked to language formulas, extraverbal direct contact with objects, and immediate intuition characterize his existence. Thus gestures, mimicry, and direct perception play a much more important role for him than for us.

I am not of the opinion that Western language interactions such as our immanent tendency to analyze ourselves and the world are of higher cultural value than the interactions common in the Third World. Moreover, it is not a language teacher's job to go about like a missionary and praise our language practice as if it were a unique achievement. On the other hand it is indispensable that we familiarize our student with specific rules of interaction in the foreign language if we expect him to be capable of mastering the communicative aspect of language.

Hence, it will be our main didactic task to teach the student to relate foreign language expressions to himself and to his environment (Osterloh 1978). First one should revise the contents of teaching material used in the Third World. Commonplace stories or those dialogues one-sidedly oriented toward European society should be replaced by contents meaningful to a given local situation. To do so successfully, one will first have to research the student's local environment, as was done by Paolo Freire before he wrote his courses for analphabets (1971). What should be reflected upon as well are the so-called geography classes (Landeskunde). "Geographic" information should not aim at the student's idealization of some far reality which might appear like a fairy tale to him. Such information has to be relevant in respect to his own local experience.

Underlining, note taking, choosing and gathering relevant information, and summarizing texts are particularly important techniques for later use of communicative processes in the foreign language. They are closely related to a series of techniques of interaction that the student should be taught so that he can verbalize his own situation. What I have in mind is to send the student out to do the following assignments: interview people, hold polls, work on statistical and other material he has found in texts of his mother tongue. As an innovation in foreign language teaching such out-of-class activities play a more important role in the Third World than in industrialized countries, since the student's environment has not yet been verbally analyzed the way we are accustomed to. In order to communicate with us successfully, the student has to satisfy communicative prerequisites considerably more difficult for him than for the student in an industrialized environment, while he remains rooted in, and is not alienated from, his own culture. Thus foreign language teaching will become directed more toward the world outside the classroom where the teacher sends the student with concrete assignments.

In order to describe the implications of intercultural differences on foreign language teaching, I started from the student's situation in the Third World. I should like to conclude by affirming that what has been said of his efforts to learn our languages naturally holds true for the reverse as well. To be able to communicate in the Arab World, [Westerners] must go through new social experiences – ones [they] have not encountered in [their] own culture. Above all [they] have to reactivate certain of [their] perceptive and communicative faculties, thus taking [them] far beyond the goals of mere linguistic language training.

Questions for consideration

1. What are some of the problems Islamic students might encounter when assigned to write a critical commentary on an author's message in an essay?
2. How would Western students have to adjust their reading and writing habits when studying in an Islamic country?
3. What new significance do you see to the cliché "It is written..." so often spoken in movies by Arab sages?
4. Given the "group agreement" philosophy cited by Osterloh, how can one account for the frequent enthusiastic vocal response of Islamic students to class discussions in classes of mixed cultural backgrounds?
5. Do you see some problems with the general application of cultural attitudes and practices to the entire Third World? How? To the entire Islamic World? How?

8 "...So near the United States"

John C. Condon
University of New Mexico

"Poor Mexico," said Porfirio Díaz, "so far from God, so near the United States." In the years since Mexico's last pre-Revolutionary President said these words the nations on both sides of the border have been greatly altered. Some might speculate on the resulting changes in Mexico's proximity to the Lord, but none would deny that geographically and commercially Mexico has never been so near the United States. The cultural distance, however, is something else, for in many respects the cultural gaps between these societies are as great as ever....

Not that there has been any shortage of contact between people of these two cultures. The fifteen hundred mile border that spans the continent is crossed in both directions by more people than in any other international border on the globe. These include millions of tourists annually who venture south into Mexico to make up more than 80 percent of that nation's primary source of revenue, tourism. It also includes the countless numbers of workers, both legally admitted and undocumented, business people, students and tourists, too, who cross from Mexico into the United States. Quite apart from this daily traffic, the cultural presence of each society is to be found across the border. The capital city of Mexico is that nation's, and soon the world's, largest metropolis; but the second largest number of Mexicans reside in Los Angeles. And it is worth recalling that scarcely a century and a half ago half of the land that had been Mexico became a part of the U.S., a fact remembered more in Mexico than north of the border. Intercultural contact is hardly a phenomenon of the jet age.

Information about and from each society has never been greater than one finds today. Studies show that the average Mexico City daily newspaper contains a greater percentage of news about the U.S. than the average New York *Times* reports about all the rest of the world combined. North American foods, fashions, products and loan words are enough in evidence in the cities of Mexico to make the casual visitor overlook some significant differences in values and beliefs. Indeed, many

Reprinted from *The Bridge* 5, 1 (Spring 1980): 2–4, 30. Used with permission from Intercultural Press, Inc.

veteran observers of relations between Mexicans and North Americans believe that the increase in superficial similarities actually contributes to culture-based misunderstandings.

Insights into contrasting cultural assumptions and styles of communication cannot be gained without an appreciation of the history and geography of the two societies. One quickly learns that where there are intersections, such as the major river that marks a good part of the border or the major war that literally gave shape to each nation, the interpretations and even the names are different in each society. The name "America" itself is one that many Mexicans feel should not be limited to the United States of America alone, particularly since culturally the "anglo" culture is a minority among the nations of the Americas. "North America" and "North American" may be more appreciated.

North Americans trace their history from the time of the first English settlers. The people already living on the continent possessed no great cities or monuments to rival anything in Europe, and they held little interest for the European colonists so long as they could be displaced and their land cultivated. The North American Indian has remained excluded from the shaping of the dominant culture of the new nations just as he had been excluded from the land. With political independence and the continuous arrival of immigrants, largely from Northern Europe, the nation took shape in a steady westward pattern. The outlook was to the future, to new land and new opportunities. The spirit was of optimism.

When the Spanish soldiers arrived in Mexico in the 16th century they found cities and temples of civilizations that had flourished for thousands of years. In what some have called a holy crusade, the Spanish attempted to destroy the old societies and reconstruct a new order on top. In religion, in language, in marriage, there was a fusion of Indian and European which was totally different from the pattern in the United States. While Cortés is no hero in Mexico – there are no statues of him anywhere in the country – the fusion of European and native American cultures is a source of great pride, not only in Mexico but extending throughout the Latin American republics. This is the spirit of *la raza* which serves in part to give a sense of identification with other Latin Americans and a sense of separateness from those of the anglo world.

There are other contrasts to be noted as well. The land that became the United States was for the most part hospitable and, for much of the country's history, seemingly endless. Less than a fifth of the land in Mexico, in contrast, is arable.

The images which the people on each side of the border hold of the other differ. Mexico's image of the United States was to a great extent shaped in Europe, formed at a time when European writers had little good to say about the anglo-American world. Even today when Mexicans speak of the ideals of freedom and democracy, their inspiration is more likely to be French than North American. The rivalry between England and Spain, compounded by the religious hostility between Protestants and Roman Catholics, influenced in a comparable way the North American's image of Mexico.

Finally, by way of introduction, we should note that regional differences are pronounced and of importance in understanding the people of Mexico. Social and economic differences vary considerably, and even in language, with perhaps 150 different languages still spoken in the country, there are truly "many Mexicos." Thus it is not surprising that for years there has been a serious interest among Mexicans to find "the Mexican." Some say this search for identity began even before the conquest, for the 16th century Spaniard was himself unsure of his identity: he arrived in Mexico less than 25 years after driving out the last of the Moors from his own homeland.

An early Adlerian analysis of "the Mexican" by Samuel Ramos found the essence of the Mexican national character in the *pelado*, "the plucked one," at the bottom of the pecking order. While the Ramos thesis has been reconsidered over the years, some of the same themes of doubt and frustration and of a tragic outlook on life continue in contemporary Mexican interpretations.

The history of relations between the United States and Mexico has not been one of understanding and cooperation, though many persons on both sides of the border are working toward those ends. Even under the best of conditions and with the best of intentions, Mexicans and North Americans working together sometimes feel confused, irritated, distrustful. The causes lie not within either culture but rather can be best understood interculturally. Here are four perspectives.

Individualism

In the North American value system are three central and interrelated assumptions about human beings. These are (1) that people, apart from social and educational influences, are basically the same; (2) that each person should be judged on his or her own individual merits; and (3) that these "merits," including a person's worth and character, are revealed through the person's actions. Values of equality and independence, constitutional rights, laws and social programs arise from these assumptions. Because a person's actions are regarded as so important, it is the comparison of accomplishments – Mr. X compared to Mr. X's father, or X five years ago compared to X today, or X compared to Y and Z – that provides a chief means of judging or even knowing a person.

In Mexico it is the uniqueness of the individual which is valued, a quality which is assumed to reside within each person and which is not necessarily evident through actions or achievements. That inner quality which represents the dignity of each person must be protected at all costs. Any action or remark that may be interpreted as a slight to the person's dignity is to be regarded as a grave provocation. Also, as every person is part of a larger family grouping, one cannot be regarded as a completely isolated individual....

Where a Mexican will talk about a person's inner qualities in terms of the person's soul or spirit (*alma* or *espiritu*), North Americans are likely to feel uncomfortable using such words to talk about people. They may regard such talk as vague or sentimental, the words seeming to describe something invisible and hence unknowable, or at the very least "too personal." The unwillingness to talk in this way only confirms the view held by many Mexicans that North Americans are insensitive. "Americans are corpses," said one Mexican.

Even questions about the family of a person one does not know well may discomfit many North Americans, since asking about a person's parents or brothers or sisters may also seem too personal. "I just don't know the person well enough to ask about his family," a North American might say, while the Mexican may see things just the opposite: "If I don't ask about the person's family, how will I really know him?"

The family forms a much less important part of an individual's frame of reference in the United States than is usually the case in Mexico. Neighbors, friends or associates, even some abstract "average American," may be the basis for the comparison needed in evaluating oneself or others. "Keeping up with the Joneses" may be important in New York or Chicago, but keeping up with one's brother-in-law is more important in Mexico City. In the same way, the Mexican depends upon relatives or close friends to help "arrange things" if there is a problem or to provide a loan. While this is by no means rare in the United States, the dominant values in the culture favor institutions which are seen as both efficient and fair.

So it is that tensions may arise between Mexicans and North Americans over what seems to be a conflict between trusting particular individuals or trusting abstract principles. In a business enterprise, the North American manager is likely to view the organization and its processes as primary, with the role of specific people being more or less supportive of that system. People can be replaced if need be; nobody is indispensable. When one places emphasis on a person's spirit or views an organization as if it were a family, however, then it seems just as clear that nobody can be exactly replaced by any other person.

Both North Americans and Mexicans may speak of the need to "respect" another person, but here too the meanings of the word respect (or *respeto*) differ somewhat across the cultures. In a study of associations with this word conducted in the U.S. and Mexico, it was found that North Americans regarded "respect" as bound up with the values of equality, fair play and the democratic spirit. There were no emotional overtones. One respects others as one might respect the law. For Mexicans, however, "respect" was found to be an emotionally charged word involving pressures of power, possible threat and often a love-hate relationship. The meaning of respect arises from powerful human relationships such as between father and son or *patrón* and *péon*, not a system of principles to which individuals voluntarily commit themselves.

Straight talk

...The ceremonial speaking of heads of state actually shows fewer differences between Mexican and North American styles than do routine conversations. It is not simply that two styles, plain and fancy, contrast; rather, persons from each culture will form judgments about the personality and character of the other as a result. The Mexican is far more likely to flatter, tease or otherwise attempt to charm another than is the North American whose culture has taught him to distrust or poke fun at anyone who "really lays it on."

Often the problem is heightened when there is a difference in the sex, status or age of the two persons in conversation. Mexicans may want to maximize these differences while North Americans often make a great effort to minimize them. North Americans may at present be most sensitive to the way in which a businessman talks to a businesswoman, lest he be accused of "sexism," but the same values apply to "making too much" of one's age or status. Thus the very style which is called for in one culture may be regarded as quite uncalled for in the other culture. North Americans are often suspicious of one who seems effusive in praise; they are also likely to make light of one who seems too enamored of titles. Mexicans, on the other hand, value one who has the wit and charm to impress another. Nor are titles or other indications of one's status, age or ability to be slighted. The owner of an auto repair shop may defer to a mechanic who is older and more experienced as *maestro*; doctors, lawyers and other professional people will take their titles seriously. To make light of them is to challenge one's dignity.

The truth

During the world congress held in Mexico for the International Women's Year, some first time visitors experienced the kind of problem that many

89

North Americans have long complained about in Mexico. The visitors would be told one thing only to discover that what they were told seemed to bear no resemblance to the facts. A delegate who would ask where a meeting was being held might be given clear directions, but upon reaching the destination she would find no such meeting. "It was not that the Mexicans were unfriendly or unhelpful – just wrong!" North American managers working with Mexicans have sometimes voiced similar complaints: an employee says something is finished when in fact it has not even been begun.

Rogelio Díaz-Guerrero, head of the psychology department at the National University of Mexico and a foremost interpreter of Mexican behavior patterns, offers this explanation. There are two kinds of "realities" which must be distinguished, objective and interpersonal. Some cultures tend to treat everything in terms of the objective sort of reality: this is characteristic of the United States. Other cultures tend to treat things in terms of interpersonal relations, and this is true of Mexico....

Viewed from the Mexican perspective, a visitor asks somebody for information which that person doesn't know. But wanting to make the visitor happy and to enjoy a few pleasant moments together, the Mexican who was asked does his best to say something so that for a short while the visitor is made happy. It is not that Mexicans have a monopoly on telling another person what that person wants to hear: perhaps in all cultures the truth is sometimes altered slightly to soften the impact of a harsh truth or to show deference to one's superior. It is the range of situations in which this occurs in Mexico and the relatively sharper contrast of "truth-telling" standards in U.S.–Mexican encounters that is so notable.

In value, if not always in fact, North Americans have given special importance to telling the truth. The clearest object lessons in the lives of the nation's two legendary heroes, Washington and Lincoln, concern honesty, while the Presidents who have been most held in disrepute, Harding and Nixon, are held up to scorn because of their dishonesty.

Francisco Gonzalez Pineda has written at length about lying. Starting from premises similar to those offered by Samuel Ramos mentioned earlier, including the idealization of manliness of the *pelado*, Gonzalez Pineda says that a Mexican must be able to lie if he is to be able to live without complete demoralization. He says that general recognition of this has made the lie in Mexico almost an institution. He describes variations of lies in different regions of Mexico, including the capital in which he says the use of the lie is socially acceptable in all its forms. He contrasts the Mexican style of lie to that which is used by North Americans. In the United States the lie is little used aggressively or defensively or to express fantasy. The more common form of defense is the expression of the incomplete truth or an evasion of truth. There are stereotyped expressions which are purposefully ambiguous and impersonal, so lacking in emotional content that they do not conflict with the emotional state of the liar.

Whether or not one supports the interpretation of Gonzalez Pineda, an examination of difficulties between North Americans and Mexicans is to be found in the broad area of matching words, deeds and intentions. The North American in a daily routine has a much narrower range of what he considers permissible than is found in similar situations in Mexico.

Time

If a culture is known by the words exported, as one theory has it, then Mexico may be best known as the land of *mañana*. Differences in the treatment of time may not be the most serious source of misunderstanding between people of the two cultures but it is surely the most often mentioned. Several issues are actually grouped under the general label of "time."

In Edward Hall's influential writings on time across culture, he has distinguished between "monochronic" (M-time) and "polychronic" (P-time) treatments of time (Hall 1966); these correspond to the North American and Mexican modes respectively. M-time values take care of "one thing at a time." Time is lineal, segmented. (American football is a very "M-time" game.) It may not be that time is money but M-time treats it that way, with measured precision. M-time people like neat scheduling of appointments and are easily distracted and often very distressed by interruptions.

In contrast, P-time is characterized by many things happening at once, and with a much "looser" notion of what is "on time" or "late." Interruptions are routine, delays to be expected. Thus it is not so much that putting things off until *mañana* is valued, as some Mexican stereotypes would have it, but that human activities are not expected to proceed like clock-work. It should be noted in this regard that the North American treatment of time appears to be the more unusual on a world scale. This writer discovered that even in Japan, a culture not known for its imprecision or indolence, U.S. business people were seen by Japanese colleagues as much too time-bound, driven by schedules and deadlines which in turn thwarted an easy development of human relationships.

North Americans express special irritation when Mexicans seem to give them less than their undivided attention. When a young woman bank teller, awaiting her superior's approval for a check to be cashed, files her nails and talks on the phone to her boyfriend, or when one's taxi driver stops en route to pick up a friend who seems to be going in the same direction, North Americans become very upset. North Americans interpret such behavior as showing a lack of respect and a lack of "professionalism," but the reason may lie more in the culturally different treatment of time.

Newly arrived residents seem to learn quickly to adjust their mental clocks to *la hora Mexicana* when it comes to anticipating the arrival of Mexican guests at a party; an invitation for 8:00 may produce guests by 9:00 or 10:00. What takes more adjusting is the notion that visitors may be going to another party first and yet another party afterwards. For many North Americans this diminishes the importance attached to their party, much as the teller's action diminishes the respect shown the customer. The counterpart of this, Mexicans' irritation with the North American time sense, is in their dismay over an invitation to a party which states in advance the time when the party will be over. This or subtler indications of the time to terminate a meeting before it has even gotten underway serve as further proof that Americans are slaves to the clock and don't really know how to enjoy themselves.

The identification of common problem areas in communication across cultures is always incomplete; there are always other interpretations and, since culture is a whole, the selection of "factors" or "themes" is never completely shown in its entire context. Nevertheless, a common effort to appreciate differences across cultures is essential, particularly in the relations between people of the United States and Mexico.

It is not an exaggeration to say that if North Americans cannot learn to communicate more effectively with Mexicans, [their] capacity to function in cultures elsewhere in the world will be doubted. Many of the well-springs of Mexican culture flow freely elsewhere, not only in other Latin American states but in such distant lands as the Philippines.

Questions for consideration

1. Are you satisfied with the author's use of the term "North American" to refer to persons of the United States of America? Where does this leave the Mexican, who geographically at least is a North American? and the Canadian? How might you explain why people of the United States are generally referred to simply as Americans?
2. How might differing feelings about individualism affect attitudes of Americans and Mexicans toward "waiting one's turn"?
3. What problems might arise in the teacher–student relationship for

a Mexican student in the United States from differing attitudes toward time and truth? for a U.S. student in Mexico?
4. How might role play be used in teaching such concepts as truth and time in a specific culture?

9 Cultural clues to the Middle Eastern student

Orin D. Parker and Educational Services Staff, AFME
American Friends of the Middle East (AMIDEAST)

"I believe, in all sincerity, that there is no substitute for direct person-to-person contacts that go deep into the heart of all the problems which invoke our common concern and capture our imagination. There is no better way to reach a profound insight of the complexity of the world we live in and grasp the immense problems we face today and are likely to encounter in the future. In the process, our opinions might differ and our views might occasionally diverge. Indeed, our culture emphasizes diversity and multiplicity as a means of reaching consensus and compatibility. What is required is not identity of viewpoints, but a genuine acceptance of each other's right to hold different opinions and entertain different ideas."

Anwar el-Sadat
President of the Arab Republic of Egypt
(In a speech to the United States Congress,
Washington, DC, 5 November 1975)

Middle Eastern students, whether Arab or non-Arab, Muslim or Christian, share many distinctive characteristics. From AMIDEAST's long experience with the area, we have selected certain characteristics that should be of particular interest to those working with Middle Eastern students on American campuses. Although descriptive primarily of Arab Muslims, they can be considered relevant to Middle Eastern students as a whole, with the exception of the Israeli student. Students from Israel, cast more from a European than a Middle Eastern cultural mold, will not necessarily reflect these patterns. However, as is true of most generalizations regarding human society, one should anticipate many exceptions to the "cultural clues" that follow.

Almost all who deal with foreign students in the U.S. agree that Middle Eastern students are among the most adaptable. They can become fully "Americanized" within a short time. Those who have seen them in the U.S. and in their own countries can only marvel at how differently they behave in each culture. A student who has become a classic student type in the U.S. will often readapt within months of his return to his own society's norms. As a common example, we all know of the numbers of

Middle Eastern students who willingly earn their support here by waiting on tables in university dining halls or commercial restaurants – a task they would not think of doing in their own countries, where social organization is highly stratified, division of labor is primarily on a class basis, and social mobility, although growing, is still difficult.

Such adaptability is not a weakness. The Middle Eastern student is not being fickle or shallow. The roots of such behavior lie within a basic characteristic of his society. Social morality prevails over personal morality; thus, concepts of right and wrong, sin and shame, derive not from an individual's determination of appropriate behavior, but from what society in general dictates as the social norm. It is self-evident that every society has its own social conscience. For behavior guidelines, the individual looks to his family, his friends, his religion – the world around him. Thus, as a student in [the Western] world, the Middle Easterner observes and adapts to [that] way of life. On his return home, he reverts to his own ways, although not necessarily without a period of adjustment.

Wherever he may be, a Middle Easterner retains a certain formality of manner, particularly in initial social relationships. He comes from a culture in which formality pervades social customs and daily routines. Even a casual encounter with a friend will begin with oft-used and elaborately formal words of greeting. In one sense, these formal patterns help keep people at a distance until one really knows them; they depersonalize relationships. In another sense they reflect the respect of one person for another. The Middle Easterner is consistently polite within his own culture, even to a person he dislikes. The Koran directs that "God loveth not the speaking ill of anyone in public." Thus, the Middle Easterner will not ordinarily "tell someone off" in public, and he expects similar consideration of others, particularly those who don't know him well. (We are speaking here of individual relationships, not of the mass media or public speeches.)

What holds true in speaking of others is equally true in writing. It would be unusual for a Middle Easterner to write down a critical judgement of anyone. The most relevant example for American educators is a letter of recommendation. A Middle Easterner will give his worst enemy a good letter of recommendation. In ten years of experience in the Middle East – in Iraq and Lebanon – I never saw a letter of recommendation from one Arab about another that discussed any negative aspects of performance or record. It is not a matter of dishonesty; on the contrary, the Middle Easterner regards as immoral our willingness to be frank in this way and to go on record regarding another's "faults."

Growing up in a paternalistic society is another factor which helps determine the behavioral characteristics of Middle Eastern students. Within the family, parents' word is final, and great respect for elders is expected and given. In his excellent book, *The Arab World Today* (1962), Morroe Berger compares the reaction of Muslims and Christians (or more broadly, Arabs and Westerners) to one of the parables of the New Testament (Matthew 21:28), in which a man asks his two sons to do some work in the vineyard. One said he would, but did not; the second said he would not, but then relented and did the work. The Westerner would give greater credit to the second son, while the Arab would consider the first, who showed respect for his father although he did not follow through, more admirable.

The paternalistic familial pattern and its authoritative hierarchy extends throughout society. This is reflected in the region's educational system, which emphasizes an *imitative* rather than a *creative* approach to learning; traditionally, students have learned primarily by memorization and imitation rather than by independent research and original work. Moreover, the individual's academic choices will often reflect his father's desires rather than his own wishes or capabilities. However, one should not assume that this method of career selection, which contrasts so sharply with our own emphasis on individual choice and fulfillment, necessarily produces unhappy people. Of course, in some cases, it does.

Hostility and suspicion may well be characteristics of the Middle Eastern student when he first arrives in the United States. Distrust of foreigners runs deep in his part of the world, where history reflects endless wars, invasions, and occupations. In addition, the region has generated three of the world's major religions; in recent centuries, Western missionary movements have returned to the Middle East in force. They have brought many major benefits to the region's peoples, particularly in terms of medical and educational development, but for some in an area predominantly Muslim, the missionary movement has increased suspicion of the West.

This suspicion can show up in matters so seemingly simple to us as completing a university application form. We have had a student argue for more than an hour over why he should enter the name of his mother on such a form. In his view, any information not absolutely relevant and essential should not be revealed. Similarly, anthropologists doing research in the Middle East quickly learn that standard Western questionnaire techniques do not work. Anyone coming into a community and asking questions may appear to the Middle Easterner to be a spy, and is thus avoided. One American researcher in Egypt wanted to conduct a survey that solicited opinions as well as facts on a certain subject. He constructed his form so that the factual information was solicited first and the opinions second. To the second section he added an explanation of the need for opinions, since his experience had indicated that while anyone will give facts, many will not give opinions without understanding the legitimate reasons for soliciting them. His Egyptian colleague looked it over and suggested he reverse the order and put his explanations with the section soliciting facts; Arabs will easily give opinions, but facts are only reluctantly divulged.

Middle Easterners hold tremendous pride in their heritage: in their historical, cultural, and religious contributions to the world. They also exhibit increasing pride in their contemporary societies and their capabilities to interact internationally as equals with other nations. Most students arrive in the U.S. with great self-confidence; it can be a shock when they do not encounter among their new American acquaintances any great awareness of their part of the world and its significance. They are sensitive to what people know and think of their region; they want an opportunity to share and be heard.

Upon arriving in the U.S., Middle Eastern students are often particularly disconcerted to encounter ignorance of Islam and to find themselves considered unbelievers. The religion of Islam has predominated in the Arab Middle East for centuries, and continues to do so today. Any attempt to define Arab "culture" must recognize Islam as its foundation. Even those who no longer observe all its tenets remain loyal to its basic concepts and give Islam its proper respect. Within Islam, Christians and Jews have held from the beginning a special place of respect as *people of the Book* – worshippers of the same God and heirs to a common religious tradition. Muslims consider their religion as the culmination of a long development process: from Judaism to Christianity to Islam. Prophets of the Old Testament are recognized as prophets within Islam; Christ is so recognized as well. Thus, it is totally surprising for a Middle Easterner to find himself considered outside the Judaeo-Christian tradition.

His religious heritage goes far to explain the Middle Eastern student's attitude of fatalism toward events in his life and in society around him. In his culture, God is revered as truly omnipotent; all things happen as God wills. Most of us know the phrase, *Inshallah* or "God willing." To many Americans, this sounds suspiciously like *mañana* or "someday," but it is not nearly so simple. Some years ago, in one of our field offices, the newly arrived American director found every instruction to his assistant acknowledged with *Inshallah*. Finally exasperated, the director stated that he expected his instructions to be followed as a matter of course, not *Inshallah*. The assistant responded that they would be, but like everything else in life, only if God were willing. One does not question the will of God.

Personal relationships are extremely important to Middle Easterners. For them, the central thing in life is people – family and friendships. They observe our rush to experience everything, and to acquire everything, as laying waste to the truly important matters of life. "Haste is of the devil," says the Koran. They see us as sacrificing people for things.

To his two or three good friends, the Middle Easterner will give generously of himself and his time. On each side there will be a sense of affection, of closeness, and of mutual obligation in time of need. Our American friendships, quickly formed and sometimes quickly ended, appear to him shallow and uncommitted.

In the Middle East, close friendships will commonly form between those of the same sex. In the U.S., the male Middle Eastern student may develop more friendships among female peers. This is not only because of the wider possibilities for female friendship that he finds here, but may also result from his inability to find American male friends willing to accept the close ties that the Middle Easterner feels true friendship requires.

Altogether, the opportunity to get to know women both personally and as fellow students can be a highly valued component of the U.S. educational experience. However, much initial confusion can be anticipated on behalf of the Middle Eastern student as he enters into male/female relationships in the U.S. His own society remains male-dominated; although influences such as education and urbanization are having their effects, women as a group still play a less prominent role than men. Relationships between men and women are surrounded with restrictions. Our more free-and-easy relationships among young men and women often lead the newly arrived Middle Easterner to unfortunate misconceptions. We should perhaps be even more aware of the pitfalls facing a young Middle Eastern woman coming here. She is unfamiliar with the life-style of young American women and unprepared for the expectations her fellow students — both male and female — are likely to have of her. An American date will raise for her a host of behavioral unknowns.

One cannot survey common characteristics of Middle Easterners without noting the significance of language in their lives. We have already noted how even a casual encounter may be surrounded with formal and specific words of greeting and departure. Proverbs and verses of the Koran are common in conversation and writing. Among traditional Islamic "sciences," one finds philology, rhetoric and criticism, lexicography, grammar, literature, and poetry. Arabs are in love with language. Men gather in coffee shops to listen for hours to poetry recitals. Important events are noted in speeches, songs, and poems. In everyday life, *how* one says something becomes almost as important as *what* one says. Words carry a weight and importance of their own. To talk, listen, and share words is important to the Arab.

With all of these cultural characteristics in mind, we turn to some of the Middle Eastern student's *needs* during his education in the United States. Based on our experience, they include the following.

— First, he needs *respect* — for himself and his people, for his country and its customs, for his religion. He is not unique in responding warmly to those with genuine interest in him as a person and in learning from him as well as teaching him about his new life here. Such matters as matching the arriving Arab student with an American roommate can be fraught with hazards if the American brings into the experience nothing more than a general willingness to share a room with a foreigner. One of our students was sure his American roommate hated him. Every night when they were studying, the American put his feet up on his desk, soles pointing directly at his Arab roommate. In most Arab countries, this is an insult – the worst kind of insult. Eventually a real friendship developed between the two, but many early misunderstandings could have been avoided if the American had been more sensitive to his new friend's reactions and had helped create an atmosphere in which the latter could begin to feel free to share his feelings.

— The Middle Easterner also needs a *close personal relationship*, or *friendship*. Those universities with well-established host-family programs can use this possible channel. American roommates may be an answer, but *only* if those Americans participating are well prepared to make the extra effort required to give this kind of exchange a chance of success. On almost any campus, students interested in this kind of outreach can be found; if they cannot be utilized in roommate situations, they can be drawn into other kinds of activities.

— Like other students, the Middle Easterner needs *casual social relationships*. Interaction with families or other groups of students in an informal way, with opportunities for relaxing, talking, listening, and sharing, can do much to help him feel at home. If one remembers the ever-present coffee shop, found on nearly every street corner in his own world, one can instantly feel the kind of informal human exchange he will miss in ours.

— Thinking again of the coffee shop, we should become sensitive to the Middle Easterner's need for *food and hospitality*. In the Middle East, they go together like mosques and minarets. It is unheard of to visit anyone, including a business visit to an office, without being served some kind of refreshment. It is a shock for a Middle Eastern student to visit someone and not be offered even a cup of coffee or a soft drink. To him, hospitality without refreshment is not complete. Its significance can be noted by the care with which food is prepared and presented. For some Middle Easterners, the assembly-line atmosphere of a U.S. cafeteria can be as much of a shock as the food itself.

— Implicit in some of the above is a need for *conversation*. The Middle Easterner's daily diet of hearty, concerned conversation may be almost as difficult for him to find here as good rice and fresh bread.

In his new bilingual world, he needs plenty of opportunity to use his English outside the classroom. But he also needs to hear his own language and to share conversation with other Arab students. It can be a mistake to have a "ghetto" of Arab students, or any other national group, living together on a campus, but nonetheless, Arab students need to get together and stay in touch with their language and culture. In a different context, the Middle Eastern student's reliance on oral communication means that a ten-minute conversation face-to-face with his advisor will be more significant for him than a two-page written analysis of his work.

— The newly arrived student in particular has a need for a *mentor from his own culture.* He is no different from others in finding that the experience of a "big brother," someone who has already gone through much of what he is encountering, can be a tremendous support. With the numbers of Middle Eastern students now on U.S. campuses, the new student takes care of this on his own, but it is useful to be aware of this need.

— With his faculty and administration advisors, the Middle Eastern student needs a *paternal relationship.* He expects to look up to his advisors and professors and receive strong guidance from them. With acclimation, he will work well within our more fraternal sets of relationships, but initially, he will thrive better in a more disciplined situation.

— And finally, he needs *to have his good deeds repaid and to have an opportunity to repay you.* There is an Arab saying, "Please don't be grateful, you will repay me." It is not intended to be self-serving, but to reflect an exchange of consideration and obligation that the Middle Easterner sees implicit in friendship. He expects a favor in return for the favor he does for you, and he expects to be able to repay you when you do a favor for him. Give him that chance.

At the outset, we suggested that many exceptions could be found to the observations we would make. Perhaps one final "clue" might be offered, and that is to avoid looking at the Arab world as a homogeneous mass from Morocco to Arabia. There are Mediterranean and mountain peoples as well as bedouin; there are Christians, Jews, Zoroastrians, and other religious groups as well as Muslims; there are city-dwellers, farmers, and nomads. The region's ethnic mosaic is rich: from Berbers and Tuaregs in the West, to Nubians in Upper Egypt, to Armenians, Druze, and Kurds in the East. While seeking the commonality among them, the variations must not be forgotten.

An awareness of the Middle Eastern student's general cultural characteristics and sympathy with his needs does not diminish the fact that the student himself must bear the major burden of adjusting to life in the United States. As with all foreign students, he must sort out *American* "cultural clues," adapt himself to American ways, and pursue his education on American terms. He is prepared to do this; on the part of Americans, a heightened sensitivity to his cultural background can ease his transition. We offer these "clues" in the hope that they will aid both students and advisors in achieving their common goal – a rewarding educational experience.

Questions for consideration

1. How might a Middle Easterner react to a society that is less formal and polite than his own?
2. In light of what the authors have told us about the attitudes of Middle Eastern students, what values and attitudes from your culture are most important to teach to these students in order for them to thrive in these environments?
3. Would a field trip for Middle Eastern students to an American or British children's school be a good idea? Why or why not?
4. How are Middle Eastern students likely to regard their teachers in a foreign land?

10 XANADU – "A miracle of rare device": the teaching of English in China

Alan Maley
The British Council

It is often said that those who visit China for a week write a book about it. Those who stay a month write an article. And those who live here a year or more – write nothing. I cannot claim the status of a China expert, having lived here for only a year and a half, yet I have the temerity to write at least an article because my work here involves me at many levels of the complex English teaching scene, because I feel it is worth the effort to try to clarify some of the issues and problems which attend the teaching of English in China, and because I shall confine myself to the impact of foreign teachers in China.

It should be said at the outset that any statement made on the subject must be open to modification or refutation because China is enormous, and it is far from being the monolith it appears from outside. Apart from geographical variation, there is a diversity of opinion and attitude at the human level which has to be experienced to be believed. This article then is an attempt to find a handhold on the slippery slopes of the mountain that is China.

In doing so, I shall be critical since there is little point in making purely cosmetic remarks, the sole intention of which is to please. My basic stance is one of a friend, and true friendship can surely withstand the expression of frank opinion. I wish then, initially, to examine a number of problems which, it seems to me, impair the efficiency of foreign teachers within TEFL in China.

Semantic problems

"When *I* use a word," Humpty Dumpty said, "it means just what I choose it to mean – neither more nor less".

And that is the first problem, since I seem to note that there are a number of key words which are interpreted differently by Chinese host

Reprinted from *Language Learning and Communication* 2(1): 97–104. © 1983 by John Wiley & Sons, Inc. Reprinted by permission of John Wiley & Sons, Inc., and Alan Maley.

and foreign guest. It is not possible to give an exhaustive list of such words or expressions, but these appear to be among the more important:

(a). *Teacher training.* Most Chinese host institutions take this to mean language improvement for their teachers. No notion of methodological improvement enters into their calculations. If their teachers "know" more English, they will teach better. This, for them, is axiomatic.

Most foreign teachers who are told they are to do teacher training tend to view the term in a different light. Better command of the target language by the teacher is a necessary but not a sufficient condition. Teacher training, for them, includes an important element of methodology, classroom observation, materials trial and development, and so on. These are two very different, if not irreconcilable, views of the same term.

(b). *Literature.* This also tends to have different connotations for different people. The teaching of English literature at most Chinese universities is set in the mould of the survey course, which gives an overview of who wrote what when and whether it is any good or not. Along with this usually goes the study of short extracts from approved authors. By contrast, the view of most foreign teachers is that the teaching of literature involves equipping the student with the tools to deal with any text; with developing critical judgment. One approach looks at the product, the other at the process.

(c). *E.S.P.* English for Special (or latterly, for Specific) Purposes is clearly one of the keys to TEFL in China. One of the main reasons for learning English is to secure access to the scientific and technical expertise available through it. Yet the understanding of the term is not at all uniform. On the one side, the view prevails of ESP as an agglomeration of specialist vocabulary to be internalised; on the other, that it consists in characteristic ways of organising thought and language for a given purpose. According to one's view of ESP, the approach to it through materials and methodology will be widely different.

(d). *Book.* For many Chinese students and teachers books are thought of as an embodiment of knowledge, wisdom and truth. Knowledge is "in" the book and can be taken out and put inside the students' heads. Hence the reverence with which books are treated, the value they are assigned, and the wish to learn by heart what they contain.

For many, if not all, foreigners, books may contain facts, opinions and ideas. The facts are open to interpretation, the opinions to dispute and the ideas to discussion. There is nothing sacred about books, which are regarded as tools for learning – not the goal of learning.

(e). *Reading.* The Chinese attitude towards books is reflected in the approach to teaching reading in English. Most foreign teachers encounter the course entitled "Intensive Reading" with some surprise. It consists in taking students through a text on a word by word, phrase by phrase basis, explaining points of vocabulary, syntax, style and content along the way – rather like the *explication de texte* in the classic French tradition. The text is used as a pretext for intensive, but *ad hoc*, examination of the language it contains.

The foreign teacher tends to find this obsessive concern with the fine detail of his language somewhat irritating since, for him, reading is something else; namely, it is teaching students to extract meaning and information from texts as rapidly and efficiently as possible, and to apply it to their current concern. This process is not, in their view, served by squeezing each text dry, since intensive reading concentrates attention on a necessarily small number of texts, rather than equipping the student with tools to deal with a wide range of texts (or indeed with any text).

(f). *Test*. The misunderstandings which arise from the use of this word are not confined to China, of course. However, even taking account of overgeneralisation, it does appear that, to the Chinese, a test is something a student passes or fails. And he does so because a pass mark in the form of a percentage has been fixed, often in a quite arbitrary fashion. There seems to be little appreciation of the fact that any score is open to interpretation, that is, that it is not an absolute. Nor is it acknowledged that there are different types of tests for different purposes, or that there are some kinds of courses which cannot be tested at all.

To the foreign teacher with even a nodding acquaintance with the theory and practice of testing, such a view is very difficult to accept. Increasingly tests are being used to diagnose the learners' language profile and assess his progress. This move away from norm-referenced to criterion-referenced testing is much more interested in what the learner can do than in what he cannot do, and it attempts to assign relative rather than absolute values to the results.

It would be possible to go on adding to this list of words which, owing to their differing interpretations, cause misunderstandings, and even conflict, between Chinese teaching institutions and their foreign guest teachers. But it is time to pass to other types of problems.

Views of the learning process and the study habits of Chinese students

It must be clear from the above that Chinese student and foreign teacher rarely share the same views on the nature of the teaching process. Even now the most widely accepted view of learning in China is that it is memory-based. The teacher, or the textbook, has the knowledge. In order to acquire it, it is sufficient for the student to commit it to memory. This inevitably condemns both teachers and students to the use of non-meaningful approaches, in which grammatical form (usually devoid of contextual meaning) takes precedence over meaningful communication.

There is likewise a heavy load of vocabulary learning (but without the range of contexts which would make it useful) and an attention to the finer points of grammar, which transforms the language being taught into a series of conundrums to be solved, rather than a vehicle for communication.

The foreign teacher is liable to regard this approach and these learning habits as misguided. His students will want to know the difference between gerunds, gerundives and participles, without being able to answer simple questions about themselves and their lives. They will spend hours on the learning of abstruse vocabulary items and idioms which they will rarely be capable of using appropriately. And they will often regard the less directive teaching methods of the foreign teacher as a waste of time.

The foreign teacher will admire the assiduity of his students, both in and out of class. But given that so often these study habits lead to knowledge about the language as an object rather than competence in using it as a tool, he will be disappointed. His students demonstrate their ability to work hard at digging a hole. But all too often, it is dug in the wrong place.

Curriculum planning and the definition of objectives

There seem to be very few courses with clearly defined objectives. Whenever questioned on the aims and objectives of a given course, the departmental head (or equivalent) is likely to answer in the vaguest of terms. "We want to upgrade the level of our teachers, improve the four skills, get some knowledge of modern English literature, improve oral English, prepare our students for study abroad, etc.". But such well-intentioned remarks are not usually accompanied by a corresponding system of minor objectives which can be mapped on to a syllabus and find its realisation in materials and teaching techniques. In most cases therefore the foreign teacher is simply left to find his own salvation without clear guidance as to what it is precisely that he is supposed to be aiming at. This often leads to a feeling on the part of the foreign teacher that, since no one else is able to tell him which way he should be going, there is no reason for him to exert himself either. He is, after all, usually paid to teach, not to do curriculum planning. If no one else can tell him what kinds of thing to teach, then clearly "anything goes".

Alan Maley

Recruitment of foreign teachers

Just as there is little guidance on the objectives of the programmes which foreign teachers are asked to teach, so there is a corresponding lack of direction in the field of recruitment.

One needs perhaps first to make a distinction between various systems of recruitment of teachers for China. There are those recruited by external agencies (such as UCLA, Georgetown University, British Council, Australian Development Aid Bureau, etc.). Given that they recruit for specific and usually well-defined projects, they will not be discussed here. Apart from these, the foreign teachers are usually recruited semi-officially (for example when a Chinese scholar returns from overseas and persuades his university to invite a teacher from the foreign university or through other kinds of personal invitation), or officially via the Foreign Experts Bureau (with the assistance of Chinese Embassies abroad).

Secondly, it is necessary to distinguish between the category Foreign Expert (directly recruited by the Foreign Experts Bureau and with return fares paid, agreed salary and perquisites) and the category Foreign Teacher (often the sort of person recruited through connections of some kind, who pays his own fare and does not get the same salary or privileges as a Foreign Expert). There is also latterly, the category of "volunteer", usually recruited by the U.N., V.S.O. [Voluntary Service Overseas], or V.I.A. [Volunteers in Asia], who gets a rock-bottom allowance and few if any privileges.

As far as the informally recruited group of teachers is concerned, it often seems that the sole criterion for employment is: "If it walks, and talks English, it is O.K.". In other words, provided the person has some sort of university qualification (in no matter what subject) and is a native speaker of English, then he is acceptable. No qualification or experience in the teaching of English as a foreign (or second) language is required.

The Foreign Experts Bureau, ostensibly at any rate, insists on the highest qualifications, and its pay scale varies accordingly. On closer examination, however, its criteria are not so very different: "If it walks, and talks English, and has an M.A. or Ph.D., it's O.K." (The Foreign Experts Bureau has on several occasions stated its preference for retired high-school or university teachers in any subject).

The recruitment scene then is beset by many paradoxes and inconsistencies. One comes across the result in terms of human wastage all over China...

— with the "see China and die" brigade, who are here for the experience, and are neither qualified for, nor capable of, doing an honest job of teaching.

106

- with teachers of history or whatever, possessing Ph.D.s or M.A.s, completely at sea, trying to come to terms with teaching their own language for the first time.
- with well-qualified TESL professionals often working well below their capacity on language improvement courses which could clearly be done by less well-qualified teachers.

Again one could prolong the list, and draw up the list of exceptions. However, the observations I have been able to make are largely subsumed under the above categories.

My, no doubt highly personal, view is that, if "friends" are preferred to "experts", if academic title is preferred to proven field experience, if the role of the foreign teacher is not thought through, and if programme objectives are not properly planned, then the result is waste – waste of state money on salaries for teachers who take half a year to find out what their job is and how to do it, waste of student energy on teachers who do not deserve the effort, waste of expertise being underused, and waste of goodwill between the teacher, the learner and the institution.

Lack of information

With reference to [curriculum planning and the definition of objectives], it is clear that few foreign teachers coming to China have any clear indication of exactly what it is they are expected to do. From their personal point of view, however, it is perhaps even more disturbing to discover that they do not even know exactly what their terms of employment are. No teacher is given a contract until, at the earliest, two months after his arrival. His salary is fixed provisionally for the first two months, after which it is supposed to be revised in the light of his performance. China must be unique in this respect. Moreover, in spite of stipulations that contracts will be negotiated, what more often happens is that the foreign teacher is presented with a document which he is expected to sign without further ado. And some teachers never succeed in obtaining a contract at all. This introduces an element of insecurity into the employer/employee relationship, which is far from healthy, and which in almost all cases builds up to conflict before the contractual period is up.

Bureaucracy

The following phrases, and others like them, will have a familiar ring to anyone who has taught in China:

107

"We are discussing the matter."
"It is not convenient."
"It will take a little time to decide."
"We need to discuss with leadership."
The foreign teacher cannot understand why even apparently innocuous and minor requests cannot be agreed to immediately, and he finds it even more frustrating to be fobbed off with temporising responses. On the other hand, he often fails to realise quite how complicated decision-making is in China, where many things are decided by an elaborate process of consensus. Nor perhaps does he realise that the responses he gets are a reflection of the embarrassment his host experiences at having to refuse a request, rather than the outright untruths he takes them to be.

The sad thing is that decisions are often taken by those least qualified to do so, and this is nowhere more true than in decisions touching upon professional matters. Furthermore, the foreign teacher is rarely, if ever, consulted while decisions which concern him or her, personally or professionally, are being made.

Isolation

Many foreign teachers feel cut off and alone. Clearly both geography and language account in part for this. It is not easy to find oneself thousands of miles from home, in the middle of an alien culture, the language of which is in most cases totally unfamiliar. But they often feel alienated socially and psychologically too. Many arrive with high hopes of integrating fairly closely with their Chinese colleagues and students. They swiftly discover that the Chinese have a different view of their presence. They tend to be regarded as tools for improving the English of the students, to be taken out of the drawer in classtime, and put away again afterwards. They are normally housed separately from their students and colleagues, often in specially-constructed foreign teachers' buildings, and they usually eat separately too. Most out of class contacts are carefully orchestrated. "Normal" person to person relationships on an individual level are frowned upon by the authorities.

A more charitable view would make the point that very few foreign teachers would survive Chinese living conditions, and that their hosts are making them as comfortable as they possibly can, often at great expense, so that they feel more at ease and can do a better job. The fact remains however that whether one regards these special conditions as a way of inhibiting unwelcome contact between the foreigner and his colleagues and students, or as an act of kindness towards the foreign teacher, the result is the same – isolation. He desperately wishes to be trusted and included, and he feels hurt that he is not.

Zenmeban?

It must be clear from the foregoing that large numbers of foreign teachers return from China with dampened enthusiasm, feelings of disappointment and in some cases bitterness and rancour. And I have little doubt that their Chinese hosts often privately feel that these foreigners are a weird lot and wonder if it is worth all the time, energy and money they expend on having them.

What could be done to improve matters? The problems fall into roughly three categories – pedagogical, recruitment/personnel, and bureaucratic/personal.

Pedagogical problems

It is a mistake for the foreign teacher to arrive thinking he has brought the good news in the form of his up-to-date methods and materials. Chinese study habits are deeply rooted and a frontal attack on them is pointless. There are ways, however, of turning these study habits to good use. For instance, by cashing in on the enormous amount of time students spend in private study. At present they most often engage in tasks which are unrewarding in learning terms, like committing the text book to memory. But properly designed self-study materials for Chinese students would have an enormous pay-off. Another idea would be to assign more out-of-class group tasks, thus harnessing the strong group solidarity. In fact one is often driven to wonder whether too much classroom teaching is done at the expense of properly organised out-of-class learning.

However, it is equally a mistake for Chinese teachers and staff to dismiss foreign techniques and materials as irrelevant. There is an inconsistency in proclaiming the policy of the Four Modernisations, while at the same time claiming that China is so different that nothing foreign can possibly work there.

This brings me to my next suggestion, which is that if more foreign teachers were involved in well-defined projects with counterpart training of Chinese staff, many of the pedagogical problems would be dealt with. One such project could involve the development of teaching materials by both Chinese and foreign teachers. This cooperation would be an excellent way to break down barriers, reduce the isolation mentioned above and come to a better mutual understanding of how to deal with the pedagogical problems.

Further, if the pedagogical objectives were better defined by the

Chinese host institutions, and if professional decisions were made by those professionally qualified to do so, some of the pedagogical problems would begin to disappear. There are after all increasing numbers of young Chinese University teachers who have qualified in applied linguistics and methodology in the United States and the United Kingdom. Unhappily, they are often considered too "junior" to use their newly acquired skills and knowledge when they return to their institutions.

Recruitment and personnel problems

If pedagogical objectives were better defined it would be possible to identify the kinds of teacher needed to achieve them.

If there were more detailed and more accurate information available to teachers before they come to China, many of the subsequent misunderstandings would never arise.

Part of this would involve bringing Chinese practice on the drawing up and issuing of contracts into line with the rest of the world. This would also save all the drawn out and often bitter wrangling which so often goes on at present.

Personal and bureaucratic problems

It would help if both Chinese and foreign teachers had slightly lower expectations. The foreign teacher is rarely likely to be the paragon of virtue, industry, brilliance and omniscience expected by his employers. Foreign teachers, for their part, should not expect within weeks to become the soul mates of students and colleagues or be acclaimed as bringers of pedagogical manna in the wilderness.

Each culture has its own time scale. In the West we tend to expect things to happen in a hurry. In China the normally expected time interval is often longer. There has to be adjustment – on both sides. Foreign teachers have to realise that, for whatever reason, things may take longer than they do back home. But there is also a need for a realisation on the part of their hosts that the Chinese time scale may not always be appropriate if the aim is an effective programme of modernisation.

There are I think hopeful signs on this front. Those teachers who stay on for a second year usually find that many difficulties simply evaporate. Is this because they no longer notice? Is it because they and their employers have effected a mutual *modus vivendi*? Or is it because they have proved themselves and are now accepted? Probably a bit of all three. However, there is little doubt that two year contracts would be better than the one year or less which most teachers serve at present. A year is not enough for foreign teacher and Chinese institution to come to terms with each other.

Foreign teachers with a problem would do well to avoid confrontations, which most often have the effect of stiffening the resistance. Patient persistence pays best. And if the assistance of a well-disposed third party can be enlisted to act as go-between, it often helps.

On the Chinese side, it would help if there were more open dialogue and less secrecy. Foreigners expect to be consulted about things which affect their lives, and are understandably upset if they are suddenly presented with decisions in which they had no hand and with which they may profoundly disagree. So, on the one hand more patience – on the other more openness.

Experience should warn us not to expect too much. To return to Alice:

... the Queen said, "The rule is, jam tomorrow and jam yesterday – but never jam *today*."

"It *must* come sometimes to 'jam today', Alice objected.

Dare we hope she was right?

Questions for consideration

1. Is there a difference in the Chinese attitude toward books described by Maley and the "Third World" – or Islamic – view described by Osterloh in Chapter 7? What is the importance of a knowledge of these attitudes to a language teacher in a class of mixed cultural backgrounds?
2. Certainly a feeling of isolation from the students would affect teachers' enjoyment of their job. How would it affect a teacher's effectiveness?
3. Time scale seems to be a problem in intercultural relations between the United States and most other cultures. How can this phenomenon be accounted for?
4. The administrator–foreign teacher relationship in China is seen to be a difficult one, perhaps understandably where two such diverse cultures are involved. Do you find similar problems, particularly with the upper administration in your own unicultural institution? How can these similarities be accounted for? What are the major differences, and how can they be accounted for?
5. How well do Maley's suggestions for improvement seem to approach a partial solution? Given the situation, how much hope do you see for his suggestions being carried out? Why?

11 Compliments in cross-cultural perspective

Nessa Wolfson
University of Pennsylvania

Communicative competence is now widely recognized as an important goal of language teaching, and a good deal has been written concerning the necessity of making knowledge about sociolinguistic rules a part of classroom instruction in ESL or, indeed, in any second language (Hymes 1972; Grimshaw 1973; Paulston 1975; Applegate 1975; B. Taylor and Wolfson 1978). At the same time, sociolinguistic studies, particularly those which take as their rhetorical framework the ethnography of speaking as proposed by Dell Hymes (1962), have made it clear that languages differ greatly in patterns and norms of interaction. Up to this point, however, there has been very little systematic comparison of languages from the point of view of speech acts and rules of speaking, and as a result, very little attention paid to describing the sorts of communicative interference which may occur as people learn second languages.

As an example of the sort of sociolinguistic information needed in order to understand the problems facing second language learners, it is useful to examine in some detail one speech act: complimenting. For the past three years, my colleague Joan Manes and I have been engaged in a thoroughgoing analysis of complimenting behavior in American English (Manes and Wolfson 1981). For the purposes of comparison, we included in our corpus a small sample of compliments collected by non-native speakers of English interacting with members of their own speech communities, both in English and in their native languages.

Examination of these data makes it clear that a single speech act may vary greatly across speech communities. In particular, what counts as a compliment may differ very much from one society to another. Even allowing for problems of translation, some of the data which were collected by non-native speakers were totally unlike those gathered by native speakers of American English. Thus, an Indonesian student brought the following examples of compliments which he had heard in Indonesian and translated:

(1) S (Husband): You must have been tired doing all the shopping.
    A (Wife): Is it so? Now you can do the cooking.
(2) S (Friend): You have bought a sewing machine. How much does it
    cost?
    A: Oh, it is cheap. It's a used one. My wife needs it badly.
(3) S: You've saved a lot of money in your account, ha?
    A: Oh, no. Please don't tease me.

Of course, one could conclude from looking at these data that the non-
native speaker had simply not understood the meaning of the term
compliment in English. This hypothesis was unacceptable, however,
since the Indonesian data, and indeed every set of data, included at least
a few examples which were immediately recognizable to the English
speaker as compliments:

(4) S (Friend): You have a nice one-room apartment.
    A: Yes. The rent is expensive. It is a burden.
(5) S (Friend invited to dinner): The food is delicious. I am full.
    A (Hostess): If you come again next time, I'll prepare the same food.

Compliments such as these which concern a nice apartment and good
food are easy for English speakers to accept as falling within the category
of compliments. It is much more difficult for us to understand why it is
complimentary in Indonesian to mention that a friend has bought a
sewing machine, saved money or done a lot of shopping. From conversation with one of the Indonesians who had collected data, it became
clear that these remarks were given and interpreted as compliments
because they implied approval of the addressee's accomplishments. Further discussion revealed that although a term for complimenting exists
in Indonesian, native speakers feel that they occur relatively rarely and
usually only among the educated who have been exposed to Western
customs. Rural people, I was assured, rarely employ this speech act form.
    In contrast with these Indonesian examples, the data collected and
translated by native speakers of Japanese exhibit a great deal of resemblance to American English compliments:

(6) S: The hat is really good. It suits you very well.
    A: Oh, is that right? It's warm.
(7) S: This is nice. Did you buy it in New York?
    A: No, it's old. There's something wrong with the strap.
(8) S: Oh, you have a nice dress on, Mrs. A.

That there is so much similarity between Japanese and American compliments must not lead us to assume that the realization of this speech

act is identical in the two societies. As in the Indonesian data, some of the material collected as compliments in Japanese would certainly not be considered complimentary by a speaker of American English:

(9) S: Your earrings are pure gold, aren't they?
    A: Yes, they are. They must be pure gold when you put them on.
    S: Money is a necessary condition to become attractive, indeed.
    A: I think so too.

For speakers of American English it is difficult to accept the idea that it is considered complimentary to suggest that another's attractiveness depends on having money. When Japanese (or indeed any non-native) speakers produce compliments which conform to the rules of speaking for American English, the assumption is that they share these rules, and their deviations. Such deviations may therefore be more harshly interpreted than might rule-breaking from a speaker who clearly follows a very different system. Thus, the very fact that such similarities exist may lead to more serious misunderstandings than would otherwise occur.

Misunderstandings, of course, work in both directions. If we look at some data from American English, we can see that some of the comments that Americans regularly accept as compliments could easily seem very insulting to someone who understood the words but not the rules for interpreting them. For example, we have compliments by which the speaker, in saying that the addressee looks unusually well, implies that the reverse is usually the case. Thus, two men meet at an elevator and one says to the other:

(10) S: Hey, what's the occasion? You look really nice today.

Or two friends meet and one greets the other by exclaiming:

(11) S: Wow! Linda! What did you do to your hair? I almost didn't recognize you. It looks great.

Although Americans do not seem to take such remarks as anything but compliments, non-native speakers are often unsure of their meaning. Indeed, when a French speaker, living in this country while doing her graduate work and fully bilingual in English, received just such a compliment from a classmate, she assumed that an insult had been intended and was quite hurt.

Another noticeable contrast between American English compliments and those collected and translated by speakers of certain other languages is the difference in the use of proverbs and other pre-coded ritualized phrases. Compliments collected by Iranian and Arabic speakers exemplify this point particularly well. In a conversation between two Jordanian women, for instance, one says about still a third woman:

(12) S: X is a nice girl and beautiful.

Her friend, in order to express the view that the speaker is even more beautiful, responds with a proverb:

A: Where is the soil compared with the star?

In complimenting her friend's child, an Arabic speaker says:

(13) S: She is like the moon and she has beautiful eyes.

And from an exchange between two Iranian friends, we have the following:

(14) S: Your shoes are very nice.
A: It is your eyes which can see them which are nice.

while an Iranian boy says to his mother:

(15) S: It was delicious, Mom. I hope your hands never have pain.
A: I'm glad you like it.

While it is true that Americans do not make use of such proverbs and set phrases in giving compliments, we do use a very restricted set of lexical and syntactic structures. And just as proverbs and ritualized phrases would have to be learned by anyone who wanted to communicate appropriately in Arabic or Farsi, so a learner of American English must become familiar with the appropriate syntactic structures and lexical items used in compliments in this society.

In order to make comparisons between the way compliments function in English and in other languages, or indeed even to begin to teach the rules of speaking for English, we must first have analyses of the patterns which govern the way English speakers use their language. In their study of complimenting behavior in American English, Manes and Wolfson (1981) discovered that one of the most striking features of compliments in American English is their almost total lack of originality. (The data upon which this analysis is based consist of 686 compliments gathered in a great variety of naturally occurring speech situations which the researchers observed or in which they participated. Careful attention was paid to recording information concerning the relationship between speakers and addressees, as well as their occupation, approximate age

115

and sex.) An initial examination of a large corpus revealed surprising repetitiveness in both the object of the compliments and the lexical items used to describe them. On closer investigation, it was discovered that regularities exist on all levels and that compliments are in fact formulas.

It is obvious that since compliments are expressions of positive evaluation, each must include at least one term which carries positive semantic load. What is not obvious and could not have been predicted is that, notwithstanding the enormous number and variety of such positive terms in English, the overwhelming majority of compliments fall within a highly restricted set of adjectives and verbs.

We may categorize 80% of all compliments in the data as adjectival in that they depend on an adjective for their positive semantic value. In all, some seventy-two positive adjectives occur in the data and there is no doubt that if further data were collected, a great many more such adjectives would appear. What is striking, however, is that of these seventy-two adjectives only five (*nice, good, beautiful, pretty* and *great*) are used with any frequency. While most adjectives occur only once or twice in the data, these five adjectives occur with such frequency that of all adjectival compliments in the corpus two-thirds make use of only these five adjectives.

The two most common adjectives found in compliments are *nice* and *good*, occurring in 22.9% and 19.6% of the data, respectively. The fact that both these adjectives are semantically vague makes it possible for speakers to use them in connection with an almost unlimited variety of nouns:

(16) Your apartment's nice.
(17) Hey, that's a nice-looking bike.
(18) That's a nice piece of work.
(19) You have a very nice wife.
(20) That's a nice blouse.

and

(21) That's a good question.
(22) You're such a good cook.
(23) You sound good on tape.
(24) Mm. The chocolate sauce is good.

The other three most common adjectives, *beautiful, pretty*, and *great*, appear in 9.7%, 9.2% and 6.2% of all adjectival compliments in the data. While *pretty* is somewhat more specific than the others, all may be seen to occur in conjunction with a great many different topics:

(25) You did a beautiful job of explaining that.
(26) You have such a beautiful baby.
(27) Your tie is really beautiful.
(28) Gosh, you have a beautiful living room.

and

(29) That was a really great meal.
(30) Your hair looks great that way.
(31) Your apartment looks great.
(32) You're doing a great job.

and

(33) You look pretty today.
(34) That suit is very pretty.
(35) Are those new glasses? They're pretty.

The extremely high frequency of these five adjectives in American English compliments may be very useful to language teachers and learners. The point is, of course, that learners may with perfect appropriateness make use of the members of this set to speak of very nearly any topic in a complimentary statement. What we have here is in effect a semantic formula and it would be well for learners to be made aware of it.

While 80% of all compliments in the corpus are of the adjectival type, compliments which make use of verbs to carry the positive semantic evaluation also occur:

(36) I like your bookcase.
(37) I really like your hair that way.
(38) I love your outfit.
(39) I really enjoyed your talk.

The only two verbs which occur with any frequency in compliments of this type are *like* and *love* and these occur in 86% of all compliments which contain a semantically positive verb. As with adjectives, most other positive verbs occur only once or twice in the data. Here again we find speakers of American English making use of what amounts to a semantic formula:

$$\begin{bmatrix} \text{like} \\ \text{love} \end{bmatrix} \text{NP}$$

117

When we turn to syntactic patterns, we see that compliment structure is even more highly patterned here than on the semantic level. *To be precise, 53.6% of the compliments in the corpus make use of a single syntactic pattern:*

NP $\begin{bmatrix} \text{is} \\ \text{looks} \end{bmatrix}$ (really) ADJ

(e.g. You look good, Your pin looks nice like that, This chicken is great, hon). In addition to this one major pattern, two others:

I (really) $\begin{bmatrix} \text{like} \\ \text{love} \end{bmatrix}$ NP

(e.g. I like your shirt, I love your blouse) and

PRO is (really) (a) ADJ NP

(e.g. That's a good system, That's a very nice briefcase) account for an additional 16.1% and 14.9% of the data respectively. Thus, only three patterns are required to describe 85% of the compliments found. Indeed, only nine patterns occur with any regularity and these nine account for 97.2% of all the data in the corpus.

The fact that in a corpus of nearly seven hundred naturally occurring compliments in American English 85% of the data fall into only three syntactic patterns is information which can clearly be put to good use in ESL classrooms. Indeed, pilot lessons have already been taught at both intermediate and advanced levels with excellent results. When learners are given the three major syntactic patterns and the five most frequently found adjectives, they have little difficulty in producing compliments which conform to the patterns used by native speakers.

Unlike other formulaic expressions such as those for thanks and greetings, the formulaic compliment is not explicitly recognized by native speakers of American English. Indeed, it is for precisely this reason that the sort of systematic ethnographic study which underlies the analysis presented here is so important. The fact is that speech act patterns – or more generally, rules of speaking – are not only very different from culture to culture but are also largely unconscious. For this reason, native speakers who themselves follow all the rules are quite unlikely to recognize that such patterns exist. It is only through the collection and analysis of large amounts of naturally occurring speech (i.e. sociolinguistic analysis) that it is possible to uncover the patterns of speaking which exist in any society, including one's own.

Speech acts differ cross-culturally not only in the way they are realized but also in their distribution, their frequency of occurrence, and in the functions they serve. In American English, compliments occur in a very wide variety of situations. They are quite frequent and they serve to produce or to reinforce a feeling of solidarity between speakers. . . . Compliments also serve other functions: they are used in greeting, thanking, and apologizing, or even as substitutes for them. They also serve as a way of opening a conversation. The frequency of compliments in American English is often remarked upon by foreigners. Comments are often heard from non-native speakers that Americans do an excessive amount of complimenting. People from cultures which are less open in expressions of approval are often extremely embarrassed by this.

Not only are there differences in frequency, but also distribution varies a great deal from culture to culture. Americans give compliments in situations where the compliment would be totally inappropriate in other cultures. A particularly interesting example of this came about recently when an American politician visiting France happened to compliment one of the members of the French government on the job he was doing. The French were very annoyed and articles appeared in the French press attributing all sorts of hidden implications to the act and condemning it as interference in French internal affairs. In reality, of course, the visiting American politician had done no more than the typical American would do when trying to be friendly to a stranger: give a compliment.

Thus we see that complimenting behavior varies cross-culturally along a number of dimensions. It may be extremely frequent, as in our own culture, or it may hardly exist at all, as among the Indonesians. It may be realized as a formula or even as a ritualized pre-coded phrase or a proverb. It may well be uninterpretable cross-culturally since the values and attitudes it expresses vary so much from one society to another.

The theoretical importance of recognizing this variation is that it points to the need for sociolinguistic descriptions of language in use. If true communication is to take place among people who come from differing cultural backgrounds, and if interference is to be minimized in second language learning, then we must have cross-cultural comparisons of rules of speaking. That is, contrastive analysis must be generalized to include not only the level of form but also the level of function.

Questions for consideration

1. A British teacher was "complimented" by a student by being told that she was old and fat. What conditions and cultural values probably underlay the remark?

2. What American or British types of compliments can you think of that should be avoided in developing countries?
3. Can you think of some compliments you have heard that have been misunderstood in your own culture, without cross-cultural interference?
4. Give some examples of ways to teach complimenting in the language you teach.
5. An example is given at the end of the article of the French misinterpreting a compliment made by an American politician. Do you know of other similar examples of cross-cultural misunderstanding of compliments?

Part III Classroom applications

Even applied linguists tend to become so involved with theories and ideas on a grand scale that they neglect the classroom – which is what all the plotting and planning is about. Theories are made and broken in the classroom, for it is here that they are found to be true or false, productive or useless, practical or fit only for the ivory tower. Out of theories come approaches, methods, and techniques to be fieldtested for validity in the classroom. The cultural component does not present an exception. The articles in the final section of this book grow out of the kind of work represented in Parts I and II.

Good techniques for teaching culture are not easy to find and need to be shared. After one has determined what values and behavior patterns need to be taught, one must determine how it may be most effectively done.

In intensive language programs, culture may be taught in a class designated for that subject, just as reading may be taught in a reading class, or writing in a writing class. Not all programs are able to devote enough time or specialized instruction to the subject, but include it in conversation classes, or reading material, listening and speaking exercises, writing topics – indeed, in virtually all areas of instruction. In foreign language classes, which typically meet from three to five hours per week, there clearly needs to be a combination of culture with other language aspects. Since one must read, speak, or write about *something*, and listen to *something*, why should not that something have a cultural content? One may listen to a passage that reveals a cultural facet of the society which speaks the target language, then read a selection on the same facet, talk about it in a discussion group, and write about it in a class or home assignment, thus learning culture while learning language. In fact, it is virtually impossible to teach a language without teaching cultural content, although it is not, unfortunately, impossible to attempt to superimpose the native culture onto the target language, particularly when the teacher is of the same cultural and linguistic background as the students. Such a hand-me-down fitting of one culture over another language must result in a gross misfit. Anyone who has read this far will surely avoid this particular trap and see it for the impasse that it is.

Once an understanding has been reached of the relationship of thought and culture to language, along with an awareness of cultural differences, distances, and similarities and how they affect language learning, the foundation has been laid for the teacher's inclusion of culture somewhere in the curriculum. However, no matter how willing, or even anxious, the teacher may be to follow through in the classroom, a lack of practical knowledge of ways and means may prevent implementation. Even knowing which aspects of the culture of the speakers of the language being taught are most important to include will not provide insight into methods of presentation. Over the years teachers have had to improvise, to follow the process of trial and error, in the effort to find effective means of making their students culturally aware and cognizant, if not unreservedly accepting, of the culture of the people whose language they are attempting to master. Today there is help for the language teacher in embarking on this quest.

The ingenuity and creative talent of many second and foreign language teachers have resulted in a wide variety of paths to follow in accomplishing the teaching of a target culture. Techniques, materials, approaches, methods, concepts, all are to be found along the paths and are eminently adaptable to any language classroom. A few of these discoveries are described in this section for the reader's use, and to point toward new trails to be blazed along the way.

12 Culture in the classroom

Nelson Brooks

...the teacher must relate language to culture if a coordinate system is to result from the learner's efforts. This is the conclusion of Robert Politzer, who says in the Georgetown University *Report of the Fifth Annual Round Table Meeting on Linguistics and Language Teaching*:

As language teachers we must be interested in the study of culture (in the social scientist's sense of the word) not because we necessarily *want* to teach the culture of the other country but because we *have* to teach it. If we teach language without teaching at the same time the culture in which it operates, we are teaching meaningless symbols or symbols to which the student attaches the wrong meaning; for unless he is warned, unless he receives cultural instruction, he will associate American concepts or objects with the foreign symbols. (1959:100–1)

Are we then to require that teachers of foreign languages take courses in cultural anthropology and that they devote a part of every class and every course to formal presentations from this discipline? If not, then how is the teacher to impart information that will be of interest and value to his students? Just as accuracy in phonology is best acquired as an incidental by-product of the learning of actual conversations, and as syntax and morphology are best learned not by analysis but by imitation and practice, in the same way knowledge of culture is best imparted as a corollary or an obbligato to the business of language learning.

Many successful language teachers habitually begin their classes with a five-minute presentation in the foreign language of a subject that has not been previously announced. The content for this simple and effective device may often be a topic that brings out identity, similarity, or sharp difference in comparable patterns of culture. For example, consider three holidays in France and the United States. In both countries Easter is essentially the same in concept and observance, but Christmas is markedly different in many ways, and the American Thanksgiving has no counterpart in the French calendar of festivals.

The point of view from which to present such topics should not be that of the deity observing the terrestrial sphere, nor a historian viewing the total experience of a civilization, nor an architect surveying the blueprint of a complicated structure. Rather, the point of view should be that of a young person of the age and status of the students being addressed, and the perspective should be that of such a person as he goes about his daily tasks.

The following list of topics (by no means exhaustive) may be considered as items for such "hors d'oeuvres" in the language classroom.

Greetings, friendly exchange, farewells. How do friends meet, converse briefly, take their leave? What are the perennial topics of small talk? How are strangers introduced?

The morphology of personal exchange. How are interpersonal relationships such as differences in age, degree of intimacy, social position, and emotional tension reflected in the choice of appropriate forms of pronouns and verbs?

Levels of speech. In what ways are age, provenance, social status, academic achievement, degree of formality, interpersonal relations, aesthetic concern, and personality reflected in the standard or traditional speech?

Patterns of politeness. What are the commonest formulas of politeness and when should they be used?

Respect. Apart from overt expressions of deference and discipline, what personages and what cultural themes, both past and contemporary, are characteristically held in sincere respect?

Intonation patterns. Apart from the selection, order, and form of words themselves, what overtones of cadence, interrogation, command, surprise, deference, and the like are borne exclusively by the dynamics of pronunciation? (For example, the French *Vous vous en allez ce soir* may be pronounced in such a way that it is clearly either a statement, a rejoinder, a question, an order, or a sentence read by a child from a book.)

Contractions and omissions. What words and intonation patterns are commonly used to enliven one's speech by way of commentary upon one's own feelings or actions, those of the person addressed, or the nature or behavior of other elements in the immediate situation?

Types of error in speech and their importance. What errors is the speaker of English likely to make in the new language? What is the relative seriousness of these errors in the new culture? (For example, in French, a mistake in the gender of a noun is deeply disturbing, but the failure to make a past participle agree, if noticed at all, is readily condoned.)

Verbal taboos. What common words or expressions in English have direct equivalents that are not tolerated in the new culture, and vice versa?

Written and spoken language. Aside from richness of vocabulary and complexity of structure, what are the commonest areas of difference between spoken language and writing?

Numbers. How are numbers pronounced, spelled, represented in arithmetical notation, written by hand, and formally printed in ways that are peculiar to the new culture?

Folklore. What myths, stories, traditions, legends, customs, and beliefs are universally found among the common people?

Childhood literature. What lyrics, rhymes, songs, and jingles of distinct aesthetic merit are learned by all young children?

Discipline. What are the norms of discipline in the home, in school, in public places, in the military, in pastimes, and in ceremonies?

Festivals. What days of the calendar year are officially designated as national festivals? What are the central themes of these occasions and what is the manner of their celebration?

Holidays. What is the usual rhythm of work days and days off? What do young people do with their days off?

Observance of Sunday. How does Sunday differ from weekdays with regard to what an individual does or does not do, may or may not do?

Games. What are the most popular games that are played outdoors, indoors, by the young, by adults?

Music. What opportunities are offered the individual for training and practice in vocal and instrumental music?

Errands. What are typical errands that a young person is likely to be asked to do, either at home or in school?

Pets. What animals are habitually received into the home as pets? What is their role in the household?

Telephone. What phrases and procedures are conventional in the use of the telephone? What is the role of the private telephone in the home? Where are public telephones to be found and how is the service paid for?

Comradeship. How are friendships and personal attachments likely to be formed and what provisions are made for fostering comradeship through clubs, societies, and other group organizations?

Personal possessions. What objects are often found decorating the bureau and walls of a young person's bedroom? What articles are likely to be discovered in a boy's pocket or a girl's handbag?

Keeping warm and cool. What changes in clothing, heating, ventilation, food, and drink are made because of variations in temperature?

Cleanliness. What is the relation between plumbing and personal cleanliness? What standards of public hygiene and sanitation are generally observed?

125

Cosmetics. What are the special conditions of age, sex, activity, and situation under which make-up is permitted, encouraged, or required?

Tobacco and smoking. Who smokes, what, and under what circumstances? What are the prevailing attitudes toward smoking? Where are tobacco products obtained?

Medicine and doctors. What are the common home remedies for minor ailments? What is the equivalent of the American drugstore? How does one obtain the services of a physician?

Competitions. In what fields of activity are prizes awarded for success in open competition? How important is competition in schools, in the business world, in the professions?

Appointments. How are appointments for business and pleasure made? What are the usual meeting places? How important is punctuality?

Invitations and dates. What invitations are young people likely to extend and receive? What formalities are involved? What is the counterpart of "dating" in the United States?

Traffic. How does vehicular traffic affect the pedestrian? What are the equivalents of traffic lights, road signs, crosswalks, safety islands, parking meters, hitchhiking?

Owning, repairing, and driving cars. Are young people interested in gasoline motors? Are they knowledgable about them? What is the role of the car in family life? What are the requirements for obtaining a license to drive?

Science. How has modern science affected daily living, inner thought, conversation, reading matter?

Gadgets. What mechanical devices are commonly found in personal use, in the home, in stores, and in travel?

Sports. What organized and professional sports are the most popular and the most generally presented for the public?

Radio and television programs. How general is the use of radio and television and what types of programs are offered, especially for young people?

Books. What are the facts of special interest concerning the printing, punctuation, binding, selling, and popularity of books?

Other reading matter. In addition to books, what types of reading matter, such as newspapers, weeklies, magazines, and reviews, are generally available and where can they be bought or consulted?

Hobbies. In what individual hobbies are young people likely to engage?

Learning in school. What is the importance of homework in formal education? What is taught at home by older members of the family?

Penmanship. What styles of handwriting are generally taught and used? What kinds of writing tools are available at home, in school, in public places? What are the conventions concerning the writing of dates, the use of margins, the signing of names?

Letter writing and mailing. How do letters customarily begin and end? How are envelopes addressed? Are there typical kinds of personal stationery? Where are stamps bought? Where are mailboxes found?

Family meals. What meals are usually served *en famille*? What is the special character of each meal, the food eaten, the seating arrangement, the method of serving dishes, the general conversation?

Meals away from home. Where does one eat when not at home? What are the equivalents of our lunchrooms, cafeterias, dining halls, lunch counters, wayside inns, restaurants?

Soft drinks and alcohol. What types of nonalcoholic beverages are usually consumed by young people and adults? What is the attitude toward the use of beer, wine, and spirits? What alcoholic drinks are in frequent use at home and in public?

Snacks and between-meal eating. Apart from the normal trio of daily meals, what pauses for eating or drinking are generally observed? What is the customary hour and the usual fare?

Cafés, bars, and restaurants. What types of cafés, bars, and restaurants are found and how do they vary in respectability?

Yards, lawns, and sidewalks. What are the equivalents of American back yards, front lawns, and sidewalks in residential and business areas? What is their importance in the activities of young people?

Parks and playgrounds. Where are parks and playgrounds located and with what special features or equipment are they likely to be provided?

Flowers and gardens. Of what interest and importance are flower shops, house plants, gardens for flowers and vegetables in town and in the country?

Movies and theaters. Where are moving picture houses and theaters to be found? What procedures are involved in securing tickets and being seated? What can be said of the quality and popular appeal of the entertainment?

Races, circus, rodeo. What outdoor events are in vogue that correspond to our auto or horse races, circuses, and similar spectacles?

Museums, exhibitions, and zoos. What types of museums, exhibitions, and animal displays are generally provided and what is their role in the education of the young and the recreation and enjoyment of adults?

Getting from place to place. What facilities for travel are provided for short distances about town or from one city or part of the country to another, by bus, rail, or airplane?

Contrasts in town and country life. What are some of the notable differences in dwellings, clothing, manners, shopping facilities, public utilities, when life in town is compared with life in the country?

Vacation and resort areas. What areas have special climate, scenery, or other natural features that make them attractive for vacation?

Camping and hiking. How popular are summer camps, camping, hiking, and cycling trips, and what organizations are especially interested in their promotion?

Savings accounts and thrift. In what ways do banks or other organizations provide for the deposit of small amounts of money by individuals? To what extent and in what ways are young people encouraged to practice thrift?

Odd jobs and earning power. What kinds of chores and odd jobs are young people expected or permitted to do? If these are paid for, how is the individual reimbursed? To what extent are regular paying jobs made available to younger persons?

Careers. What careers have strong appeal for the young? How important is parental example and advice in the choice of a career? What financial help is likely to be forthcoming for those who choose a career demanding long preparation?

It is culture in this technical, scientific sense that has been so misunderstood and so inadequately presented in our classrooms. Once the necessary distinctions are made and this meaning is clearly conceived, its usefulness and worth to the youthful student are only too apparent. There is little danger that culture in its other two meanings of *refinement* and *artistic endeavors* will be slighted; all the influence of literature and textbooks, travels and traditions will inevitably orient both teacher and student in this direction. The focal point of the presentation of culture in all its meanings should be the view of life as seen from within the new speech community, especially by individuals who are in circumstances comparable to those of the student. The teacher, by means of the incidental talks suggested above, by means of behavior traits as speaker and hearer that are authentic and typical in the new community, by establishing in the classroom a cultural island made up of both material and nonmaterial elements, and especially by identifying and commenting upon references in literature that are culturally significant, may convey to his students the concepts which make language learning invaluable and are at the same time accompanied by many other important learnings.

Questions for consideration

1. How might Brooks's list be used in a class of mixed cultural backgrounds?

2. Select ten categories from the list to which you would give priority. Why did you select them?
3. Select three of the categories to discuss. What is the importance of the entries? What do they tell us about the culture?
4. How many of the categories could you handle in another culture? In a subculture of your own environment?
5. Suppose a spy came to your country with native-sounding speech and knowledge of the answers to all the above questions. What are some ways the spy could still be tripped up and revealed?

13 Newspapers: vehicles for teaching ESOL with a cultural focus

Charles H. Blatchford

At some time most ESOL teachers have probably decided to enliven their classes by turning to the newspaper as a resource for variety, contemporaneity, or relevance, but they have likely found themselves having to explain a lot of the cultural allusions which block their students' understanding and thereby reduce the effectiveness of the newspaper's use. The newspaper can be used in ESOL, however, but to better effect if the emphasis is shifted from language teaching to an acknowledged and overt focus on culture. In this context I am speaking of culture as "a bundle of patterns of behavior, habits of conduct, customs, laws, beliefs, and instinctive responses that are displayed by a society," a definition taken from Henry Steele Commager (1970: 161). Especially in an ESL setting, students spontaneously ask questions about puzzling aspects of the society as reflected in the newspaper, they take part in real tasks that the newspaper provides, and they learn useful information about how to exist in their new English-language surroundings. All the while, language is the vehicle for communication either among themselves or with the teacher, and both the sense of threat and the level of self-consciousness are reduced from what may exist in a strict language classroom.

In my conduct of an experimental, two-week workshop for university-level, volunteer students, my assumptions were in part that the newspaper would reveal Americans in their own cultural setting and provide insights of interest to foreigners, and that practical tips to their understanding of us would accrue to them in their arduous process of acculturation. This article is a report of some of the ideas that worked in the workshop and some of the notions I learned not to take for granted. Let's look at some aspects of culture revealed in a newspaper and some questions which might elucidate our cultural patterns of behavior.

1. *Ann Landers / Dear Abby.* Many English teachers have used this

feature to pose a problem; they then ask students to supply answers which can be compared with Ann's. With a focus on culture, however, it is the topics that Ann's readers submit that are of most interest. What bothers Americans? Why do they write to an impersonal party for professional advice? Why can't people discuss problems openly with family, friends, ministers, or colleagues and get immediate help? What is it in our society that makes some subjects taboo? If there were a similar type of column in the student's country, what would the topics be? Would their culture even permit some of the topics to appear in print?

2. *The horoscope.* Why do seemingly pious people read the horoscope? What is revealed about our patterns of beliefs in the supernatural? To what extent do people ascribe the day's events to these prophecies?

3. *The front page.* What is worthy of the front page? What do editors feel will most tempt a reader to buy and read their paper? What are the events of concern to a reader's life? What cultural mores do crime, war, danger, or threat transgress to make stories newsworthy?

4. *Commentators and columnists.* Why are the information they reveal, the innuendoes they cast, or the interpretations they render of interest to Americans? Is this type of writing the same as what a student would find at home?

5. *Classified.* How do Americans categorize – what are the different classifications? What is it people treasure so much that they advertise in "Lost and Found" to get it back? What do people find that they feel others want back? What personal belongings are most advertised for sale; what do people want to sell? Do the ads give reasons for selling? For example, what prompts "garage sales"? Does this reveal the mobility of Americans? In the ads, how do people generally like to be contacted? Do most people list their telephone number, or their address? (Incidentally, what can you learn about the place of sale from the telephone exchange?) What concerns are revealed in the personals? In other cultures do parents advertise for their errant children? What does this reveal about a "generation gap"? What is Alcoholics Anonymous? Would you infer that drinking is a significant problem? "Find help in the Lord Jesus Christ." Help for what? Why? Call the Rev. Downs and find out what the recorded message says; what type of appeal is he making?

6. *Miss Fixit.* In this column which cuts through official red tape, what sorts of problems do people pose? In what areas of government are they given the run-around? Why are they afraid to ask designated official agencies, and why do they work through this third party? Do people exhibit any cultural fears – of police, for example? What complaints are typical? What cultural patterns do the complainants

report have been violated? Why are people so ignorant of where they could find the answers themselves? Why do people seek anonymity in submitting their complaints?

7. *Letters to the editor*. What causes people to write such letters? What is the point of view usually expressed – disagreement with the paper, with another letter writer, or just expression of a cause?

These features or the bridge column or the crossword puzzle are some of the features a reader might turn to first. But there are many other cultural indicators which can fruitfully be discussed. Are these indicators universal or culture-specific?

Cartoons: Jib Fowles' article (1970) proved very helpful in getting at a workable analysis of cartoons. *Caricature*: What are the features that identify specific people or types of people? *Graphs and charts*: Are the symbols used the same as those in the student's culture? What type of information is most effectively presented in graphs? *Advertising*: What does the amount of display advertising indicate about the consumerism of Americans? What information is presented in an ad that will cause an American to buy – are hard facts about a product important? If an item is on sale, what is the reason for the sale? What are the special events around which sales revolve? Why should people buy things just because it's the Fourth of July? What is a coupon in an ad? What does *swift* mean in a premium bacon ad?

While talking about the cultural aspects described above, language will inevitably be intertwined. *Demonstrators are like mosquitoes – you just have to put up with them* didn't make any sense to one Japanese student, because flies, not mosquitoes, are his culture's symbol of annoyance. Though I like to keep the focus on culture, the inadvertent question on a language problem provides an apt opportunity for comment. For example, a student asked, "Isn't *a January 31 launch* wrong?" Some uses of punctuation, symbols and abbreviations may be unfamiliar and hinder comprehension. For example, what is the use of single quotation marks: *he was 'cautiously optimistic'* or *into a 'very good year'*? What is the use of the colon: *Kernell: Fasi weighs all views*? What words are these abbreviations for: *ofc, secy, secty, bkpr, hr., exper.*? What does *thru* mean? Does the plus sign mean the same in *$300+* and *$1.60 hr. + free cottage*?

In order to include as many answers as possible to who, what, when, where, why, and how in the lead paragraph, journalists may use appositives. While students may have studied apposition in grammar books, they may need to be reminded of it. Nominal phrases may be fully packed: *its dry cargo west-bound container freight rates*; alliteration may signal levity: *Canny Cannon's Cannon Canon*; ellipses may indicate taboo words (what words are culturally taboo, anyway?).

Within any newspaper is a variety of styles. There is the very formal editorial, the argument of the news analysis, the slang or the sarcasm in a letter to the editor, the elliptical phrasing of some columnists, the truncated style of the headline, the dialect of the comic strip. There are allusions from literature or mass culture, including puns, e.g. *Out damn scribe! Out I say; Like ships passing the bight* (caption for a picture of two ships passing in San Francisco Bay); and *Babes in Nurseryland* (What's the effect of change from *Babes in Toyland?*).

In terms of language skills, there is plenty to talk about or recognize in the different registers of English and the appropriate use of each. Activities which emanate from a newspaper class can center around a cultural theme, but give practice in the language. The discussion of cultural differences practices speaking, the discussion itself involves comprehension; understanding the topic under discussion involves reading. Assignments or activities can include writing: write a letter to the editor about a story you read in today's paper, expressing disagreement along some cultural line; write an ad to sell a hi-fi and remember that every word costs; read the first 10 "help wanted" ads, determine which ones you would qualify for and write an application letter; write a "position wanted" ad describing yourself and your skills. Another activity of interest is to look at newspapers historically and see not only the changes in popular culture and social history but also the changes in formats, use of photographs and type faces.

So far, the discussion has noticeably omitted the news. With culture in mind, wire service news stories seem to be of least relevance as they do not reveal anything unique about our culture. (Of course news stories can be slanted and can reveal a bias which a particular newspaper may have; the fact that newspapers are permitted to have a bias, under the First Amendment, may reveal a cultural pattern unfamiliar to readers of a more circumscribed national press.) Students may need to be taught how to identify such stories from local news where there are indications of local patterns of behavior.

A disadvantage of starting off with news in the newspaper is that it often does not spark much discussion and news usually leads to the teacher's interpretation of events and a consequent lack of involvement on the part of the students. An alternative way to approach news, however, is to work on the assumption that students know what it is and assign them a task of writing some news. What happened to them? Can they write it in a newsworthy style? For example, getting the class to transform the submitted raw data, "I bought a bicycle that cost $52 the other day" into a newsworthy sentence such as "Genkyu Hamamoto of 3468 Aala Street bought a $52 bicycle September 14, but it has been worthless" not only illustrated the use of the 5 WH-words, but also involved the students in something about themselves. From this approach, it appeared easier to make up headlines; they felt how they had to cut away words and this task proved more useful than taking raw headlines and trying to discover the deletions that had already been made.

One assignment that didn't work was each student's reporting of ten first paragraphs he read at home. It was a waste of time and meaningless. By the next day, the stories were old, and not every student had read the same ten. A more appropriate task might have been an in-class decision on the single word that might best capture a lead paragraph. (My colleague, Ted Plaister, offered this suggestion.)

News stories are admittedly a source of vocabulary in context. If one follows a news story over a period of days, he will find the same words recurring in slightly different contexts. And the same words may occur in connection with different stories: during the 10-day course headlines gave *tax hike*, *rate hike*, and *fare hike*. Good reinforcement! But vocabulary also occurs in other sections of the paper, and in ads, it is frequently illustrated. I asked students to jot down 10 new words they learned each night. If there were problems, they asked questions the next class. Since many students consider vocabulary the quintessence of language learning, I capitalized on their desire as a motivator, even though it wasn't necessarily connected with my goal of teaching about culture.

A newspaper is fresh daily; there is interest and a challenge in dealing with a new text each day; if the newspaper is to be used in an ESOL course, it may be best not to work at it intensively, but to use it as an alternate activity for a day, after you feel that you've had enough pronunciation or pattern drill. In any case, when you use it, use that day's paper to get the most out of the resource; don't ask students to keep bringing it back day after day. A few other do's and don'ts:

— Don't try to cover the whole paper each day; select just one or two features. Consider the rest of the paper a resource which your students may be motivated to try to read on their own at home.

— Don't get stuck on headlines. Guide students to read the lead sentences of a story first; the headlines should then become clear. Students can practice writing their own headlines.

— Each time you use the paper, select another type of feature.

— Take a good dictionary to class with you. In most cases, you won't have had much chance to prepare ahead of time. You won't be able to explain everything; ESOL teachers can't be expert in everything the newspaper covers. You may not be interested in sports, but you'll learn! You may not read columnists, but you'll become aware of their points of view pretty quickly.

— Let each student have his own newspaper. Teach him how to fold his

paper in fourths, subway-style, to reduce the awkwardness of holding
it fully spread out.
— If you have an overhead projector, you can focus students' attention
on a certain point you want to discuss. You may be more certain
that all of the students know what you are talking about than if you
orally direct them to page C–8, column 4 – although that's a good
exercise in aural comprehension.

The appropriateness of the newspaper as a resource depends upon
the situation you face. One might question the wisdom of dealing with
the newspaper in an academic situation where the student's first problem
is to get through his courses; is the newspaper going to help him tackle
his texts? In an adult education setting where the students come together
more informally for conversation, the newspaper may spark a good deal
more interest, and may prove ideal in providing topics for conversation.
Immigrant adults, living in the community, are more apt to face the
necessities of finding good buys, of dealing with housing officials or
landlords, of operating in the society whose culture the newspaper
presents.

The newspaper is not easy to teach from; it puts a considerable strain
on the teacher to deal with an unfamiliar text without some advance
preparation. It humbles us to be faced with not knowing all the answers
to all the student's questions, but we are thereby more human. In this
regard, in our role as representative of the culture and friend, we can
learn a lot about our student's acculturation problems. I think of one
student who wrote about a contretemps in a grocery store where the
clerk rang up $5.15 worth of groceries. Having only $5, he asked
whether he could return a can of guava juice. The check-out girl said
he could not without asking the manager. He then asked whether he
could borrow 15¢ from her. Again she denied him but suggested he ask
the lady behind him who did lend him the money. So humiliated and
embarrassed, he could get himself out of the bind only by giving the
kind lady the guava juice in return. When the newspaper elicits such
personal outpourings and you as the teacher can empathize and smooth
over such cultural misunderstandings, a kind of communication develops
that gets at real language situations the student faces. This is what
language in culture is all about.

In sum, a newspaper is mammoth and to tackle one in a foreign
language is a great task. Alone, a student gets discouraged because there
is so much cultural interference, let alone language difficulty. He needs
to be guided and taught. I have suggested some aspects of the newspaper
which can help students understand us and our ways and help him get
around better in his new life here. And in addition, we should feel that
we have given him lots of practice in the language as well as some

instruction in how the newspaper fulfills its social role of informing, advising, helping, and entertaining.

Questions for consideration

1. What specific types of issues might appear in an advice column in a United States newspaper that would be shocking to Middle Eastern students? to Asians? How should such a situation be handled?
2. How can letters to the editor be used to illustrate the limitations on freedom of speech as proscribed by society?
3. How might the obituaries be used to teach culture?
4. How could Blatchford's ideas be used with a newspaper in another culture, such as German, Japanese, or Brazilian?

14 Culture in literature

Joyce Merrill Valdes
University of Houston – University Park

The statement that literature may be used to teach culture is probably so widely accepted as to be almost a cliché. When the audiolingual method appeared on the scene, the teaching of literature was glowered upon, as was everything else contained in the still alive but possibly moribund grammar-translation method. Most objections, however, were linguistically based and did not attempt to deny the usefulness of literature as a medium for teaching culture. As others have done a fine job of refuting the linguistic objections, both in the early years of the controversy (Marquardt 1967; Povey 1968, 1984) and more recently (Widdowson 1975, 1982; McKay 1982), there is no need to review the justifications. It is simply accepted as a given that literature is a viable component of second language programs at the appropriate level and that one of the major functions of literature is to serve as a medium to transmit the culture of the people who speak the language in which it is written. Perhaps it would not go amiss, however, to include a warning against teaching literature solely as a means of presenting cultural slices of life. Certainly literature is culture in action, but it is much more than that, and to ignore the wealth of benefits to be accrued from its study in order to concentrate on one aspect only, no matter how valuable, is to deprive the students. This caveat attended to, we can now devote our full attention to the specific purpose of this article.

Both second language readings and literature may be used to teach culture, but they are not the same thing. As Povey points out,

> Yet if we have to accept the primacy of language, we cannot make this our only concern, otherwise the most effective ESL reading material would be those items we created ourselves to the specific linguistic architecture of levels of difficulty. Such works more often become readers without any element of literature in them. The simplified stories from the classics are justified by a similar appeal to language necessity, but they are usually only a thin reminder of what was once a significant book. (Povey 1968: 188)

Since Povey made those remarks it has become less necessary for language teachers to create their own readers. Many readers have appeared on the market, with the linguistic level for which they are intended clearly

137

designated in the introduction and the subject matter obviously selected for the teaching of culture as well as language. However, even an appeal to linguistic demands cannot justify the "simplification" of the classics, for any purpose at all. To go beyond glossing difficult words in original literary texts is a disservice to students, who have the mistaken idea that they have read the work and are deprived of the experience of reading the original when their language proficiency improves, as well as receiving a distorted impression of the work itself. In the 1940s that mammoth work of Melville's, *Moby Dick*, was reduced to less than 60 pages for students of ESL. One wonders if this travesty even allowed room for the whale. Fortunately, today there are few "simplifications" and an abundance of good original work for readers in ESL.

What, then, is literature? "If we say that language is oriented essentially toward a restatement or symbolic transformation of experience, we may say that literature is oriented toward the conscious creation of an illusion of reality" (Brooks 1960: 99). That statement is perceptive but perhaps elusive for the present purpose. Since literary scholars have a long history of attempting to define what it is that they are scholars of, it would seem to be wise merely to produce a working definition: Literature is unabridged fiction, drama, poetry, or essay written for an educated audience of native speakers of the language in which it is written, purporting to represent life as it really is. While this definition may seem to exclude fantasy and science fiction from the realm of literature, actually such works, regardless of time and place, fit the definition; could anyone deny *Alice in Wonderland* a place in literature – or deny that its underlying theme of life as it really is forms the basis for its time-proven popularity?

This definition automatically places the teaching of literature at an upper-intermediate to highly advanced level. Readings are appropriate for and effective in beginning and lower-intermediate levels and will not be a part of this discussion.

An understanding of literature depends upon discernment of the values inherent, but not necessarily specifically expressed, in the work. The values of any cultural group, even if the author's own values differ from those of the group to which he or she belongs, underlie plots and become the theme in virtually all works of literature. Obviously, values are not universal even within cultural groups, or there would be nothing to write about, but there are certain concepts in each cultural group that carry general consensus, despite dissenting minorities. Perhaps the reason that the Ten Commandments have withstood scrutiny for so many years and through so many cultures is their universality, geographically as well as chronologically. No major cultural groups condone killing, stealing, or coveting a neighbor's wife, and honoring one's parents seems natural and proper anywhere and at any time, though the degree of approval or disapproval of these and other commandments may differ considerably from group to group. Less obvious values must be recognized in literature as well as those that stand in the rank of commandments.

Presumably students of a second language have been taught – to the extent that such concepts can be taught – to respect both their own and other cultural values before they have reached the level at which they are introduced to literature in the second language. The task of the classroom teacher, then, aside from teaching the literature for all the other good reasons literature should be taught, is to make clear the values that underlie the behavior of characters and points of view of the authors, not in order for students to judge these values but to understand them and the literary works that contain them. Comparisons to other cultures are not idle, however, as they often result in real consideration of one's own cultural values where blind acceptance has existed before – for students and teachers alike.

Clearly teachers, whether native speakers of the language being taught or not, must have a broad awareness of the values in the literature they are teaching as well as a depth of understanding. For the ESL teacher, few significant differences in values exist between American and British cultures that would create a problem for the reader; although certainly many different customs have developed from the same underlying values, these rarely meet the earlier qualification of "significant." Students of literature are far beyond the need to know that magazines may be purchased at a supermarket in the United States, or that newsagents in Great Britain may have branch post offices; these things they learned at lower levels, from "readings" and other materials.

Although the principles put forth in this article apply to the teaching of culture through the literature of any language, examples will be from American literature and my many years' experience of teaching a course I have named "American Life Through Literature," for sophomore non-native speakers of English at the University of Houston – University Park. It is the aim of the course to teach literature for the same reasons that literature is taught to sophomore native speakers of English, but also to teach American culture by observing the behavior of fictional and real Americans from the time of the earliest colonial settlers to the present day, and by noting the influences that have shaped that behavior throughout our history. Teachers of other foreign languages may adapt the principles to the languages they teach and select the works that best exemplify the values they perceive to be significant.

It is a mistake to consider the identification of American values to be a facile matter. How we appear to others and how we see ourselves may be vastly different. Probably the most frequent opinion of American values expressed by non-Americans is that Americans care only for money – a view we frequently share, as can be seen by such expressions as "the almighty dollar" and the ironical "What's good for General Motors is good for the country." Other expressions, such as "God and country" and "Mom and apple pie," represent the opposite pole. All these attitudes exist in various individuals and groups in America, but what is the norm? A commercial of a few years back expressed it very well: "Baseball, hot dogs, apple pie, and Chevrolet." In this motto are symbols of clean, wholesome living, simple pleasures in life that represent "the American Way," but the grand finale is General Motors all the way. It is this tempering of the commercial with more spiritual attitudes that is desirable in the teaching of United States culture to "native speakers of other cultures," and that must be detected in the literature and explained to give a clearer picture of who and what Americans are.

In American literature the values will be apparent to the teacher, provided the teacher is well versed in American culture. A full consideration of American values has been presented by various sociologists, anthropologists, linguists, and combinations thereof. Perhaps the most valuable for the language teacher is Stewart (1972), with its extensive discussion of each value and the resultant behavior, and Condon and Yousef (1975). For the purposes of this discussion, it will suffice to mention one or two of the most prevalent values and how they appear in literature, and then to allow specific literary works to exemplify values.

Probably the most important value to present to students of American English is that of independence, which subsumes the notion of individual rights. Americans, typically, hold their individual independence in high esteem and will defend their right to maintain it. So basic is this concept to Americans that they assume it is a universal attitude, although in many other countries it is society or family that comes first, not the individual, and independent thought, far from being encouraged or admired, may be dangerous to one's welfare. Once ESL students understand the American reverence for individual independence, they are halfway to an understanding of most American literature.

The most obvious example of this American reverence for independence is in Emerson's essay "Self Reliance," in which he extols that virtue and explicates its value. From the same period and genre, Thoreau's "Walden Pond" also speaks directly to the matter of selecting one's own drummer, as do other works of these authors. A little later Mark Twain's Huck Finn exemplifies what Emerson and Thoreau were talking about. The American reader admires Huck's resourcefulness throughout the novel as well as his reluctant decision to help Jim find his own independence, and at the same time the reader envies somewhat Huck's determination not to allow himself to be "civilized" again. Contemporary works are so rife with examples of individualism that it would be possible to select a title almost at random, but we may cite as an example John Updike's short story "A&P," in which a youth quits his job at a supermarket in protest over the manager's treatment of a young customer. He will not change his mind even though he probably regrets his action, because he feels that backing down after making the grand gesture would be sacrificing his individualism.

Almost as strong as the attitude toward individualism in American culture is the concept of competition and fair play. This is related to individualism in its concern for where one person's rights end and the next person's begin. How is this value portrayed in our literature? The most obvious application would be in sports, but sports stories are rarely classified as "literature," even in our rather loose definition. Competition and fair play are seen throughout life, however, in the workplace, in the family, in human relations everywhere. In Stephen Crane's "The Bride Comes to Yellow Sky" we have a drunken gunman who challenges the marshall in order to prove his superiority in the quick-draw, but he gives up and goes away out of a sense of fair play when he learns that the marshall is unarmed and is accompanied by his new bride. In a fine satirical short story, "The Top," George Sumner Albee describes a company housed in a building shaped like a pyramid, with employees climbing to the top over the backs of their colleagues, with fair play conspicuous for its absence. In "Roman Fever" Edith Wharton presents two matrons reflecting on the years of their close association. The story ends with the revelation that foul play in the past had not paid, and the American reader rejoices in the proper "comeuppance" that the vicious, underhanded woman receives.

Understanding these unspoken values and presenting them to second language learners is an absolute requirement for the teacher. Rather than coming up with a value and trying to find a literary work to exemplify it, however, one should select a work because of its interest to the students, the level of proficiency it requires, and what it has to say. Then one should extract the values and include them in the teaching process. A valuable aid is Walter P. Allen's *Cultural Checklist* (1973: 12–24), which provides a chart for determining what cultural items are included in a given work. Allen gives an impressive number of cultural elements to search for in any given literary work, to determine its cultural value for nonnative speakers of English. The four main topics are general patterns in American culture, man and nature, man and man, and values in the culture, with dozens of subtopics, from eating habits to attitudes toward artists. It is an excellent guide to the parsing of a literary work for its cultural content. The native teacher frequently needs to have cultural items pointed out, as their very familiarity blinds one to their cultural significance.

Patently, literature that is appropriate for upper-intermediate students must be relatively simple in structure and style, be free from abstruse vocabulary, and contain valuable cultural content. For example, essays and short stories by James Thurber may be used at this level, with some glossing and considerable explication by the teacher of the cultural content. Such familiar essays as "The Night the Ghost Got In" and "The Night the Bed Fell" give the teacher the opportunity to approach the subject of humor, for while humor is universal, what constitutes humor in different societies offers considerable variety and contrast. Both of these essays point to the fact that Americans are amused by someone who makes fun of himself, especially if the reader can identify with the experience and thus feel more comfortable about having done or felt something equally silly. In some other cultures making fun of oneself is no laughing matter; it is seen as destructive of one's dignity and is taboo. Thurber's brief piece "The Unicorn in the Garden" and his short story "The Secret Life of Walter Mitty," on the other hand, concern another ancient American tradition, the battle of the sexes – a concept that is not really puzzling to those of many other cultures, although students often profess to believe that women of their own cultures never nag but are always properly subservient to their husbands.

It is wise to introduce the topic of humor at an early stage, as the understanding of what is funny in another language and culture is one of the last attainments of language students, who tend to sit in classes for years wondering what the teachers are laughing about. Learning that the most widespread basis for humor in most English speaking countries is a sense of the incongruous or the unexpected can help the nonnative speaker at least to understand humor when it is pointed out, if not to recognize it independently or to appreciate it with any degree of sincerity. The incongruous and the unexpected can easily be discerned, for example, in all the Thurber works cited here.

Other works appropriate to students at the upper-intermediate or lower-advanced level include various short stories by Ernest Hemingway and some plays by Tennessee Williams. Hemingway's "The Killers," for example, is almost all dialog, and while the language is informal, there is little dated slang that would stand as a barrier to the student. As most of the characters have little education, the syntax and vocabulary are simple. At the same time, the story is suspenseful, has characters in whom the students are interested – American gangsters – and concerns the values of individual rights and fair play. Williams's *The Glass Menagerie* has many of the same characteristics as "The Killers" – easy dialog, uncomplicated plot line (in spite of the complication of the theme of the play), and a concern with individualism and fair play, among other values, such as Tom's sense of responsibility to his mother and sister and the values inherent in American family relationships. Also at this level but very different in style and content is John F. Kennedy's essay "Waves of Immigration," which is written in a smooth, flowing style and with uncomplicated syntax. The vocabulary, though not excessively difficult, would probably need some glossing, and the content, concerning the various groups who have immigrated to America over the centuries and the experiences they encountered here, gives students much to identify with.

By the time ESL students pursuing academic studies reach sophomore literature courses in North American colleges or universities, they should be prepared to read almost any level of literature but should still be in separate classes for nonnative speakers of English, because an entirely different teaching approach is required for them, aside from the obvious one of different selection of materials. For example, if a mixed class of native and nonnative speakers is studying a work in which one character accuses another of being puritanical and the teacher takes the time to explain the background and meaning of the term to the nonnative speakers, the native speakers roll their eyes in disgust and take a nap. On the other hand, if such terms are not explained to the nonnative speakers, they have little chance of understanding the material. Obviously much more is involved when a conscious effort is made to teach the foreign culture through the literature.

Certainly there are some works that are, perhaps, beyond the easy reach of even such advanced students as those in sophomore literature classes. Emerson's style and vocabulary are so abstruse (for native speakers of English in sophomore classes, too!) that it would be wise to omit his essays, with the exception of "Self Reliance," which is worth the strain because of its cultural importance.

Some other works recommended for their content and linguistic clarity are Willa Cather's *O Pioneers!* and *Death Comes for the Archbishop,* which reflect early American values that persist to the present day; *Huckleberry Finn* (the dialect is more of a help than a hindrance at this level); Nathaniel Hawthorne's *The Scarlet Letter* or "Young Goodman Brown," which present Puritan philosophy and attitudes that pervade contemporary thought; William Dean Howells's "Editha," the anti-war theme of which has resurfaced in recent years; and works by or about minority groups, particularly blacks, Chicanos, and Jews. Followups are helpful, such as an excerpt from Frederick Douglass's "A Slave's Life," then William Faulkner's "That Evening Sun," and finally Donald Barthelme's "Margins" to trace the development of the relations between blacks and whites in America, along with selections by black writers. The real problem, in all honesty, is to keep the reading list to a manageable length.

Is the teaching of poetry to be avoided with nonnative speakers? Many believe it is, even if they advocate teaching of other genres of literature in ESL. The objections are obvious: The syntax is often distorted, the images are elusive, the vocabulary is convoluted, and the meaning is often obscure. These charges are valid with some poems and, indeed, with some poets, though of course such generalities cannot be accepted as a rule to live by and, as with other genres, the selection process overcomes the obstacles. Do we throw out Robert Frost's "Stopping by Woods on a Snowy Evening" because John Donne's religious poetry is difficult to grasp? It is permitted to omit Donne from the reading list. Frost's "Home Burial," however, with its flowing conversational style and diction, the universality of its topic of human suffering and shared or separate grief of parents for the loss of a child, is both appealing to and reasonably easy reading for advanced nonnative speakers. The added advantage is the opportunity it gives to discuss not only burial customs but attitudes toward the handling of grief over the death of someone who has been loved. Comparisons with other cultures bring out much that is immensely interesting to students and certainly to teachers.

The task of listing poets whose poems are suitable to ESL classes is not so important as an understanding of ways of approaching the teaching of poetry. One avoidable snare is the assignment of poems with the assumption that they will be understood by the students because they are clear to the teacher. After a poem has been read by the students it should be explained holistically; then read aloud so that the meaning can be clarified through pitch, stress, and intonation; then explicated bit by bit, though not necessarily line by line. Both during and after this process the cultural content and meaning can be approached. Even Edgar Allan Poe becomes less formidable through this method. Epic poems of considerable length cannot be given this thorough treatment and should be avoided.

A fallacy that has been prevalent for many years is that students from other lands, particularly those who are in technical disciplines, are alienated by poetry because they are not interested in it. Of course some are not, but neither are some native speakers – a fact that has not deterred us from exposing them to it. As a matter of fact, poetry is held in high esteem in many cultures and is consequently of special interest to many foreign students.

Some novels have been included among the recommendations here. It may be considered difficult to hold the attention of nonnative speakers over a sustained period, but it should be remembered that these students are able to read the language with considerable ease. The opportunity a novel gives to follow the effects of specific cultural patterns and mores through the lives of the characters over a period of time is invaluable in learning a second culture. For instance, *The Scarlet Letter*, despite Hawthorne's archaic style, which slows down the reader somewhat, not only reveals the Puritan attitude toward adultery, which still has its place in many circles of our society in spite of the sexual revolution, but also goes into great detail on the Puritan belief in the basic sinfulness of human beings. Hawthorne ruminates on and reveals the *degrees* of sin, from the weakest (spur-of-the-moment, atoned for, and victimless) to the moderate (spur-of-the-moment, not atoned for, and allowing someone else to suffer for one's deed) to the ultimate (premeditated, deliberate, vindictive, intended to destroy the immortal soul of the victim). Obviously there is much material here for discussion, both in a historical and contemporary setting, in strictly American or cross-cultural perspectives. Students write well on such topics, as well as on church and state, and many other topics suggested by this great novel.

Plays are an obvious choice because of the presentation through language that represents real speech among real people, clear enough to reveal the characters and the interactions of the plot. Still the cultural aspects will be no more obvious to the reader than in other genres, and the students will need no less guidance from the teacher. Full-length plays give a more complete treatment of cultural patterns and mores than do shorter works, though less than the novel usually does, since it also generally carries the informative contributions of the author and covers a longer period of time.

The short story, on the other hand, is valuable for almost opposite reasons from the novel: It generally presents a few characters over a short period of time in a situation that encapsulates a cultural attitude, with probably minor cultural values also to be uncovered and discussed. The aforementioned stories of Thurber, Updike, and Wharton exemplify this circumstance.

It is clear, then, that all genres of literature lend themselves to study by upper-intermediate to advanced second language students, giving them much greater insight into the culture and leading to greater understanding – and therefore appreciation – of literature, possibly of their own as well as that of the second language. Expansion of horizons is the aim of all education.

For best effect, students should be warned frequently to keep up in their reading. Because they cannot benefit fully from class discussion if they have not read the assignment before coming to class, pop quizzes may sometimes be needed to keep them honest. Teachers should give manageable assignments for each class and should not confuse the students by discussing parts of a work that have not yet been assigned – students like to have the suspense sustained.

All of this is presented as a guide to teachers, but another caveat is in order here. As the Knower in the cultural context, the teacher may be tempted to follow the format of straight lecture, which does provide the students with information but deprives them of the depth of understanding and enjoyment that is derived from class discussion, through the reactions of the students to what they have read, to what the teacher has said, and to what their classmates have contributed in a cross section of cultural attitudes. Be the Knower, point out and explain cultural matters, but do not attempt to be the Oracle. Your thesis should never be "This is the way it is in the United States of America and the way it ought to be everywhere," but "This is the way it is in the United States – how is it in your culture, and what do you think about it all?" It is equally important to attempt to overcome student prejudice, but only by leading students to consider all sides of an issue.

How should teachers arrange the literary material? A simple chronological arrangement is probably best, as it provides a historical perspective and a satisfactory structural frame. On the other hand, the selections may be grouped according to the values or themes they reveal. The theme arrangement can be effective, so long as the lesson to be gleaned does not begin to pall before the examples are completed. The value, or theme, of independence, for example, could have many selections listed, since the theme is a pervasive one, and the category itself could occasion too much stressing of a single point. Many values may be revealed in one work, and categorization has the effect of minimizing other equally important themes. An arrangement by genres is neat and easy, but sacrifices the variety that is achieved by mixing the genres together and could result in a loss of student interest.

Wilga Rivers has said,

Our students need literature, poetry, music, and other artistic manifestations, not only of a literate elite, but also of the common people in oral traditions, folklore, the arts of the people, the history and stories that make small pockets of cultural identity unique. Through this content they can share the culture and the concerns of many times and many peoples, faraway and close at home. The preoccupations change and interweave, but societies and groups have had to face basically the same issues. (Rivers 1983a: 33)

Indeed, the teaching and discussion of literature in a second language is an exciting cosmic experience. Enjoy it.

Questions for consideration

1. What distinctions are made between readings and literature? Are these distinctions valid?
2. How does the author justify the assignment of such a difficult essay as Emerson's "Self Reliance"? What are the pros and cons of such a selection?
3. Select a short humorous work that you enjoy. How would you present such a work to a class of nonnative speakers? What situations or remarks would require cultural explanations?

4. What poets in the language you teach are particularly suitable for teaching to nonnative speakers? Why?
5. What are the dangers, or limitations, of teaching cultural matters strictly as points of information? What can you add to what the author has said?

15 English language teaching from an intercultural perspective

Stephen C. Dunnett
SUNY Buffalo

Fraida Dubin
University of Southern California

Amy Lezberg
Massachusetts College of Pharmacy

Techniques

... Implementation of an intercultural perspective within an English language program can be made explicit by setting up courses or activities that focus on culture-related themes. At the same time, an intercultural view inevitably will be implicit in the materials utilized for instructional purposes. But beyond these explicit and implicit means of teaching intercultural communicative competence, the vital element which gives language courses a tone of cultural understanding is the teachers' own attitudes toward their students' backgrounds as well as toward the materials utilized. This section will consider these several ways in which teachers deal with intercultural communication in English language teaching.

No matter how intercultural attitudes come into an EFL course, all of those professionals concerned – teachers and administrators – must possess certain basic understandings about language and culture. If they have this awareness, the programs they plan, the courses they create, the syllabi they construct and the materials they write can foster an intercultural point of view.

Some of the most basic of these understandings are as follows: (1) Languages cannot be translated word-for-word. All languages have idiomatic expressions which carry connotations that are above and beyond the meanings of the separate words themselves. (2) The tone of a speaker's voice (the intonation pattern) carries meaning. All languages have

Reprinted by permission from *Learning Across Cultures*, edited by Gary Althen, pp. 57–69. © 1981 by National Association for Student Affairs.

different "tunes" or patterns of intonation. Similarly, the degree of loudness/softness used by speakers is a characteristic of the language itself. (3) Each language-culture employs gestures and body movements which convey meaning. Gesture and body movements are not necessarily the same for all languages. (4) We also understand that languages use different grammatical elements for describing all parts of the physical world. (5) All cultures have taboo topics. Part of knowing a language is knowing what one can and cannot say to whom on what occasions. (6) In personal relationships, the terms for addressing people vary considerably among languages. Even in informal American culture, there are commonly agreed-upon rules indicating when people are addressed by their first name and when they are called by a title such as Mrs., Mr., or Dr.

The most explicit format for presenting these and other intercultural elements in English language programs is through courses designated as "Intercultural Communication" or "Intercultural Conversation." It is useful to describe how such courses have been presented in the past. Teachers, of course, will want to adapt these suggestions to their own particular settings. One successful plan for an intercultural communication course includes participation by American students. In some cases, the Americans receive academic credit for their contribution to the group. In others, the EFL institute, center or department recruits Americans through work-study or similar programs, or through "freshman English" classes. American volunteers may also be graduate students enrolled in masters' programs in TEFL/TESL. Usually, American participants are required to do outside reading in the field and to attend periodic meetings with the course coordinator.

Criteria for selecting the American student-facilitators include factors such as sensitivity to the language learning problems of foreign students, an active interest in exploring and understanding cultural differences in a nonjudgmental way, experience in group discussion leadership and, above all, a friendly, open manner with people from other cultures.

At some large universities that have a high enrollment of foreign students, the intercultural program is part of a 25-hour per week intensive English program. Students enrolled at this level typically score between 300–400 on the TOEFL (Test of English as a Foreign Language) and are ranked as low intermediates. The intercultural class meets for two hours a week with a coordinator. The enrollment in each section is approximately 12–15 foreign students and four to five American students. A feature of the so-called class is that it does not meet in a classroom. Considerable effort is made to secure a comfortable, homelike meeting place.

At the beginning of the semester, the coordinator decides on a list of conversation topics. Possible topics include Parents and Children; Getting Older/Getting Old; Divorce: American Style; The Largest Minority: Women; Drugs and Society; Childhood Fantasies; Stereotypes; Personal and Public Behavior; Gestures and Non-Verbal Communication; Interpersonal Sharing; and City Life and Its Problems.

For each topic the coordinators write a set of questions to focus students' attention on the cross-cultural aspect of the issue. For example, in the discussion on parents and children the following points were brought up:

In your country:
    When do people become adults?
    When do people move away from their parents' home?
    What conflicts do parents have with children?
    What conflicts do children have with parents?

In this particular discussion, one of the important insights for the American facilitators was that the topic itself held the built-in message for Americans that somehow conflict between generations is to be expected. This was not always the case for other cultures.

Intercultural themes can also be the basis for spoken English in classes where one of the course objectives is to foster freer communication. A variety of techniques have been developed through which to present structured communication activities that ensure everyone's taking part in the discussion. For example, the following procedure for conducting a class discussion on the topic of stereotypes has been successful (adapted from Batchelder and Warner 1977):

1. Students list four or five stereotypes or preconceived ideas they had before coming to the United States about life in the United States and/or in other countries represented in the group.
2. The facilitator writes these stereotype statements on the blackboard or distributes them on a handout at the next class meeting.
3. The facilitator leads discussion by mentioning stereotypical statements English speakers often make about other languages, e.g., "French is for romance, German is guttural, Italian sounds like music."
4. Each group represented responds to the stereotypes about life in the U.S. and elsewhere. "Where did you hear that . . . ?"

Presenting a problem for students to solve is a particularly effective technique for evoking discussion about cultural differences. Participants read or hear briefly about a real-life problem. The problem should illustrate the topic or theme of the discussion. The problem can be set out quite elaborately with a number of points to discuss. Or, the lesson can be done by simply offering alternate endings to the story. The discussion then centers on deciding which solution to adopt.

An example of a problem-solving situation is the lifeboat scene: the descriptive paragraph gives biographical details concerning eight to ten individuals who have survived a catastrophe and are now in a lifeboat. But there is only food and water for so many days. Or, there are only life jackets for so many people. The writer, of course, is free to create dramatic elements that sustain interest, always remaining within the language capabilities of the participants. The problem in this case is: Who should be allowed to survive?

Another technique is called the "culture assimilator." In this approach, an incident containing a misunderstanding between a non-native speaker of English and an American is described. Then there are questions which embody varying interpretations coming from culturally different points of view. The students choose the statement that they think most accurately interprets the event. They then look to see if their interpretation is the correct one. If it is not, they are told why it is not, and then are asked to try again.

The process of brainstorming is a freer format through which to discuss cross-cultural themes while, at the same time, the participants are gaining practice in using the new language. Sound materials for cross-cultural discussions should be constructed with the learners' language abilities in mind. Vocabulary lists are always extremely helpful.

Among additional techniques are the following: (1) The role play: Students take on the parts of typical members of host and native cultures. (2) Value hierarchies: Students put random lists of items into a preferred order. For example, the most important/prestigious/valued professions are ——. (3) Compare and contrast: Students fill in blanks with their choice. For example: Who is responsible for the following household tasks in your country? mother / father / both parents / servant / children / no one.

In using each one of these techniques, it is vital that a full and open discussion take place following the activity.

An effective technique for stimulating cross-cultural introspection is the use of personal journals in conjunction with the intercultural communication class. Since this type of writing gives the language learner more freedom, students often experience their own understanding of the cross-cultural element in a class discussion when they reflect on the session while writing up their reactions and feelings in a weekly journal report.

A final example of an explicit technique is the lecture-discussion format. Often offered as a credit-bearing course about American culture, it can serve multiple purposes: (1) The course creates a context through

151

which students strengthen their skills in listening comprehension, note-taking, examination writing, etc. (2) The course serves as a bridge between the EFL program and regular classes in the university. (3) When presented by a skilled lecturer, the course can focus on cross-cultural themes.

Topics included in the syllabus for such a course could include the following (*American Language Institute Manual* 1979):

1. The United States – The Melting Pot Society
   – diagram of American ethnicity
     emphasize the melting pot idea – has it succeeded?
   – discuss "mainstream America"
2. Mexican Culture
   – attitudes of and toward Mexican-Americans
   – Spanish and Mexican influences in many parts of the United States
3. Blacks in America
   – attitudes of and toward
   – Martin Luther King and the Civil Rights movement
   – Uncle Tom's Cabin excerpt / short stories written by Black Americans
4. Native Americans
   – contributions of
   – Indian folk stories
   – American Indians as depicted by films
5. Religion in America
   – attitude toward
   – different kinds
   – effects on culture
   – cults and organized religion
6. Women in America
   – contributions of
   – attitudes of and toward
   – ERA and anti-abortionists
   – anti-abortionists
7. The American Family
   – structure
   – values
   – level of closeness
   – dependence/independence
8. American customs
   – multiplicity of
9. The American Character
   – stereotypes

- myths
- various types
10. Big Cities vs. Small Towns
    - ways and attitudes
11. American Business
    - how does it affect relations and attitudes?
    - commercialization: Christmas and Easter
12. Pop Culture
    - poetry
    - abstract painting / Andy Warhol's "Campbell Soup Can"
    - rock music
    - disco music
13. American Attitudes
    - toward themselves
    - toward the world
14. A View from the Outside
    - looking at the arts and literature from abroad, how are Americans viewed in other countries?

Materials

Most if not all of the materials used in language teaching convey cultural biases. These materials implicitly communicate attitudes concerning the culture of the target language and the learner's native language-culture. It is possible to find materials for English language teaching which encourage an intercultural point of view. They treat culture-related themes from at least two contrasting perspectives. We can designate them as two-dimensional materials.

But it is more often the case that typical English language instructional materials communicate cultural messages from a one-dimensional view. Social scientists point out that it is as impossible to escape from one's own culture as it is to get out of one's own skin. So, it is probably to be expected that textbook writers continually convey culture-bound ideas in at least every other exercise of each lesson. More often than not it is up to the instructor to alter materials to express a two-dimensional or multi-dimensional outlook.

In order to realize the implicit cultural message in almost all language teaching materials, it is helpful to separate out what has been called cultural habits and customs – elements that are broadly recognized as not being universally the same – from the less transparent themes. The following aspects of American culture are frequently reflected implicitly in English language instructional materials (Kraemer 1973):

- Individualism: The belief that each person is a distinct entity and ought to assert and achieve independence from others.
- Egalitarianism: The belief that all human beings are equal in their intrinsic worth.
- Action orientation: Doing is more important than being.
- Perception of interpersonal encounters primarily in terms of their immediate utility and downgrading of the social significance of such encounters.
- Universalism: The value attached to being guided in one's action in a given situation primarily by an obligation to society (i.e., by general standards of conduct – laws, regulations, rules, established procedures, etc.).
- Definition of persons (including oneself) in terms of their work and their achievements.
- The belief that the collective wisdom of the group is superior to that of any individual.
- The idea that the process of decision making requires evaluation of the consequences of alternative courses of action, and selection of the one that, on balance, seems most advantageous.
- The belief that competition is a good way to motivate people.
- The idea that there is usually a best way of doing something, which should be determined and then followed.
- The idea that knowledge gained through observation is superior to knowledge gained in other ways.
- Unnecessary qualification: The tendency to quantify aspects of experience.
- Placing a higher value on utilitarian aspects of experience than on aesthetic ones.
- Problem orientation: The tendency to perceive "problems" in the world and in one's existence in it, and to look for "solutions."
- The belief that thought cannot directly influence events.
- Reasoning in terms of probability.
- Impatience: The tendency to be annoyed by the pace of activities, if it is slow by one's own standard.
- The tendency to make comparative judgments.
- The willingness to offer one's services for the benefit of the "common good."
- The belief in the existence of a behavior pattern called "self help."
- The use of absurd suppositions to communicate ideas or to elicit ideas from other persons.

One way by which to evaluate the culture sensitivity quotient of English language texts is to view them in the light of this list of American culture characteristics. To what degree does the language in the text reflect deep aspects of the culture of the target language? In order to answer this question, one must analyze the text in terms of what people in the book say and do. In typical beginner's level materials, stick or cartoon figures introduce themselves. (My name is ———. What's yours?) They talk about their possessions. (Is this your book? Yes, it's mine.) They locate objects. (Where's your raincoat? It's in your bedroom.) They indicate their likes and dislikes. (Do you like carrots? Do you like chocolates? Do you like bananas?) They talk about the time of day. (Excuse me. What time is it? It's one o'clock.) They buy and sell things. (What's she buying? She's buying a banana.) They talk about their occupation. (This is Mr. Jenkins. He's a postman.) They talk about their recreational activities. (Jim likes skating. What does Mary like? She likes skiing.) (Mellgren and Walker 1973).

The examples are not meant to match exactly with the list of culture characteristics. However, even the most superficial scanning of standard language texts, particularly those at the beginning of elementary level, indicate a strong motif of deeper American culture themes, with few opportunities to introduce a two-dimensional view unless the teacher injects a question such as: "This is what Americans do. What do you do?" Or, "This is the American view. What is your view?"

It is important for the teacher who wants to stress culture themes in the language course to evaluate materials carefully. As an example of the kind of elements teachers need to be aware of, we next look at three different texts designed for reading, writing, and discussion practice at the intermediate and advanced levels. In these three texts, it is possible to trace different approaches to the elucidation of intercultural themes.

A text which encourages and stimulates an intercultural approach is *Living Language: USA Culture Capsules for ESL Students* (Johnson 1979). In the introduction, the author states:

The purpose of these capsules is not to teach you one specific way of thinking about any particular aspect of United States culture. Rather, they are designed to help you analyze different areas of culture in the United States and compare them with your native language... The capsules do not attempt to make any value judgments with regard to U.S. culture. You may make these judgments for yourself after some investigations and thinking of your own.

In this book, the author treats the following topics in "culture capsule" lessons: unemployment, singles' life, shopping, education, urban development, divorce, family unity, racism and the position of women.

A somewhat different and a provocative approach to learning about and from cultural differences is presented in another text, *Points of View* (Pifer and Mutoh 1977). With this book the instructor must bring out the intercultural possibilities in the materials, since the intercultural emphasis is not as explicit as it is in Johnson's book. Using case studies for analysis and problem solving, the authors give students and instructors the following comments:

Reflecting on individual and cultural values. All decisions in these case studies, as in real life, are based on peoples' frames of values. These activities cause students consciously to consider their own values. In bi- or multi-cultural groups, this presents an excellent occasion for cross-cultural learning.

A third text is a good example of a one-dimensional approach. *Read On, Speak Out* (Ferreira and Vaie 1979) also encourages students to read, think and discuss topics of current interest to educated adults. In this text, though, the orientation is strongly towards an American point of view. For example, in Lesson Six, "Gray Power: It's *In* to Be Old," the title tells us something about the value system of Americans today. Contained in the lesson are readings and discussion questions concerned with the United States older population: The gray revolution. Changing U.S. population trends. Prejudice towards older people in jobs. Problems of the retired. Is there life after 65? What's it like to be free, gray, and 65? Should workers be forced to retire at age 65?

In the final section, "In your opinion," students answer two questions about the entire six pages of text regarding attitudes in their own countries towards older people. From the point of view of an instructor who wants to emphasize an intercultural point of view in a reading/discussion course, this text would be less appropriate than either of the two mentioned above because it is heavily weighted towards cultural attitudes in the U.S.

Teachers who are sensitive to an intercultural approach would probably be successful using any of these materials if they did a great deal of adapting, changing and augmenting. For it is true that an intercultural ethos can be brought into any classroom when teachers stop to consider their students' values and attitudes towards topics under discussion. Similarly, in less advanced classes, the teacher can inject a two-dimensional view towards the subjects and topics practiced in drill and exercises. But some teachers still express concern over where they should place emphasis. What should receive the most attention? They ask, "How can there be time to deal with culture when students must pass examinations, gain entrance into degree programs and get ready to find jobs in an English-speaking community?"

Those teachers who do spend some time with intercultural themes usually find real satisfaction in their experiences with students. They say that they find they themselves learn as much as their students. Above all, they feel that their own lives have been enriched when they listen to their students' point of view.

Issues and implications

The implementation of an intercultural perspective or approach within an English language program raises several issues and has implications for EFL program administrators and teachers.

To implement an intercultural approach would require some curricular revision for most EFL programs, which in practice devote the major portion of their instructional time to the four basic language skills. This immediately gives rise to several curricular issues.

The first issue is how much of the core curriculum can be devoted to the teaching of culture. Or, in the case where the teaching of culture is integrated with language materials and methodology, to what degree can culture learning be successfully integrated? It is often difficult to convince many EFL teachers that teaching of a culture is not a secondary goal. Given the time constraints that EFL teachers face, it is understandable that they might view the integration of culture learning as interfering with basic English language teaching. In such situations it might be best to present intercultural elements in separate courses similar to those we described earlier in this chapter.

Whether cultural instruction is integrated or taught separately, it is important that it not be approached in a haphazard manner. Intercultural activities and courses must be given the same importance in the curriculum as all other language activities. If this is not done students will consider intercultural activities as secondary to language instruction and teachers will, even in an integrated approach, give only passing attention to cultural components.

Curricular coordinators should make every effort to relate cultural topics to appropriate language learning activities while controlling vocabulary and grammar content. A detailed, long-range instructional plan should be developed incorporating carefully selected cultural topics in items with assigned dates and contract hours. If an integrated approach is chosen, EFL program administrators should provide their teachers with an instructional plan or syllabus and suggested strategies for teaching about culture.

The implementation of an intercultural approach in EFL teaching requires not only a re-examination of traditional EFL program curricula but also the content of teacher training programs. Although many EFL teachers in the field are sensitive to issues of intercultural communication and have received professional training in this area, there are teachers who come to the field with different professional backgrounds. Some are former foreign language teachers, others are secondary or elementary school teachers, and still others have little or no formal training.

TEFL training programs are providing a good preparation in theoretical backgrounds to second language teaching, applied linguistics, and in-class practice teaching, but very little in the way of intercultural training. The contemporary EFL teacher requires a thorough background in comparative/contrastive analysis (especially in non-Indo-European analysis) and cultural anthropology in order to deal competently with today's diverse student population. In addition to training students for appropriate linguistic performance, EFL teachers must also make their students aware of the proper linguistic performance in diverse types of intercultural settings.

The sophisticated EFL teacher, while introducing foreign students to some aspects of American culture, must also encourage students to maintain their own cultural identity. To achieve this, the teacher must be trained to talk about cultural relativism as well as the universality of certain components shared by different cultures. The teacher should guide cultural discussions so that they do not become judgmental and lead to conclusions that some cultures are superior or inferior.

Students in TEFL training programs should be provided with opportunities to gain culture-teaching experience by working closely with foreign students and other non-native speakers from the very beginning of their degree programs. They should also be required to observe experienced teachers in their classrooms. Additional practical experience may be gained by volunteer service in foreign student advisers' offices, international living centers and other student service offices. Finally, student teachers should be encouraged to study a non-Indo-European language to gain better appreciation of the problems of foreign students from non-Western countries.

If it is not possible to add a specific course in intercultural communications or comparative cultures to the TEFL training program, student teachers should be strongly encouraged to participate in workshops or training sessions organized on other campuses, such as the Stanford Institute in Applied Intercultural Communication that is held every summer.

Finally, TEFL training program administrators should assist their students in the ultimate intercultural training experience – teaching or studying abroad.

For EFL teachers already in the field it may not be possible to engage in the types of academic training activities we have just described. They can, however, receive in-service professional training through participation in a number of professional associations such as the Teachers of English to Speakers of Other Languages (TESOL); NAFSA's [the National Association for Foreign Student Affairs] professional section for

English as a second language teachers, called the Association of Teachers of English as a Second Language (ATESL); Foreign Language Teachers Association; and the Society for Intercultural Education, Training and Research (SIETAR).

Through subscriptions to the journals and other publications of these professional associations and attendance at their regional and national workshops and conferences, EFL teachers can obtain valuable in-service training.

Through NAFSA's Field Service Program, EFL teachers may apply for special in-service training grants to visit postsecondary institutions or related community organizations. Grantees may observe day-to-day operations, activities and classes of established EFL institutes and programs. In-service training grants cover modest expenses of such visits to confer with EFL colleagues and explore ideas which may prove applicable for use in one's own setting. It is our hope that through the curricular modification of both EFL programs and EFL teacher training programs to add an intercultural perspective, we shall enable our students to achieve true communicative competence in English. . . .

All EFL training programs, in order to strengthen their intercultural perspective, should strive to implement the following recommendations:

1. Hire teachers with a strong background in comparative analysis, and/or comparative cultures and/or training in intercultural communications.
2. All other qualifications being equal, give preference to EFL teachers with overseas training experience and familiarity with non-Indo-European languages.
3. Provide in-service training opportunities in intercultural communications for teachers currently on staff.
4. Provide an orientation each semester to both faculty and staff on linguistic and cultural backgrounds of current student population in EFL programs.
5. Integrate intercultural education with language instruction through carefully designed syllabi.
6. Select EFL materials which encourage an intercultural point of view.
7. Develop specific strategies for teaching culture in the English program.
8. Establish a specific course to focus on culture-related topics.
9. Provide students with a comprehensive program of extracurricular activities such as excursions, tours, lectures, films, conversation groups led by American students, a sports program, and a homestay with an American family.
10. Establish programs to help break down the ghettoization of foreign students which may take place in the university residence halls. . . .

As stated earlier..., there are no perfect textbooks which completely and successfully integrate language instruction with cultural components. However, EFL teachers can improve upon textbook selection by following these guidelines:

1. Examine each new textbook carefully to determine whether it takes an intercultural point of view.
2. Try to identify the cultural aspects inherent in the textbook and list them by chapter or units. Are they positive or negative? Mixed?
3. Examine the exercises carefully. Determine if they will assist you in drawing students into intercultural activities.
4. Check to see if the vocabulary items, examples, grammar structures, drills, etc., are placed in some meaningful cultural context.
5. Examine photographs and illustrations, if any, to see if they are culturally related.
6. Carefully examine dialogues, if any, for their cultural content.
7. Go back and re-examine those textbooks which take a strong intercultural point of view for possible cultural bias. Are they objective? Do they stereotype or overgeneralize about U.S. or foreign cultures?

Conclusion

Most practitioners in international educational interchange believe that intercultural experiences have beneficial results for individual participants and, over time, for their respective societies. Studying and living abroad are seen as ways of fostering broadmindedness, tolerance, and the ability to deal constructively with people who are different. These attributes are seen as increasingly necessary in a world where international interactions and mutual dependencies are growing in scope and importance. For EFL students in the U.S., these attributes can be fostered by EFL teachers who embody them, who use materials that focus attention on them, and who use techniques that help their students learn them. It is our hope that readers of this chapter have found it helpful in providing ideas for EFL teachers and administrators who want to bring culture learning to the EFL classroom.

Questions for consideration

1. In the United States, how much someone weighs is not an acceptable question. Can you name five more taboo topics in U.S. culture? Are they equally taboo in another culture that you know well?

2. What arguments can you make against culture courses only at the intermediate level of intensive language programs?
3. In Kraemer's list of aspects of American culture, which ones would you have believed to be universal? common to all Western cultures?
4. How can the majority of what is said in this article be applied to a foreign language course in an English speaking country? to an English course in a non-English-speaking country?

16 An argument for culture analysis in the second language classroom

George H. Hughes
University of Kansas

The focus of culture study

Should culture study in the second language classroom try to achieve an understanding of an individual's motives, intentions, desires, and reasons for behavior? Or, should the focus of our material and discussions concern forms of organization, concepts, customary beliefs, and patterns of behavior seen in relation to each other? For example, should we be concerned with the actual behavior of members of a culture (their desires and interests) or simply rely on what many have called abstractions from actual behavior (that is, beliefs, patterns of social organization, political organization, etc.)? It is the contention of the writer that the first type of question is what is of major concern to the second language student.

To make this point clear, the types of questions which deal with needs, motives, desires, and purposes can be referred to as *individual* or *psychological questions*; those which inquire into ideas, beliefs, customs and forms of organization can be called *institutional questions*. Psychological questions can aid us in sensitizing our students to cultural differences. Institutional knowledge is widely applicable to the culture as a whole, but it is factual knowledge that students can usually look up on their own. In contrast the study of psychological questions should be carefully guided by a skilled teacher in order to help our students relate to the target value system and reach personal decisions about their own values.

Models for the analysis of culture

Brooks' Key Questions

Now, let us examine several models which have been proposed for the analysis of culture. It should be worthwhile to mention a format sug-

This article is excerpted from George H. Hughes, "An Argument for Culture Analysis in the Second Language Classroom," pp. 38–50, originally published in 1984 in the *American Language Journal* 2(1): 31–51. It is reprinted here by permission.

gested by Nelson Brooks (1975), which exemplified the practical use of distinguishing between individual and institutional aspects of culture. Brooks suggests that when observing and studying a culture it is important to have key questions in mind. This helps promote systematic observation. Here is a sample list of questions that serve to highlight the individual aspects of culture:

How do you think and feel about your family?
How do you tell right from wrong?
How do you appear in public?
How do you act toward a stranger?
How do you treat a guest?
How do you view the opposite sex?
How do you answer a child's question about God, birth, sex, and myth?
How do you look upon minority groups?
What are you superstitious about?
What is your greatest ambition, your chief regret?
Of what organizations are you a member?

These individual questions which Brooks suggests are certainly relevant and interesting to the teenage learner. Contrast these with the following sample which represents the type of questions that Brooks distinguishes as being of the institutional kind:

What schools and colleges can you go to?
Under what system of government do you live?
What laws must you obey? Who makes them?
What churches or religious organizations may you join?
What publications can you buy?
What is the money system you use?
How do you get from place to place?
What must you obtain a license for?
What public recreational facilities are available to you?
For what do you get your name in the papers?
What military organizations may you or must you serve in?

Getting the students to ask themselves such questions concerning their own society is a good start in cultural study. Moreover, this is an excellent chance for the instructor to orient the students to be aware of cultural differences and understand basic anthropological concepts. However, exclusive use of these types of questions will consume valuable class time that could have been more efficiently used. They will promote interesting discussions but will inevitably lead to answers that students could have discovered independently, outside of class.

George H. Hughes

Murdock's Seven Facets

One of the most extensive models for the analysis of culture is that of George Murdock who bases his classification on the assumption that any one element of culture may have seven facets upon which to be classified. These seven facets are (1) a patterned activity, that is, "A customary norm of motor, verbal or implicit (covert or ideational) behavior"; (2) the appropriateness of such an activity under certain circumstances such as time or place; (3) the particular subject of the behavior; (4) the object toward which the behavior is directed; (5) some means external to both the subject and the object of the behavior; (6) the purpose of the activity; and (7) the result of the activity. The resulting outline for examining a culture has a total of 888 categories (Murdock et al. 1971).

Hall's Ten Primary Message Systems

Edward T. Hall derives one hundred categories from ten primary message systems. The criteria upon which these ten forms of human activity were chosen are the following:

1. Rooted in a biological activity widely shared with other advanced living forms. It is essential that there be no breaks with the past.
2. Capable of analysis in its own terms without reference to the other systems and so organized that it contains isolated components that can be built up into more complex units.
3. So constituted that it reflects all the rest of culture and is reflected in the rest of culture.

The Primary Message Systems are Interaction, Association, Subsistence, Bisexuality, Territoriality, Temporality, Learning, Play, Defense, and Exploitation (Hall 1959).

From these ten primary message systems, Hall has created an interrelated *Map of Culture* (Hall 1959: 222–3). The order of the ten systems is supposed to represent theoretically the evolution of culture. For example, we begin with the first primary message system, *Interaction*, which is a primary characteristic of all life. "Ultimately, everything man does involves interaction with something else." (Hall 1959: 46). *Association*, which has its roots in the joining of two cells, is the basis for the structurizing of societies. *Subsistence* has to do with the nutritional requirements of man and the way in which these are met in a particular society. *Bisexuality* is the answer the human race has invented to meet the need of a mixed genetic background. *Territoriality* (space) and *Tem-*

164

porality (time) help man to define himself. *Learning* is important as an adaptive mechanism. *Play* includes humor. *Defense* includes religion, war, law enforcement, and medicine. Finally, *Exploitation* is the extension man makes of his body to utilize the environment (Hall 1959: 46–60).

Hall's *Map of Culture*, which crosses lines of various theoretical orientations, can be utilized by second language instructors to obtain a comprehensive and comparative view of their native and target cultures. Such crosscultural analyses, using Hall's map, help the instructor to pinpoint where students may have difficulties in understanding the target culture – that is, the areas which show the most contrast, making transference unlikely.

Taylor and Sorenson's Model

Darrel Taylor and John Sorenson (1961: 351) propose a model on which to base culture capsules, so that while analyzing one element at a time, the student eventually derives a unified picture. The categories in this outline are technology, economy, social organization, political organization, world view (religion and philosophy), esthetics, and education. As with Hall's system, the order in which the categories are derived is significant. In this model one starts with the concrete and proceeds to more abstract considerations. There is also a subcultural category including biological, geographical, and historical elements. The model given in their article is based on Mexican culture specifically, unlike those of Hall and Murdock, which are not geared to one particular culture. The categories are subdivided into precise topics which makes observational and data-gathering processes easier. One category's subdivisions are included here for the purpose of example:

II. Technological category
   A. Food-getting and using
      (Cultivating and the major crops; preparing, serving, and eating typical foods)
   B. Shelter-Housing
      (the patio form, barred windows, fronting on street)
   C. Clothing
   D. Tools
   E. Transportation

Nostrand's Emergent Model

Another popular model used for the analysis of culture is Howard Lee Nostrand's *Emergent Model*. Nostrand looks for patterns in the "feelings, beliefs, and thought process" of members of the target culture. It is assumed that certain ingredients are characteristic of a culture member's behavior. The procedure is to combine experience of the people's way of life with descriptive knowledge about the people, so that the resulting study is an examined experience of the target culture.

Nostrand based his model on four levels of societal organization: the human organism (personality), social relations, culture patterns and ecology. He emphasized three cultural elements – values, traits, and world view – as concrete manifestations of the *ground of meaning* on which culture members base their lives. That is, all the concrete manifestations of the target culture are somehow contained within these categories. Furthermore, if one adds to the values of the culture the traits and assumptions of fact (world view) which are necessary in order to understand the value, one arrives at the culture's main themes. Each culture has its own themes and no culture has more than twelve. The twelve themes of French culture, according to Nostrand (1974), are the following:

1. The art of living: enjoyment of the lifestyle one has chosen
2. Intellectuality and *être raisonnable*
3. Individualism and civil liberty (including acquisitive ambition)
4. Realism and good sense (including health care and sensitivity to material conditions and conveniences)
5. Law and order (including retributive justice)
6. Distributive justice (including an increasing humanitarian concern and sensitivity to the deteriorating environment)
7. Friendship
8. Love
9. Family
10. Religion
11. The quest for community (with a subculture), and loyalty to a province or region
12. Patriotism and its object, *la patrie*

In conclusion, models for the analysis of culture offer an opportunity for culture study to proceed in a systematic, comparative, and comprehensive manner. Although no cultural models can function to isolate cultural elements, they demonstrate the integrative aspect of culture. Most important, various models cut across cultural boundaries; therefore, they can be applied to any culture (including comparative analysis). Moreover, cultural models, as well as the concepts on which they are based, also cut across time barriers. That is, models are consistent designs that allow for the incorporation of new and changing data. However, models that present an empty taxonomy – those which need to be filled in for each culture – are of little use unless the language teacher has acquired an orientation to the concepts and processes involved....

Techniques for teaching cultural awareness

There are numerous expert language teachers and teacher trainers who have written extensively about the many vehicles that have proven successful for the teaching of cultural awareness. Only a very brief sketch can be included here of those deemed most practical:

1. *Comparison method*. The teacher begins each discussion period with a presentation of one or more items in the target culture that are distinctly different from the students' culture. The discussion then centers on why these differences might cause problems.
2. *Culture assimilators*. Developed by social psychologists for facilitating adjustment to a foreign culture, the culture assimilator is a brief description of a critical incident of crosscultural interaction that would probably be misunderstood by the students. After the description of the incident, the students are presented with four possible explanations from which they are asked to select the correct one. If they make the wrong choice, they are asked to seek further information that would lead them to the correct conclusion.
3. *Culture capsule*. This technique is somewhat similar to culture assimilator, but cannot be assigned as a silent reading exercise. The teacher gives a brief presentation showing one essential difference between an American and a foreign custom. It is accompanied by visuals which illustrate the difference, and a set of questions to stimulate class discussion.
4. *Drama*. This technique is especially useful for directly involving students in crosscultural misunderstandings by having selected members act out in a series of short scenes a misinterpretation of something that happens in the target culture. The cause of the problem is usually clarified in the final scene.
5. *Audiomotor unit or Total Physical Response*. Primarily designed as a listening exercise, this method employs a carefully constructed list of oral commands to which students respond. The commands are arranged in an order that will cause students to act out a *cultural experience*.
6. *Newspapers*. Many aspects of culture that are not usually found in a textbook are present in the newspaper. The teacher asks students to compare a certain item in the foreign newspaper with its equivalent in their newspapers. Good cultural insights can readily be found in headlines, advertisements, editorials, sports pages, comics, even the

167

weather report. The humor found on the comic page is especially revealing.

7. *Projected media.* Films, filmstrips and slides provide cultural insights as well as providing a welcome variety of classroom activities. Excellent filmstrips on culturally related subjects are available commercially, and slides that teachers have collected in their travels can be worked into short, *first-hand* cultural presentations.

8. *The culture island.* The teacher maintains a classroom ambiance that is essentially a *culture island* through the use of posters, pictures, a frequently changing bulletin board, all of which are designed with the purpose of attracting student attention, eliciting questions and comments.

Foreign language teachers or superscholars?

With this new emphasis in second language study, that of training students to understand and interpret the culture, and to function in that new environment, the burden placed upon language instructors has greatly increased. Since we cannot expect them to be linguists, psychologists, philosophers, and cultural anthropologists (and, perhaps, geographers, historians, philologists, and literary critics) we can, at least, suggest that a basic course in cultural change and cultural universals would be of most use to the second language teacher. Even more helpful would be an anthropology course that is ethnographic in character. Ethnographic courses concentrate on the study of a particular culture or culture area, utilizing the theories and concepts of cultural anthropology. It is not even essential that this course focus on the particular culture the language instructor intends to teach. The significance of such study is to familiarize the instructor with the application of anthropological theory. Of value also would be a course in intercultural communication or anthropological linguistics.

Questions for consideration

1. In Brooks's list of institutional questions (page 163), which question provides the greatest contrast between your culture and that of another culture with which you are familiar?
2. To become familiar with the method, apply the Taylor and Sorenson Technological category (page 165) to the culture that you know best.
3. How does Nostrand's Emergent Model differ in approach from Hall's Ten Primary Message Systems?

4. Can you supply suggestions for vehicles for the teaching of cultural awareness other than those supplied by the author?
5. How does the information in this article better prepare a teacher for direct teaching of culture?

17 Culture bump and beyond

Carol M. Archer
University of Houston – Houston Park

Rare is the ESL teacher who has not heard or told a variation of the story about the student who comes to his office, bringing a friend to translate. The message this enterprising student wishes to convey is something to the effect, "Please teacher you must to move me to high level." The story elicits groans of recognition and prompts listening ESL practitioners to roll their eyes heavenward. Other such stories universally recognized by members of the TESL profession pertain to the student who inevitably comes late, interrupting the class while entering; the student who promises daily to bring her paper "tomorrow"; the shy student who refuses to participate despite the teacher's best efforts; and, of course, the student who talks incessantly during the class. In each of these cases, the individual who suffers the most is the teacher.

On the other side of the coin, there is the Asian student who sits in shock as his teacher bounces into the room and announces familiarly, "Hi, my name is Karen! I'm your teacher and I'm sure we're going to have a great time together!"; or the Arab who is bewildered by his teacher's angry outburst when he politely tries to explain why he was late to class – again – before taking his seat; or, of course, the Latin who is genuinely puzzled that his next door neighbor doesn't even let him into her apartment when he drops by, giving the excuse that she has to study, when only last week she had told him to come by "anytime." When Hong sits with his Asian friends and relates the story of his extraordinary teacher, they smile and nod and tell about their equally outrageous teachers (or some that are even worse!). Arab eyes roll when Hassan tells his tale to his friends, and groans of recognition greet Joaquin's story to his friends.

All across North America, little culturally homogeneous groups gather and recount their encounters with "them," nod in agreement that "they" are weird, cold, aggressive, pushy, too shy, not friendly, too friendly, clannish, rude – and go on their way with a leery eye on "them." Thus are the seeds of cultural stereotypes sown.

What has happened in each of these cases is a *culture bump* followed by a mirroring process (discussed on p. 176). A culture bump occurs when an individual from one culture finds himself or herself in a different, strange, or uncomfortable situation when interacting with persons of a different culture. This phenomenon results from a difference in the way people from one culture behave in a particular situation from people in another culture. Since the purpose of this article is to inform teachers, most of the focus will be on the teacher rather than on the student, with explication of what happens to the student in the process.

Certain situations (e.g., arriving late to class) exist in all but a few cultures, and each culture develops particular responses that are labeled "polite" for these situations; for example, North American culture teaches university students who are late for class to enter quietly without knocking and sit down, while Chinese culture teaches university students to knock, offer an explanation, and wait for the teacher's permission to enter. A culture bump occurs when an individual has expectations of one behavior and gets something completely different. The unexpected behavior can be negative (as in the examples at the beginning of this article) or neutral (as when an individual has become accustomed to a behavior) or positive (as when a North American is pleasantly surprised by being kissed on the cheek when greeted by a Latin American). Unlike culture shock, which extends over an extended period of time, culture bumps are instantaneous, usually over within minutes or even seconds, though the effect may be long-lasting, and can occur any time one is in contact with members of a different culture. One does not have to leave one's own culture in order to experience a culture bump. Certainly the ideal is gradually to eliminate the negative culture bumps, leaving the neutral and positive ones.

Indeed, culture bumps provide a gold mine for the international educator. They lead teacher and student alike to an awareness of self as a cultural being and provide an opportunity for skill development in extrapolating one cultural influence on everyday life, expressing feelings effectively in a cross-cultural situation, and observing behavior. The entire process is language in action, leading to general improvement in communication in the target language.

In order to illustrate how a culture bump is analyzed, let us take the example of the teacher who has a culture bump with a student who talks incessantly in class. This bump, taken from the teacher's point of view, can be processed in the following steps:

1. Pinpoint some time when I have felt "different" or noticed something different when I was with someone from another culture.
   I notice Joséfina talking in class at the same time that I am talking.
2. Define the situation.
   A university classroom in which I am lecturing.
3. List the behaviors of the other person.
   Joséfina leaned over to Maria and spoke in a whisper for 30 seconds.

171

4. List my own behavior.
   I looked at Joséfina, faltered in speaking, looked at my notes, looked back at her. I said, "Joséfina, do you have a question?"
5. List my feelings in the situation.
   I felt angry, uncertain (that I was doing a good job), humiliated (that she did this in front of the other students), disrespected.
6. List the behaviors I expect from people in my own culture in that same situation.
   I expect students not to talk when I am talking.
7. Reflect on the underlying value in my culture that prompts that behavior expectation.
   In American concepts of time, the idea of monochronic time is dominant. In other words, only one thing at a time can be done comfortably. Taking turns is important in all situations, from people talking to stopping at four-way stop signs, and is associated with polite behavior.

   (If one wants to teach the concept of culture bump in class, step number eight would be to take this new-found cultural insight and apply it in designing role plays or lectures for teaching others about their cultures.)

The teacher now has the base for asking two critical questions. The first is asked of Joséfina: "Why did you talk while I was talking?" Upon receiving the answer, "I hadn't understood what you said and I didn't want to be impolite and interrupt you, so I asked my friend," the teacher reflects: "How do students in my culture handle that situation in a polite way?" The teacher then teaches the answer to Joséfina, reassuring her that she knows that Joséfina was attempting to be polite and showing Joséfina how to express her intention of politeness in this culture. Both parties are now in a position to begin to comprehend the other's behavior. In many cases, this mere comprehension will be sufficient to defuse the incident and clear the way for better understanding in the future. The key to the interaction is that the teacher approaches the student rationally certain (even if not emotionally certain) that the student's reaction was cultural and not personal, thereby giving the student the benefit of the doubt.

The teacher has now moved beyond the culturally biased judgmental stage (example: Joséfina is rude) to the "comprehension of other" stage (example: She did that because she is polychronic and because she was trying to be polite to me) and to the "self-comprehension" stage (example: I reacted because I am monochronic and am oriented to different behavior). By moving through these three stages, the teacher is able to comprehend the situation as it becomes depersonalized and is placed within a cultural context.

Normally when people from differing cultures interact and some type of conflict results, they do not have the vocabulary to express that conflict in an objective way. In fact, the conflict would probably not be mentioned out loud. If a teacher were to describe the situation, it would be a personal evaluation of the student's behavior, as in "He's always talking out loud in class and driving me nuts." The words used to characterize the other person in such situations are frequently pejorative. Once the teacher perceives these encounters as culture bumps, however, he can distinguish and categorize his experience in a new way. Whereas before, the incident could only be categorized as a personal conflict, it is now removed from that level and eased into a cultural level. Not only is the objective view more rational, but this cultural level is safer emotionally, and at best it even invites further exploration. This depersonalization of an incident allows, even encourages, an individual to seek more and more interaction with members of the other culture. Rather than moving through their midst with a leery eye, he begins to move among them with an eager eye – looking for culture bumps.

Paradoxically, by first depersonalizing the situation, the individuals can approach one another on a truly personal level, much more intimate than typically (if ever) occurs in a short time span for people in cross-cultural situations. In our example, the teacher, rather than having an unconscious assumption that Latin Americans talk during class, now has a conscious assumption that Latins are polite, and that most of them are not aware of the appropriate way to express that politeness in an American classroom.

Depersonalization makes possible the expression of emotions in such a way that neither participant is damaged; rather, both experience an increase of trust and willingness to communicate. The individual begins by revealing his reactions, making it evident that he is aware that he, himself, is responsible for his feelings. Rather than saying, "Your rudeness made me feel angry" or "You hurt me," he simply states, "I feel angry, frustrated, and hurt." This acknowledges his feelings without placing blame for those feelings on the other, and allows both to take a major step forward in the communication process. The controlled sequence ensures not only that emotions are expressed but that the incident is accurately defined. That is to say, the individual must describe his and the other's actions as observable behavior. His own interpretation and evaluations have no place in processing the culture bump. This ability to separate observable behavior from personal interpretation and then to label it accurately, as exemplified in step number three, is fundamental to being able to depersonalize the incident and express emotions.

Once a teacher has learned to analyze his role in the culture bump process, he is ready to use culture bump with the students as a way of teaching cultural awareness and language simultaneously. The teacher is the obvious "knower" of the target language and through experience and/or study should have garnered numerous instances of discrepancies between the target culture and the cultures of the students. He may elicit further examples through discussion sessions in which students are queried about what bothers them in the behavior of people in the target culture. Armed with this information, he explains the culture bump process to the students, making sure that they understand the reason for what may seem to them a purposeless game that consumes valuable time which should be devoted to more obvious language learning exercises.

Using what he knows of disparate cultures, or taking the example supplied by a student, the teacher devises a situation that is sure to result in conflict, and assigns the selected students to role-play the situation. Clearly, the controlled culture bump must be based on observable behavior, but it must also include the expression of reactions of the participants and of other members of the class. Here is an example taken from a heterogeneous class studying English. Two women students, one South American and one Asian, are told to assume that after being in the same class for several weeks, they happen to meet socially at a party. They are simply told to greet each other. Typically, the South American is effusive and rushes over to kiss her classmate on the cheek. The Asian's inclination is merely to stand where she is, smile, and say "Hello," and possibly "How are you?" The result is predictable. Led to express their reactions openly and objectively, through the steps described in the culture bump analysis, the South American feels rejected, disliked, cold-shouldered, while the Asian feels set upon, her space violated, the victim of aggressive behavior. The instructor then opens the discussion to the whole class in a search for the meaning of the incident. The teacher plays the role of moderator, attempting to lead the discussion in the right direction, but may have to provide further explanation if class discussion does not achieve the desired conclusion. The question that arises, naturally enough, is "What should be done to avoid the negative results?" If all goes well, this should lead to an acceptance of one another's cultural bias, and a willingness to try to meet somewhere in between. Humans being what they are, results are not always what one plans, but the percentages are very good.

If there are no representatives of the target culture in the class, the teacher would also explain what the behavior of someone from that culture would probably be, given the same situation. At other times, the teacher will take part in the role play in order to demonstrate target culture behavior.

The linguistic advantage to the controlled culture bump process is clearly to be seen in the requisite exchange of ideas that students are anxious to communicate.

Another way of processing culture bumps is through ethnic group dramatizations, which lead to the same sort of discussions that the one-on-one role play produces. After dividing the class into cultural groups, the teacher assigns situations, or scenes, for each group to work out and present for the class. After each group reaches a consensus on what "typical" behavior of their culture would be in the circumstances and presents its version of the scene, the entire group discusses similarities and differences, and learns from the teacher what the target culture presentation would probably be like, if it differs from all the others. An example is a classroom in the native culture. The set-up is to have one student enact the teacher, the others enact the students, and one student assigned to arrive late. The scene is not too different from one group to another before the arrival of the teacher, with the students chatting among themselves, but differences occur upon the arrival of the teacher. To use the Asians as an example, all conversation ceases and the students all rise and remain standing until the teacher reaches the lectern and indicates that they may be seated. Complete silence is maintained as the teacher calls the roll, except for responses as names are called. The tardy student arrives at the door and knocks, waiting for permission to enter. The teacher nods and the student comes in and respectfully tells the teacher why he is late and asks to be excused. The teacher tells him to avoid such tardiness in future and allows him to sit. As he calls on each student, the student stands to recite and sits again when the teacher's nod gives permission. All is based on a rote form of learning. A student who is not prepared and cannot give a correct answer is admonished and meets with disfavor from the other students, as well as from the teacher. The students do not leave until the teacher exits.

After the group concludes its performance, other students ask questions about what they have seen, eventually getting to the values that underlie the behavior. After all the presentations are completed, the class discusses the differences without making value judgments. When all the groups have played their scenes – possibly only one per class period – a further discussion ensues, including a comparison with the target culture, resulting in an understanding of what would be expected of the student in the target culture and how misinterpretation could occur if a student used his own classroom behavior in the target culture classroom. In other words, the students conceive the likelihood and nature of culture bumps.

Other examples of situations for dramatic presentation are arriving at someone's home for a dinner party; a group of friends together at dinner in a restaurant; a group reacting to someone mistreating an animal, or to a robbery; a husband and wife and their children deciding to move or stay where they are (to note differences in involvement of various members of the family); businessmen gathering for a meeting; women at a social event for women only; students who feel their professor has graded their tests unfairly and want something done about it; a family at the dinner table; a political rally.

Role plays can be videotaped or tape-recorded and, once the cultural analysis has been made, can be used for teaching language. Using an adaptation of the Community Learning method, the teacher makes a script of the role play, which is used to teach vocabulary and idioms in context, grammar, and pronunciation. In this way the learning of the target language is placed within the total context of the students' personal experiences as well as the all-pervasive cultural influences. One could hardly find a method for teaching language more communicatively.

The mirroring process, in which the individual checks out his experience of the other person with members of his own culture, assumes a new, more positive role. Rather than being the breeding ground for cultural stereotypes, the classroom becomes the laboratory for testing the validity of a culture bump; that is, Was my reaction a cultural one or a personal one? If members of one's own culture all agree with the individual's reaction, there is a good chance the reaction was cultural. This process works for the teachers, too; thus those "war stories" told in the teacher's lounge assume new shapes – they now hold the possibility of reflection and new personal and professional growth. In fact, those "outrageous" behaviors that everyone experiences become candidates for serious cultural analysis.

I have emphasized the teacher in this article because I believe very strongly that the culture bump should first be rigorously applied to the teacher's experiences before it is applied to those of the students. Without a visceral as well as rational knowledge of it, there exists the risk of the culture bump being used as a club over the head of the student or as a subtle method of having students give up their "bad" behavior and learn how to "do it right." The teacher's own involvement in the culture bump process, both in the formal, controlled role plays and in the unstructured cross-culture experiences both in and out of the classroom, is quite likely to result in an almost embarrassing realization of himself as a cultural being. It seems that almost always the insight one has of oneself as a cultural being is accompanied by a feeling of embarrassment or of being "found out." The teacher can watch for this both in himself and in his students and point it out as a very good sign, leading to a new, more profoundly based appreciation, not only of cultural differences, but of one's own cultural characteristic that has been uncovered.

In implementing this method there are several concerns that the facilitator should take into consideration:

1. Being sensitive to how different cultures learn, both in methods and in time needed to integrate new learning, and to the processing of what may be very personal, emotional experiences for the individual student.

2. In a class with students from varied cultural backgrounds, an awareness of how they respond to high-student-involvement learning methods, such as the culture bump. This can mean the difference between success and failure. Generally speaking, Western cultures will readily adapt to self-analysis and role play. Since these methodologies are familiar ones to them, the teacher will need only to explain what he expects of them and spend a minimum of time giving feedback and motivating them. Experience has revealed that students from Asia take a longer time than Western students to participate fully, but once they do begin the process their involvement is profound and they produce extremely effective results. Middle Easterners tend to require a longer period of time than the other two to become truly involved.

3. How the culture bumps are initiated. Because the method frequently relies on the student choosing an incident that stands out in his memory, it has the potential for psychological harm. Great care must be taken that the teacher, as facilitator, never belittles or rejects the student's choice nor permits other students to do so. If a student chooses it, it is valid – even if it causes misgivings.

4. Stereotyping. The teacher must make it abundantly clear that all Asian classrooms are not exactly the same, that all businessmen of a certain culture do not behave in just the same way when gathering for a meeting, and all Americans do not ask their children whether they would prefer to move across town or stay where they are. The best antidote to stereotyping may be found in the difficulties each ethnic group encounters in agreeing on their own ethnic behavior.

After all the tocsins are sounded, the culture bump remains an effective and pleasurable method for teaching both culture and language.

Questions for consideration

1. Have you ever experienced a culture bump? Describe it, and its consequences.
2. How does the culture bump help one to understand one's own culture?
3. How can the culture bump be used to reduce prejudice? Is it usable between subcultures of the same main culture?

4. Is the culture bump more suitable for use with children or adults? Why?
5. What are the dangers of the culture bump in the classroom if discussion is not properly guided?

18 The culture test

Rebecca M. Valette
Boston College

As the teaching of culture has become an accepted part of the second-language course, teachers are realizing how broad and how complex this subject matter really is.

Culture in the broad sense has two major components. One is anthropological or sociological culture: the attitudes, customs, and daily activities of a people, their ways of thinking, their values, their frames of reference. Since language is a direct manifestation of this phase of culture, a society cannot be totally understood or appreciated without a knowledge of its language. The other component of culture is the history of civilization. Traditionally representing the "culture" element in foreign language teaching, it includes geography, history, and achievements in the sciences, the social sciences, and the arts. This second component forms the framework for the first: it represents the heritage of a people and as such must be appreciated by the students who wish to understand the new target culture.

As language teachers strive to introduce their students to a second culture so as to free these young people from the strait jacket of mon-oculturalism, some specialists are beginning to warn of the dangers of immersion into the great tradition of a second high culture. Margaret Mead writes:

When students saturate themselves deeply and meaningfully in one other culture and language, and that in a high culture with whose members they can engage in sophisticated discourse, they tend to become locked into a kind of we-they position, in which one language and culture tends to become better, higher, than the other.... There is no doubt that learning a second language is a releasing activity and is much more difficult than learning subsequent languages. But we need to go further and consider how to rescue students from the various traps that lie in the intense immersion in a second high culture, whether it be the trap of romanticism, of finding a counter culture, of excessive guilt over past imperialism and western chauvinism, or the development of a kind of double personality, complete with kinesics. (Mead 1974: 14–15)

She suggests increased cooperation between teachers of the commonly-taught languages and the anthropologists who work with primitive cultures and unwritten languages. The study of a third language and culture could help avoid the dangerous polarization that bilingualism and biculturalism may produce.

General considerations

Although most foreign language teachers do not deny the importance of culture in their course curriculum, few teachers actively test whether students are attaining their cultural goals. The problem seems to be that many teachers are uncertain as to what specifically their goals are and how they may be evaluated.

For many years, the New York State Regents Examinations in modern languages contained a "culture" section. This part of the text asked the student to respond to ten out of fifteen questions in a multiple-choice format. Here are some typical examples (taken from the University of the State of New York Regents High School Examination: *Comprehensive Examination in French: form B*, June 24, 1975):

1. Orly et le Bourget sont deux aéroports situés dans la banlieue
   A. du Havre
   B. de Lille
   C. de Marseille
   D. de Paris
2. Aujourd'hui la population de la France est d'environ
   A. 20.000.000
   B. 50.000.000
   C. 80.000.000
   D. 100.000.000
3. Louis XIV fit construire l'Hôtel des Invalides pour y
   A. enterrer Napoléon
   B. abriter des reliques
   C. présenter des spectacles
   D. soigner les militaires

1. *Orly and Le Bourget are two airports located in the suburbs of*
   A. *Le Havre*
   B. *Lille*
   C. *Marseilles*
   D. *Paris*
2. *Today the population of France is about*
   A. *20,000,000*
   B. *50,000,000*
   C. *80,000,000*
   D. *100,000,000*
3. *Louis XIV had the Hotel des Invalides built in order to*
   A. *bury Napoleon*
   B. *shelter relics*
   C. *give shows*
   D. *give medical aid to soldiers*

4. Au théâtre, les Français sifflent parfois pour exprimer leur
   A. enthousiasme
   B. impatience
   C. dissatisfaction
   D. reconnaissance

4. *At the theater, the French sometimes whistle to express their*
   A. *enthusiasm*
   B. *impatience*
   C. *dissatisfaction*
   D. *appreciation*

Correct responses: D, B, D, C

These items test the knowledge of discrete cultural facts and are therefore relatively easy to prepare and score. The disadvantage of such items on broadly administered tests is that students are likely to cram lists of names, places, dates, and facts as a last-minute preparation for the examination. In explaining why the Regents Examinations were dropping the Culture Section as of June 1976, Paul Dammer of the New York State Education Department wrote:

In essence, then, the type of questions most suitable, from the technical point of view, for inclusion in the Regents examinations has encouraged the pursuit of pedagogically unsound practices which, while retarding pupils' intellectual growth in understanding how discrete cultural items function and interact, in most cases assured pupils of a high grade in this part of the examinations – provided, of course, that they could readily recall the facts with which they were confronted.... Therefore, the Bureau decided to recommend removal of the culture section from the Regents examinations in modern foreign languages in order to stimulate a greater interest on the part of teachers in making cultural understanding a more meaningful learning experience for pupils. (Dammer 1975: 6–7)

For the classroom teacher, cultural goals may be divided into four categories: developing a greater awareness of and a broader knowledge about the target culture; acquiring a command of the etiquette of the target culture; understanding differences between the target culture and the students' culture; and understanding the values of the target culture. Each of these goals will be treated in a separate section of this chapter.

However, before considering cultural goals, the teacher must define his or her view of the target culture. For example, in a French class, is the emphasis on the culture of Paris? of a village in Auvergne? of Guadeloupe? of Québec? of Dakar? or of the Franco-American community in Manchester, New Hampshire? In the Spanish class, is the course to focus on Spain? Argentina? Mexico? Cuba? the Puerto Ricans? the Chicanos? the Cuban-Americans? Probably the teacher will want to convey the complexity of the target culture in its many facets, or perhaps focus on one regional variation of the target culture (the one with which the teacher is most familiar through travel, residence, research, and/or study) while discouraging overgeneralization. The actual choice of testing techniques will depend on the goals of the course.

Rebecca M. Valette

Cultural awareness

As students progress through a foreign language program, it is expected that they will increase their awareness of the culture or cultures characteristic of the speakers of the language under study. This broadened awareness may touch on all aspects of culture: the people's way of life as well as the geographic, historical, economic, artistic, and scientific aspects of the target society.

Tests of cultural awareness are generally built around items measuring cultural knowledge. The student who is aware of American history can identify people like Washington and Lincoln. These bits of knowledge constitute the general background of members of the target culture, and the student who shares this knowledge demonstrates an increased awareness of the parameters of that target culture.

Cultural awareness tests are typically administered in pairs: pretests and posttests. The pretest establishes the baseline or point of departure: how great is the students' cultural awareness before entering a course of study? The posttest allows the teacher to determine the degree of progress that the students have made.

The geographical parameters of the target culture

One goal in the area of cultural awareness is bringing students to realize the breadth and variety of countries and areas where the target language is spoken.

SAMPLE ITEM TYPE 1   GEOGRAPHIC LISTS

List the countries and places where Spanish is spoken.
Correct responses: Spain, Mexico, United States, Argentina, Cuba, etc.
Note: At the end of a course, the students probably have a much more accurate picture of where the target language is used.

SAMPLE ITEM TYPE 2   MAP IDENTIFICATION

Identify the French-speaking countries and places on the map of the world (facing page).
Correct responses:
1. l'Algérie, 2. la Belgique, 3. le Cambodge, 4. le Cameroun, 5. le Congo-Brazzaville, 6. la Corse, 7. la Côte d'Ivoire, 8. la France, 9. le Gabon, 10. la Guadeloupe, 11. la Guinée, 12. la Guyane, 13. Haïti, 14. le Laos, 15. le Liban, 16. le Luxembourg, 17. le Madagascar, 18. le Mali, 19. le Maroc, 20. la Martinique, 21. la Mauritanie, 22. le Niger, 23. Québec, 24. la République Centrafricaine, 25. la Réunion,

182

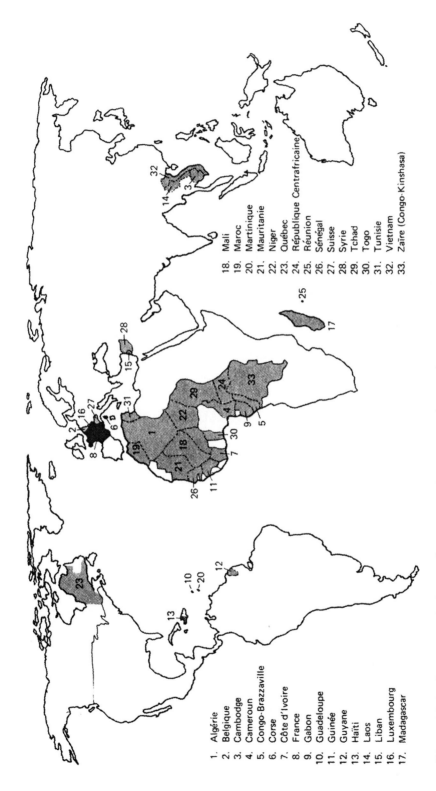

1. Algérie
2. Belgique
3. Cambodge
4. Cameroun
5. Congo-Brazzaville
6. Corse
7. Côte d'Ivoire
8. France
9. Gabon
10. Guadeloupe
11. Guinée
12. Guyane
13. Haïti
14. Laos
15. Liban
16. Luxembourg
17. Madagascar

18. Mali
19. Maroc
20. Martinique
21. Mauritanie
22. Niger
23. Québec
24. République Centrafricaine
25. Réunion
26. Sénégal
27. Suisse
28. Syrie
29. Tchad
30. Togo
31. Tunisie
32. Vietnam
33. Zaïre (Congo-Kinshasa)

Figure 18.1   Pays et territoires où l'on trouve des groupes francophones

26. le Sénégal, 27. la Suisse, 28. la Syrie, 29. le Tchad, 30. le Togo, 31. la Tunisie, 32. le Vietnam, 33. le Zaïre (Congo-Kinshasa).

Contributions of the target culture

This category includes an awareness of the contributions of the target culture to world civilization in general and to the history of the students' home country, where appropriate.

SAMPLE ITEM TYPE 3   ORIGINS OF PLACE NAMES – IDENTIFICATION

Explain the origins of the names of the following United States cities:
1. Germantown, Pennsylvania
2. Detroit, Michigan
3. Santa Barbara, California
Correct responses:
1. Germantown was the first settlement of Germans who arrived in America in 1683.
2. Détroit in French means strait: the city is situated on a strait between Lake Saint Clair and Lake Erie.
3. Santa Barbara is the name of a Spanish mission founded in 1786.

SAMPLE ITEM TYPE 4   FAMOUS PEOPLE – MATCHING

Match the following persons with their contributions:
1. Rochambeau   a. poet and president of Sénégal
2. Senghor   b. feminist writer
3. De Beauvoir   c. pioneer aviator and novelist
4. Curie   d. discoverer of radium
                    e. commander of French troops during the American revolution
Correct responses: 1e, 2a, 3b, 4d

Note: In items of this sort it is better to ask the students to match two lists of unequal length. This reduces the opportunity for guessing.

Differences in way-of-life patterns

One goal of many foreign language classes is to sensitize the students to the existence of differences in daily life patterns between the target culture and the native culture. The first step is increasing student awareness of the existence of these differences.

Imagine you are living with a family in Germany. List outward cultural differences you would be likely to observe.

Correct responses: different ways of making beds, different ways of setting the table, tendency to keep all doors closed, etc.

Differences in values and attitudes

Students learning a new language learn that the target culture and the native culture do not always have identical values and attitudes. At first, students are made aware of the existence of these differences. Then, an effort is made to develop an understanding of these new values.

SAMPLE ITEM TYPE 6   IDENTIFYING PATTERNS – TRUE-FALSE FORMAT

Indicate whether the following statements are true or false.
1. French young people may earn money by baby-sitting.
2. Most French parents encourage their teenage children to find part-time jobs.
3. Most French young people would like to earn their own money.

Correct responses: 1. true   2. false   3. true

Command of etiquette

Most foreign language programs introduce the students to the polite behavior expected of persons living in the country or countries where the target language is spoken. The command of etiquette may be tested either with written tests or through role-play activities.

Knowledge of etiquette

Each target culture has different etiquette patterns. French etiquette in Paris, for instance, differs from patterns in Sénégal or Québec or Tahiti. As the students learn about certain polite codes of behavior, they should also know when and under which conditions such behavior is appropriate.

SAMPLE ITEM TYPE 7   DESCRIBING ETIQUETTE

What is the traditional American pattern when a man and woman are walking down a city street?

Correct response: The man always walks on the curb side.

Rebecca M. Valette

SAMPLE ITEM TYPE 8   INTERPRETING CODES OF BEHAVIOR –
MULTIPLE-CHOICE FORMAT

Imagine you are in France near a school. You observe a teenage girl meet a boy and watch them kiss each other on the cheeks. What should you conclude? Explain your answer.
a. They are going steady.
b. They are friends.
c. They are cousins.
Correct response: Either *b* or *c*. Members of a family (including distant family) tend to kiss each other upon meeting. Often teenagers also greet friends this way. Of course, *a* is also a possible explanation, but not the only one.

It should be noted that multiple-choice items of this sort are difficult to prepare. The options should all be equally plausible to a person who is not aware of the meaning of a specific behavior pattern. At the same time, the item should be validated by asking native speakers to take the test. Often the test writer will find that native speakers do not all agree to one correct response (see Seelye 1974).

Ability to adopt patterns of etiquette

The ability to react appropriately to situations in the target culture is frequently taught through role-play activities and "culture capsules." If desired, students can be evaluated informally on their participation in such activities. In a more formal test, each student would be expected to carry out specific instructions or demonstrate specific behaviors.

SAMPLE ITEM TYPE 9   GREETINGS

Demonstrate how you would greet the parents of a French friend.
Correct response: The student should use the phrases "Bonjour, Monsieur" and "Bonjour, Madame" and should shake hands.

SAMPLE ITEM TYPE 10   TABLE MANNERS

Imagine you are eating in the home of a French family. Show how you would behave.
Correct response: The student should keep his or her hands on the table rather than in the lap. When eating meat, the fork is kept in the left hand both while cutting and while putting the food in the mouth. Pieces of bread may be used for pushing food and for soaking up sauce.

SAMPLE ITEM TYPE 11 LEVELS OF LANGUAGE

Imagine that you had written the following persons, indicating that you were unable to meet them as planned, but the letters were not received. How would you excuse yourself?

a. Monsieur Boutron, professor
b. Marc, a close friend

Correct responses:

a. Je suis désolé, Monsieur, que vous n'ayez pas reçu ma lettre.... (use of formal language and the pronoun *vous*)
b. Ça m'embête que t'aies pas reçu le mot que j'ai laissé.... (use of informal language and the pronoun *tu*)

Note: Items of this type combine linguistic and cultural goals. The emphasis is on communication in a cultural context.

Understanding of outward cultural differences

Many facets of daily life are organized differently in another culture. In the foreign language course, the students should learn how to interpret unfamiliar cultural conventions and realia. This understanding will help those students who travel to the foreign country to function more easily. Even students who are unable to travel will be better able to understand foreign films and magazines.

Unfamiliar conventions

Often the foreign culture has a different way of indicating dates and times. Meals may be served at different hours, and foods may be served in different combinations or at unexpected times of day. Driving codes and street signs may be different in the foreign culture.

SAMPLE ITEM TYPE 12 READING TIMETABLES

Answer questions about the arrival and departure times of French airplanes according to the following timetable:

Rebecca M. Valette

| AÉROPORT | PRINTEMPS · ÉTÉ 76 |
| DE CLERMONT-FERRAND/AULNAT | jusqu'au 31-10-1976 |

TÉL. 91.71.00 - 92.28.28 et Agents de voyages
Télex 390024

I.C.A.A
MEMBER

Lignes Directes à destination de :	Heure Départ	Heure Arrivée
Service en Caravelle	07.55 (1)	08.50 (1)
→ PARIS	11.00 (2)	12.10 (2)
	18.30 (3)	19.40 (3)
Service en Caravelle	21.30 (1)	22.25 (1)
→ LYON	08.20 (6)*	09.00 (6)
	18.45 (1)	19.25 (1)
→ TOULOUSE	10.35 (1)	11.35 (1)
→ BORDEAUX	21.00 (3)**	22.15 (3)
→ TOURS	21.05 (1)	22.00 (1)
→ NANTES	10.30 (1)	11.50 (1)
→ MENDE \ a/c du 12/4 /	08.05 (1)	08.55 (1)
	21.35 (1)	22.25 (1)
→ MONTPELLIER a/c du 12/4 via MENDE	08.05 (1)	09.50 (1)
→ LA ROCHELLE du 1/8 au 4/9	21.05 (1)	22.25 (1)
→ GENEVE	08.10 (1)***	08.00 (1)*
	18.35 (1)***	18.25 (1)*
→ LONDRES a/c du 02/5	19.00 (4) du 19/5 au 15/9	20.10 (4) du 19/5 au 15/9
	19.00 (5)	20.10 (5)
	du 20/6 au 12/9	du 20/6 au 12/9
	18.10 (5)****	18.30 (5)
	du 2/5 au 13/6	
	et du 19/9 au 24/10	
	16.10 (4)****	16.30 (4)
	du 22/9 au 20/10	

(1) Q. sf Sa et Di - (2) Sa - (3) Q sf Sa - (4) Me - (5) Di - (6) Q. sf Di
* Sa 08.30   * Compte tenu décalage heure légale
** Di 21.05
*** Arr. GENEVE 1 h plus tard a/c du 26/9
**** Dép. CLERMONT-FERRAND 1 h plus tôt a/c du 26/9

ATTENTION ! Les horaires ci-dessus indiqués peuvent être modifiés
sans préavis. De même certaines lignes fonctionneront à des fréquences
réduites ou seront supprimées de fin juillet à fin août.
Se renseigner auprès des agences de voyage.

If you leave Clermont-Ferrand a little after 9 p.m., when will you arrive in Tours?
Correct response: At 10 p.m.

SAMPLE ITEM TYPE 13   READING NEWSPAPER ANNOUNCEMENTS

Look at the following schedule of movies from an American newspaper. Which one is appropriate for an eight-year-old child? Which one is restricted to adults?

188

Regent, 7 Medford st. 643-1197.
EARTHQUAKE (PG)★
Through Tues. Shows at 7 and 9:15 p.m.
Also Sun. at 4:45.
Burlington — Cinema, Rte. 128, exit 42.
272-4410.
BLACKBEARD'S GHOST (G)
Through Feb. 12. Shows at 1, 3, 5, 7 and 9.
DOG DAY AFTERNOON (R)★★★★
Through Tues. Shows at 1:45, 4:25, 7:20
and 9:40 p.m.
Danvers — Sack Danvers, Liberty Tree Mall.
777-1818 or 599-3122.
CUCKOO'S NEST (R)★★★★
Due Wed. Call theater for times.
STORY OF O (X)★
Through Tues. Shows at 7:30 and 9:30
p.m. Also Sat.-Sun. at 1:30, 3:30 and 5:30.

Correct responses: Blackbeard's Ghost; Story of O

Linguistic cultural referents

In order to understand a conversation among speakers of the target language or an article in a target language magazine it is frequently necessary to interpret cultural referents. The state of Florida, for instance, is not just one of the fifty states, nor is it simply a southern state: it is a place where elderly people retire and where college students go for spring vacation. Therefore, an American would interpret a reference to Florida differently than a reference to Alabama or South Carolina.

SAMPLE ITEM TYPE 14 INTERPRETING REFERENTS –
MULTIPLE-CHOICE FORMAT

A French student mentions that she will be visiting her grandparents in "Bretagne" during the "Toussaint" holidays.
1. She will be traveling from Paris toward
    a. central France
    b. the Mediterranean
    c. the Atlantic
2. She plans to be with her grandparents on
    a. October 15
    b. November 1
    c. December 24
Correct responses: 1c, 2b (*Toussaint* is All Saints' Day, November 1).

Rebecca M. Valette

A German pen pal writes that his sister is attending a boarding school and is in "Unter Sekunda." About how old do you think she is?
Correct response: About 15 (Unter Sekunda is the tenth year of schooling)

Performing according to unfamiliar conventions

Items of this type are appropriate for courses that are preparing the students for residence in the target culture. As part of the course objectives, students might learn how to fill out hotel forms, how to write business letters, how to buy train tickets, and so on.

SAMPLE ITEM TYPE 16 WRITING CHECKS

Demonstrate your ability to write checks in France by completing the blank check below. Request that Jean-Michel Vergne be paid one thousand francs.

Correct response:

Understanding of cultural values

A major aim in the teaching of culture is to bring the students to the realization that the target culture may have a system of values that differs from their own. While we may expect students to imitate the social conventions of this target culture, we do not normally expect them to adopt a new set of values. However, students should understand the foreign system of values and come to respect it.

Interpreting behavior of members of the target culture

In items of this sort, the student is presented with an example of behavior in the target culture. For a French course, for example, the teacher might describe a situation, or project a situation via video or film clips. The American students would interpret the situation in terms of the French system of values. (It should be remembered that there is no single system of values in the target culture, but rather a range of value systems that varies according to social position, age, sex, region, etc.)

SAMPLE ITEM TYPE 17 OPEN INTERPRETATION

Mireille plans to invite an American student to her home. She tells her parents that this new friend is "très cultivé" and they react by saying they look forward to meeting him. What is meant by "cultivé" and how do you explain the parents' reaction?

Correct response: The French respect culture and admire people whom they consider "cultivés" or cultured, that is, people who can express themselves easily on a wide variety of subjects – especially art and literature. The French tend to stereotype the Americans as "uncultured." Mireille knows that her parents will react favorably to the idea of meeting a student who represents the exception: the cultured American.

It should be noted that the described situation reflects a predominantly urban and middle-class to upper-middle class attitude. As a variation to such an item, the students might be asked to transfer the situation to their native culture. For example: What would you tell your parents about a visiting French student so that they would wish you to invite him to your house? Or would you simply invite him without even asking your parents?

SAMPLE ITEM TYPE 18   MULTIPLE-CHOICE INTERPRETATION

The film "Amarcord" has several scenes that take place in a classroom. How would a middle-aged Italian probably view these scenes?
a. As examples of very poor teaching, reminiscent of the Fascist period
b. As examples of very undisciplined students, whose parents failed to inculcate in them the proper sense of respect
c. As examples of classroom situations with which he or she easily identifies.
Correct response: c

Multiple-choice interpretation items are extremely difficult to prepare. Either the distractors are so wrong as not to attract the students, or the distractors contain an element of truth and become ambiguous. In his validation of test items about Guatemalan culture, Seelye discovered that test items that did work were multiple-choice questions referring to the understanding of outward cultural differences (how stores indicate whether fresh meat is available or whether tamales are being sold). Multiple-choice items requiring interpretation of behavior frequently gave ambiguous results (Seelye 1974: 147–152). John Clark in his description of culture tests also points out the problems involved in multiple-choice items of this type and suggests that teachers use free response techniques similar to Sample Item Type 17 (Clark 1972: 140).

Interpreting behavior of members of the native culture

Here the students are expected to anticipate aspects of their own culture that would strike a foreign visitor as strange. In items of this type, the teacher would specify, for example, which segment of the target culture the foreign visitor represents: is the Spanish speaker a businessman from Madrid? a student from Peru? a farm worker from Mexico?

SAMPLE ITEM TYPE 19 ANTICIPATING REACTIONS

Robert Duroc is staying at the home of an American family in a Boston suburb. The family consists of Mr. Paul Brand, a business associate of Monsieur Duroc's; Mrs. Margaret Brand; and Mary, Mrs. Brand's daughter by a previous marriage. Which of the following behaviors would probably shock Monsieur Duroc? Explain.
1. Mary calls her stepfather Paul.
2. Mary phones home after school to tell her mother that she will not be coming home for supper.
3. Mary kisses her parents goodnight before going to bed.
Correct responses: 1. (because French children do not call parents or step-parents by their first names); 2. (because French children are expected home for supper, and if there were an invitation to eat elsewhere they would ask their mother's permission, rather than simply inform them of a decision)

Analysis of the target culture

The analysis of the target culture is as challenging as the investigation of one's native culture. As students begin to study various facets of the target culture in depth, they will begin to realize that their own culture incorporates a complexity of patterns they were never aware of. They will also discover that a culture is not a static but an ever-changing phenomenon. In the United States, for instance, the hair length that symbolized revolt and rebellion in the mid-1960s became the accepted style for most adults in the mid-70s.

In testing the students' ability to analyze the target culture, teachers will probably adopt evaluation techniques that parallel those employed in their classroom approach to the topic. The following sections suggest some directions that have been explored in recent years.

Beaujour and Ehrmann: the semiotic approach

In the semiotic approach to culture the objective is to interpret natural language signs, such as "mercredi" (Wednesday), in terms of their implicit cultural signs (a school holiday for French children).

Beaujour and Ehrmann (1967) stress the semiotic analysis of raw cultural data, such as interviews, pictures, television commercials, and magazine ads.

193

Rebecca M. Valette

SAMPLE ITEM TYPE 20   ANALYZING AN AD

Look at this ad prepared by the Club Méditerranée. Discuss the following topics:
1. The visual impact of the ad and the choice of images.
2. The text of the ad: what impression does it create in the reader?
3. The role of vacations for the French: how are they organized? what possibilities are open to the individual? how does the individual view vacations? does the ad fit this general vacation picture?
4. The role of vacations in an industrial society: is there a conflict between advanced technology and the happiness of the individual? what solution does the ad offer? is the Club's main concern the happiness of the individual or the financial profit of the organization? Explain.
5. Would such an ad be appropriate for an American readership? If so, why? If not, what changes would you suggest and why?

Scoring: Detailed instructions of this type permit a more objective scoring system than a simple one-line statement, such as "Analyze the following ad." The teacher would assign a specific number of points to each part of the essay. Then the teacher would read the responses to question number 1, and place the essays into four piles: outstanding response, good response, average response, and poor response. These scores would be recorded on the backs of the test papers. Then the papers are shuffled, and the teacher would read the responses to question number 2, and so on.

Nostrand: the thematic approach

Nostrand (1967) has found it possible to summarize the shared patterns of a culture into about a dozen major "themes," which are defined as the pervading concerns that make up a culture's value system. For French culture, he has identified the following main themes: l'individualisme, l'intellectualité, l'art de vivre, le réalisme, le bon sens, l'amitié, l'amour, la famille, la religion, la justice, la liberté, la patrie. For Hispanic culture, he suggests: individualism, dignidad, orientation toward person, serenidad, beauty, leisure valued over work, human nature mistrusted, "cultura" despite "la realidad del medio," rising expectations. Students who are aware of the underlying themes of the target culture are more likely to react appropriately or, at least, to appreciate the reactions of members of the culture, to stimuli such as jokes, cartoons, television programs, movies, songs, and even literature.

SAMPLE ITEM TYPE 21   IDENTIFYING CULTURAL THEMES

The student is shown an unfamiliar cartoon, or listens to a popular song that he or she may have heard before but never analyzed.

Read the lyrics of Georges Moustaki's well-known song "Le Métèque" as you hear it played. Then study the lyrics and identify the underlying themes of French culture. Explain how each theme is exemplified in the song, and give a second example of the same theme from a play, comic book, film, ad, song (etc.) studied in class.

Correct response: The students would probably identify individualism, love, and liberty.

Santoni: the contextual approach

For Georges Santoni (1976; Rey and Santoni 1975), the language used by an individual in society is not only an expression of that person's thought but also of his or her culture. The culture of a worker is not that of an intellectual or a high school student, and this difference in culture is also reflected in a difference in language. Santoni stresses the complexity of the target culture and insists on a careful study of relevant cultural data: facts, descriptions, interviews, and documents. Most questions do not have clear-cut answers, and the students should learn to analyze possible options in the light of the data they have been working with.

SAMPLE ITEM TYPE 22   THE CULTURE GRID

Read the following statement and the suggested explanations. In the light of the data you have studied, indicate which option (or options) are most likely to be true. Then indicate which option (or options) are probably false. Substantiate your choices by referring to material studied in class or other cultural data.

L'absence de toute communication entre les parents et les élèves est assez rare...

Parce que:
A. En France, la famille joue toujours un rôle important et l'heure du repas est un moment privilégié pour la discussion en famille.

It is rare to find that there is absolutely no communication between high school students and their parents...
Because:
A. In France, the family still plays an important role and mealtime is a special part of the day set aside for family discussion.

B. La morale a beaucoup changé depuis quelques années et les jeunes se sentent plus libres de s'exprimer ouvertement.

C. Les jeunes sont tous d'accord avec la manière de vivre de leurs parents.

D. Les jeunes Français reçoivent une éducation très sévère et profondément catholique. Ils sont obligés de se confier à leurs parents.

B. *Morals have changed a great deal in recent years and young people feel freer to express themselves openly.*

C. *Young people are all in agreement with their parents' life style.*

D. *French young people are brought up in a strict and profoundly Catholic setting. They feel obliged to confide in their parents.*

Correct responses: A and B tend to be true, C and D tend to be false. However, the essential feature of the answer is the explanation.

Scoring: This type of item is scored on how effectively the students justify their choices. In a more informal setting, small groups of students may be asked to pool their reactions and information and arrive at a consensus. In this case, scoring would reflect each individual's participation in the discussion.

Applying an unfamiliar model

After the class has spent a given amount of time, from one unit to an entire semester, studying the target culture, the teacher might suggest analyzing aspects of that culture through the framework of a model unfamiliar to the class. For instance, if the students in a French course had not worked with Nostrand's cultural themes, the teacher might describe the parameters of selected themes and ask the students to find illustrations for each from material studied in class. The following sample item type introduces the viewpoint of a psychologist.

SAMPLE ITEM TYPE 23 ANALYSIS ACCORDING TO A NEW MODEL

In preparation for the test, the American teacher of a course on German culture explains Maslow's five Basic Needs to the students (Maslow 1954). Here are the five Basic Needs determined by Maslow:
1. comfort and survival
2. safety
3. belongingness and love
4. self-esteem and the esteem of others
5. self-actualization
Determine in what way the Germans meet these needs and to what extent the German pattern differs from the American pattern. Give examples.

Scoring: The students' replies are scored on appropriateness and on the ability to substantiate their interpretations. In an informal test, pairs or small groups of students can discuss their views and submit a joint oral or written response.

Questions for consideration

1. What is the validity of the argument propounded by Dammer for removing the culture section of the Regents examination?
2. What is the importance to the traveler of a command of the etiquette of the culture? What priorities would you suggest for this area?
3. Of the test types outlined in this article, which seem the most effective? Why?
4. What are the possible pitfalls in the use of multiple-choice items for a culture test?
5. Devise a 20-minute test on the culture of the speakers of the language you teach. Avoid ambiguity.

Bibliography

Aarons, A. C., B. Y. Gordon, and W. A. Stewart (eds.). 1969. "Linguistical Differences and American Education." *Florida FL Reporter* special anthology issue 7(1).

Acton, William R. 1979. *Second Language Learning and Perception of Differences in Attitude.* Unpublished doctoral dissertation, University of Michigan.

——— 1985. "Affect in the Communicative Classroom: A Model." In *On TESOL '84*, pp. 63–74.Washington, D.C.: TESOL.

Adams, John B. 1965. "On Expressive Communication in an Egyptian Village." In Dell Hymes (ed.), *Language in Culture and Society.* New York: Harper & Row.

Adams, Parveen (ed.). 1972. *Language in Thinking.* London: Penguin.

Adler, Peter S. 1972. "Culture Shock and the Cross-cultural Learning Experience." *Readings in Intercultural Education*, vol. 2. Pittsburgh: Intercultural Communication Network.

Albert, Rosita D., and John Adamopoulos. 1977. "An Attributional Approach to Culture: The Culture Assimilator." *Cross Currents* 4(2): 97–114.

Allen, Edward D., and Rebecca M. Valette. 1977. *Classroom Techniques: Foreign Languages and ESL.* New York: Harcourt Brace Jovanovich.

Allen, J. P. B., and S. Pit Corder. 1973. *Readings for Applied Linguistics. The Edinburgh Course in Applied Linguistics*, vol. 1. London: Oxford University Press.

Allen, P. 1975. "The Sacred Hoop: A Contemporary Perspective on American Indian Literature." In A. Chapman (ed.), *Literature of the American Indians: Views and Interpretations.* New York: Meridian.

Allen, Walter P. 1973. *A Cultural Checklist: A Technique for Selecting Reading Materials for Foreign Students.* Portland, Oreg: English Language Services.

Althen, Gary (ed.). 1979. *Students from the Arab World and Iran.* Based on a seminar held March 1978. Washington, D.C.: National Association for Foreign Student Affairs.

——— (ed.). 1981. *Learning Across Cultures.* Washington, D.C.: National Association for Foreign Student Affairs.

Altman, Howard B., and Victor Hanzeli (eds.). 1974. *Essays on the Teaching of Culture: A Festschrift to Honor Howard Lee Nostrand.* Detroit: Advancement Press.

American Language Institute Manual. 1979. Los Angeles: American Language Institute, The University of Southern California.

Applegate, Richard B. 1975. "The Language Teacher and the Rules of Speaking." *TESOL Quarterly* 9(4): 271–81.

Argyle, Michael. 1975. *Bodily Communication*. New York: International Universities Press.

Argyle, Michael, and Mark Cook. 1976. *Gaze and Mutual Gaze*. Cambridge: Cambridge University Press.

Aronoff, Joel. 1967. *Psychological Needs and Cultural Systems: A Case Study*. Princeton: Van Nostrand.

Asante, Molefi, Eileen Newmark, and Cecil A. Blake. 1979. *Handbook for Intercultural Communication*. Beverly Hills/London: Sage.

Ausubel, David. 1968. *Educational Psychology – A Cognitive View*. New York: Holt, Rinehart & Winston.

Ayisi, Eric O. 1972. *An Introduction to the Study of African Culture*. London: Heineman.

Bagnole, John W. 1976. *TEFL, Perceptions, and the Arab World; With a Case Study of the University of Garyounis*. Washington, D.C.: AFME.

Banks, Ann. 1975. "French Without Language." *Harvard Today* 18(1): 4.

Bannai, Hideko. 1981. "Sociocultural Influences on the Communication Development of Asian ESL Students." *On TESOL '80*. Washington, D.C.: TESOL.

Barnlund, Dean C. 1975. *Public and Private Self in Japan and the United States: Communicative Styles of Two Cultures*. Tokyo: Simul Press.

Barry, Herbert III, and Alice Schlegel (eds.). 1980. *Cross-cultural Samples and Codes*. Pittsburgh: University of Pittsburgh Press.

Barton, Francis B., and Edward H. Sirich. 1933. *New French Review Grammar and Composition*. New York: F. S. Crofts.

Basso, Keith. 1970. "To Give Up on Words: Silence in the Western Apache Culture." *Southwestern Journal of Anthropology* 26(3): 213–30.

Basu, A. K., and R. G. Ames. 1970. "Cross-cultural Contact and Attitude Formation." *Sociology and Social Research* 55:5–16.

Batchelder, Donald, and Elizabeth G. Warner (eds.). 1977. *Beyond Experience: The Experiential Approach to Cross-cultural Education*. Brattleboro, Vt.: The Experiment in International Living.

Bates, Elizabeth. 1976. *Language and Context*. New York: Academic Press.

Bateson, Gregory. 1972. *Steps to an Ecology of Mind*. New York: Ballantine.

Beaujour, Michel, and Jacques Ehrmann. 1967. "A Semiotic Approach to Culture." *Foreign Language Annals* 1(2):152–63.

Becker, Tamar. 1971. "Cultural Patterns and Nationalistic Commitment Among Foreign Students in the United States." *Sociology and Social Research* 55 (July): 467–81.

Benedict, Ruth. 1934. *Patterns of Culture*. Boston: Houghton-Mifflin.

Berger, Morroe. 1962. *The Arab World Today*. New York: Doubleday.

Birdwhistell, Ray L. 1960. "Kinesics and Communication." In Edmund S. Carpenter and Marshall McLuhan (eds.), *Explorations in Communication*. Boston: Beacon Press.

1970. *Kinesics and Context*. Philadelphia: University of Pennsylvania Press.

1974. "The Language of the Body: The Natural Environment of Words." In

Albert Silverstein (ed.), *Human Communication: Theoretical Explorations*. Hillsdale, N.J.: Erlbaum.

Boas, Franz. 1911. "Linguistics and Ethnology." In Franz Boas (ed.), *Handbook of American Indian Languages*. Washington, D.C.: Smithsonian Institute. Reprinted in Dell Hymes (ed.), *Language in Culture and Society*. New York: Harper & Row, 1964.

Bochner, Stephen. 1976. "Problems in Culture Learning." In Stephen Bochner and P. Wicks (eds.), *Overseas Students in Australia*. Sydney: The New South Wales University Press of Hawaii.

(ed.). 1981. *The Mediating Person: Bridges Between Cultures*. Boston: Hall.

(ed.). 1982. *Cultures in Contact: Studies in Cross-cultural Interaction*. Oxford: Pergamon Press.

Bolinger, Dwight. 1980. *Language – The Loaded Weapon*. New York: Longman.

Bouraoui, Hedi. 1980. "Creaculture in the Classroom: A Rationale for the Cross Fertilization of Culture and Literature Studies." *Canadian Modern Language Review* 36(4): 654–8.

Bourque, Jane M. 1974. "Study Abroad and Intercultural Communication." In Gilbert Jarvis (ed.), *The Challenge of Communication*, pp. 329–51. Skokie, Ill.: National Textbook.

Bourque, Jane M., and Linda Chehy. 1976. "Exploratory Language and Culture: A Unique Program." *Foreign Language Annals* 9: 100–16.

Briere, Eugene J. 1973. "Cross-cultural Biases in Language Testing." In John W. Oller, Jr., and Jack C. Richards (eds.), *Focus on the Learner*. Rowley, Mass.: Newbury House.

Brislin, Richard W. 1970. "Back-Translation for Cross-Cultural Research." *Journal of Cross-cultural Psychology* 1(3): 185–216.

Brislin, Richard W., and Paul Pedersen. 1976. *Cross-cultural Orientation Programs*. New York: Gardner Press.

Brister, Louis E. 1978. "Exploring German-American Culture in the Community." *Die Unterrichtspraxis* 11(2): 48–52.

Brooks, Nelson. 1960. *Language and Language Learning*. New York: Harcourt Brace Jovanovich. 2nd ed. 1964.

1975. "The Analysis of Foreign and Familiar Cultures." In Robert Lafayette (ed.), *The Culture Revolution in Foreign Language Teaching*. Skokie, Ill.: National Textbook.

Brown, H. Douglas. 1973. "Affective Variables in Second Language Acquisition." *Language Learning* 23(2): 231–43.

1980. *Principles of Language Learning and Teaching*. Englewood Cliffs, N.J.: Prentice-Hall.

Buchanan, William, and Hadley Castril. 1953. *How Nations See Each Other: A Study in Public Opinion*. Urbana: University of Illinois Press.

Bundesarbeitsgemeinschaft Englisch an Gesamtschulen. 1978. *Kommunikativer Englischunterricht*. Munich: Langenscheidt-Longman.

Burling, Robbins. 1970. *Man's Many Voices: Language in Its Cultural Context*. New York: Holt, Rinehart & Winston.

Bursack, Lois. 1970. *North American Nonverbal Behavior as Perceived in Three*

Overseas Urban Cultures. Unpublished dissertation, University of Minnesota.

Butler, Jack H. 1964. "Russian Rhetoric: A Discipline Manipulated by Communism." *Quarterly Journal of Speech* 50(3): 229–39.

Carmichael, L., H. P. Hogan, and A. A. Walter. 1932. "An Experimental Study of the Effect of Language on Visually Perceived Form." *Journal of Experimental Psychology* 15: 73–86.

Casse, Pierre. 1981. *Training for the Cross-cultural Mind.* Washington, D.C.: SIETAR.

Cave, George N. 1970. "Some Sociolinguistic Factors in the Production of Standard Language in Guyana and Implications for the Language Teacher." *Language Learning* 20(2): 249–63.

Chang, Hwa-Bao. 1973. "Attitudes of Chinese Students in the United States." *Sociology and Social Research* 58: 66–77.

Chastain, Kenneth. 1976. "Teaching Culture." In Kenneth Chastain, *Developing Second-language Skills: Theory to Practice.* Chicago: Rand-McNally.

Chihara, Tetsuro, and John W. Oller, Jr. 1978. "Attitudes and Attained Proficiency in EFL: A Sociolinguistic Study of Adult Japanese Speakers." *Language Learning* 28: 55–68.

Christie, Agatha. 1955. *Hickory Dickory Death.* New York: Dodd, Mead.

Clark, John L. D. 1972. *Foreign Language Testing: Theory and Practice.* Philadelphia: Center for Curriculum Development.

Clark, Leon E. 1970. *Through African Eyes: Cultures in Change,* Units I–VI. New York: Praeger.

Clarke, Mark. 1976. "Second Language Acquisition as a Clash of Consciousness." *Language Learning* 26(2): 377–89.

Cole, Michael, John Gay, Joseph A. Glick, and Donald W. Sharp. 1971. *The Cultural Context of Learning and Thinking: An Exploration in Experimental Anthropology.* New York: Basic Books.

Collett, P. 1971. "Training Englishmen in the Non-verbal Behavior of Arabs." *International Journal of Psychology* 6(3): 209–15.

Colwell, James L. 1971. "German Students View the American Character." *International Educational and Cultural Exchange* 7(1): 1–9.

Commager, Henry Steele. 1970. *Meet the U.S.A.* New York: Institute of International Education.

Condon, E. C. 1973a. *Human Relations in Cultural Context, Series C: Teacher Training Materials.* New Brunswick, N.J.: Rutgers University Press.

1973b. "Introduction to Culture and General Problems of Cultural Interference in Communication." *Introduction to Cross-cultural Communication* no. 1. New Brunswick, N.J.: Rutgers University Press.

Condon, John C. 1972. "Language in Reasoning and Rhetoric." In S. Sakurai (ed.), *Studies in Descriptive and Applied Linguistics,* pp. 62–75. Tokyo: International Christian University.

1975. *Semantics and Communication,* 2nd ed. New York: Macmillan.

Condon, John C., and Mitsuko Saito (eds.). 1974. *Intercultural Encounters with Japan: The Proceedings of the 1972 Conference on Intercultural Communication.* Tokyo: Simul Press.

1976. *Communicating Across Cultures for What?* Tokyo: Simul Press.

Bibliography

Condon, John C., and Fathi Yousef. 1975. *An Introduction to Intercultural Communication.* Indianapolis: Bobbs-Merrill.

Conklin, Harold C. 1959. "Linguistic Play in Its Cultural Context." *Language* 35(4): 631–6.

Cope, Corinne. 1980. "Supervision in ESL." Paper presented at the 14th Annual TESOL Conference, San Francisco, Cal.

Croft, Kenneth. 1971. "Language and Categories: Some Notes for Foreign Language Teachers." *The English Record* 21(4): 1–12.

Cüceloglu, D. M. 1970. "Perceptions of Facial Expressions in Three Different Cultures." *Ergonomics* 13: 93–100.

Cummins, James. 1981. "The Role of Primary Language Development in Promoting Educational Success for Language Minority Students." In California State Department of Education, *Schooling and the Language Minority Student: A Theoretical Framework*, pp. 3–30. Los Angeles: Evaluation, Dissemination and Assessment Center.

Curran, Charles. 1976. *Counseling-Learning in Second Languages.* Apple River, Ill.: Apple River Press.

Dabaghian, Jane (ed.). 1975. *Mirror of Man.* Boston: Little, Brown.

Dammer, Paul. 1975. "A Rationale for the Elimination of the Culture Section from the Regents Examination in Modern Foreign Languages." *Language Association Bulletin* 27: 2.

Darrow, Kenneth, and Bradley Palmquist (eds.). 1975. *The Trans-cultural Study Guide.* Palo Alto, Cal.: Volunteers in Asia.

Davis, A. L. (ed.). 1969. *Culture, Class, and Language Variety.* Urbana, Ill.: NCTE.

Davis, Flora. 1973. *Inside Intuition: What We Know About Non-verbal Communication.* New York: Signet.

DeCamp, David. 1965. "Training English Teachers in the Far East." *Language Learning* 15(3, 4): 119–27.

Dil, Anwar S. (ed.). 1972. *Language, Psychology, and Culture: Essays by Wallace E. Lambert.* Stanford, Cal.: Stanford University Press.

Dodd, Carley H. 1982. *Dynamics of Intercultural Communication.* Dubuque, Iowa: William C. Brown.

Dodge, James H. (ed.). 1972. *Other Words, Other Worlds: Language-in-Culture. Reports of Working Committees, Northeast Conference on the Teaching of Foreign Languages.* New York: MLA Materials Center.

Dunnett, Stephen C. 1977. *The Effects of a 6-Week English Language Teaching and Orientation Program on Foreign Student Adaptation at SUNY at Buffalo.* Buffalo: SUNY at Buffalo.

Durkheim, Emile. 1897. *Le Suicide.* Paris: F. Alcan.

Dye, Joan. 1977. *Use of Body Movement to Facilitate Second-language Learning for Secondary School Students.* Unpublished doctoral dissertation, New York University.

Eberhard, Wolfram. 1970. "Problems of Students Returning to Asia." *International Educational and Cultural Exchange* 5(4): 41–9.

Efron, David. 1941. *Gesture and Environment.* New York: King's Crown. Later published as *Gesture, Race and Culture.* The Hague: Mouton, 1972.

Eibl-Eibesfeldt, I. 1972. "Similarities and Differences Between Cultures in Expressive Movements." In R. A. Hinds (ed.), *Non-verbal Communication*. Cambridge: Cambridge University Press.

Eide, I. (ed.). 1970. *Students as Links Between Cultures*. Oslo: Universitetsforlaget.

Eisenberg, Abne M., and Ralph R. Smith. 1971. *Nonverbal Communication*. Indianapolis: Bobbs-Merrill.

Eisenstadt, S. N. 1949. "The Perception of Time and Space in a Situation of Culture-Contact." *Journal of the Royal Anthropology Institute* 79: 63–8.

Ekman, Paul. 1971. "Universals and Cultural Differences in Facial Expressions of Emotion." In J. Coles (ed.), *Nebraska Symposium on Motivation*. Lincoln: University of Nebraska Press.

Ekman, Paul, and Wallace V. Friesen. 1972. *Emotion in the Human Face: Guidelines for Research and Integration of Findings*. New York: Pergamon.

Ekman, Paul, Wallace V. Friesen, and Silvan S. Tomkins. 1974. "Facial Affect Scoring Technique: A First Validity Study." In Shirley Weitz (ed.), *Nonverbal Communication*. New York: Oxford University Press.

Elkins, Robert J., Theodore B. Kalivoda, and Genelle Morain. 1972. "Teaching Culture Through the Audio-motor Unit." *Foreign Language Annals* 6(1): 61–7.

Erassov, Boris S. 1972. "Concepts of 'Cultural Personality' in the Ideologies of the Third World." *Diogenes* 78:123–40.

Feather, N. T. 1975. *Values in Education and Society*. New York: Free Press.

Ferreira, L., and M. Vaie. 1979. *Read On, Speak Out*. Rowley, Mass.: Newbury House.

Fersh, Seymour (ed.). 1974. *Learning About Peoples and Cultures*. Evanston, Ill.: McDougall, Littell.

Fieg, John P. 1975. *There Is a Difference: 12 Intercultural Perceptions*. Washington, D.C.: Meridian House International.

Figge, Richard C. 1977. "The Use of Film in Teaching German Culture." *Die Unterrichtspraxis* 10(2): 88–94.

Firth, Raymond. 1953. "The Study of Values by Social Anthropologists." *Man* 53: 145–53.

Fisher, Glen. 1979. *American Communication in a Global Society*. Norwood, N.J.: Ablex.

Fishman, Joshua A. (ed.). 1968. *Readings in the Sociology of Language*. The Hague: Mouton.

1977. "Knowing, Using and Liking English as an Additional Language." *TESOL Quarterly* 11(2): 157–71.

Fleming, Gerald. 1971. "Gestures and Body Movement as Mediators of Meaning in Our New Language Teaching Systems." *Contact* 16: 15–22.

Foa, U. G. 1964. "Cross-cultural Similarity and Difference in Interpersonal Behavior." *Journal of Abnormal and Social Psychology* 68(5): 517–25.

Ford, Clellan S. (ed.). *Cross-cultural Approaches: Readings in Comparative Research*. New Haven: HRAF Press.

Ford, J. F. 1978. "The Prospective Foreign Language Teacher and the Culturally and Linguistically Different Learner." *Foreign Language Annals* 11(4): 381–90.

Bibliography

Foster, George M. 1962. *Traditional Cultures and the Impact of Technological Change.* New York: Harper & Row.

Fowles, Jib. 1970. "Ho Ho Ho: Cartoons in the Language Class." *TESOL Quarterly* 4(2): 155–9.

Franklin, James C. 1980. "Teaching Culture Through Film: *Der letzte Mann.*" *Die Unterrichtspraxis* 13(1): 31–8.

Freire, Paulo. 1971. *Pädagogik der Unterdrückten.* Berlin.

Fries, Charles C. 1955. "American Linguistics and the Teaching of English." *Language Learning* 6(1, 2): 17.

1970. *An Anatomy of Values: Problems of Personal and Social Choice.* Cambridge: Harvard University Press.

Gandhi, R. S. 1970. "Conflict and Cohesion in an Indian Student Community." *Human Organization* 29(2): 95–102.

Gardner, Robert C. 1979. "Social Psychological Aspects of Second Language Acquisition." In H. Giles and R. St. Clair (eds.), *Language and Social Psychology.* Oxford: Blackwell.

Gardner, Robert C., and Wallace Lambert. 1972. *Attitudes and Motivation in Second Language Learning.* Rowley, Mass.: Newbury House.

Garfinkel, Alan, and Stanley Hamilton (eds.). 1976. *Designs for Foreign Language Teacher Education.* Rowley, Mass.: Newbury House.

Gatbonton, Elizabeth C., and G. Richard Tucker. 1971. "Cultural Orientation and the Study of Foreign Literature." *TESOL Quarterly* 5(2): 137–43.

Giglioli, Pier Paolo (ed.). 1972. *Language and Social Context.* London: Penguin.

Gleason, Henry A. 1961. *An Introduction to Descriptive Linguistics*, rev. ed. New York: Holt, Rinehart & Winston.

Gleeson, Patrick, and Nancy Wakefield (eds.). 1968. *Language and Culture.* Columbus, Ohio: Merrill.

Glenn, Edmund S. 1966. "Meaning and Behavior; Communication and Culture." *Journal of Communication* 16(4): 248–72.

Goffman, Erving. 1966. *Behavior in Public Places.* New York: Free Press.

Goodman, M. 1962. "Values, Attitudes, and Social Concepts of Japanese and American Children." In B. Silberman (ed.), *Japanese Character and Culture.* Tucson: University of Arizona Press.

Gordon, Raymond L. 1974. *Living in Latin America: A Case Study in Cross-cultural Communication.* Skokie, Ill.: National Textbook.

Grabe, William, and Denise Mahon. 1983. "Teacher Training in China: Problems and Perspectives." *On TESOL '82*, pp. 47–60. Washington, D.C.: TESOL.

Green, Jerald R. 1968. *A Gesture Inventory for the Teaching of Spanish.* Philadelphia: Chilton.

Greenberg, J. H. 1971. *Language, Culture, and Communication.* Stanford, Cal.: Stanford University Press.

Grimshaw, Alan D. 1973. "Rules, Social Interaction, and Language Behavior." *TESOL Quarterly* 7(2): 99–115.

Griswold, W. J. 1975. *The Image of the Middle East in Secondary School Textbooks.* New York: Middle East Studies of North America.

Grittner, Frank M. (ed.). 1976. *Careers, Communication and Culture in Foreign Language Teaching.* Skokie, Ill.: National Textbook.

204

Gudykunst, William B., and Yun Kim Young. 1984. *Communicating with Strangers: An Approach to Intercultural Communication*. Reading, Mass.: Addison-Wesley.

Guiora, Alexander. 1972. "Construct Validity and Transpositional Research: Toward an Empirical Study of Psychoanalytic Concepts." *Comprehensive Psychology* 1(2): 139–50.

1976. "Are Symbols Universal? A Psycholinguistic Perspective." Paper presented at the Major Conference of the Department of Psychiatry, University of Michigan, March 3.

Guiora, Alexander, and William R. Acton. 1979. "Personality and Language Behavior: A Restatement." *Language Learning* 29(1): 193–205.

Gullahorn, John T., and Jeanne E. Gullahorn. 1963. "An Extension of the U-Curve Hypothesis." *Journal of Social Issues* 19(3): 33–47.

Gumperz, John J., and Dell Hymes (eds.). 1972. *Directions in Sociolinguistics: The Ethnography of Communication*. New York: Holt, Rinehart & Winston.

Gumperz, John J., and Ceila Roberts. 1978. *Developing Awareness Skills for Interethnic Communication*. Middlesex: National Centre for Industrial Training.

Hall, Edward T. 1959. *The Silent Language*. New York: Doubleday.

1966. *The Hidden Dimension*. New York: Doubleday.

1974. "Making Sense Without Words." In Seymour Fersh (ed.), *Learning About Peoples and Cultures*. Evanston, Ill.: McDougall, Littell.

1976. *Beyond Culture*. Garden City, N.Y.: Doubleday.

Hamayan, Else, Fred Genesee, and G. Richard Tucker. 1977. "Affective Factors and Language Exposure in Second Language Learning." *Language Learning* 27(2): 225–41.

Hamilton, Vernon. 1983. *The Cognitive Structures and Processes of Human Motivation and Personality*. Chichester: Wiley.

Hannerz, Ulf. 1973. "The Second Language: An Anthropological View." *TESOL Quarterly* 7(3): 235–48.

Hansen, Thomas S. 1980. "Myth in the German Curriculum: An Interdisciplinary Approach to the Culture Course." *Die Unterrichtspraxis* 13(1): 25–30.

Harms, L. S. 1973. *Intercultural Communication*. New York: Harper & Row.

Harrison, Randall P. 1974. *Beyond Words: An Introduction to Nonverbal Communication*. Englewood Cliffs, N. J.: Prentice-Hall.

Hatch, Evelyn (ed.). 1978. *Second Language Acquisition*. Rowley, Mass.: Newbury House.

Haugen, Einer. 1966. "Dialect, Language, Nation." *American Anthropologist* 68(4): 922–35.

Hayes, Frances C. 1940. "Should We Have a Dictionary of Gestures?" *Southern Folklore Quarterly* 4(4): 239–45.

Henderson, Ingeborg. 1980. "Cultural Strategies in Elementary College Language Classes." *Modern Language Journal* 64(2): 190–6.

Hendon, Ursula S. 1980. "Introducing Culture in the High School Foreign Language Class." *Foreign Language Annals* 13: 191–9.

Henle, Paul (ed.). 1958. *Language, Thought, and Culture*. Ann Arbor: University of Michigan Press.

Bibliography

Heringer, H. J. et al. 1977. *Einführung in die praktische Semantik*. Heidelberg: Quelle & Meyer.

Hewes, Gordon W. 1955. "World Distribution of Certain Postural Habits." *American Anthropologist* 57(2): 231–44.

1957. "The Anthropology of Posture." *Scientific American* 196(2): 122–32.

Hill, J. C. 1978. "Curriculum Development: Cultural Modules." *Canadian Modern Language Review* 34(4): 731–4.

Hirschmann, Rudolf. 1975. "An Intensive Approach to Culture and Civilization: The German Semester at USC." *Die Unterrichtspraxis* 8: 78–81.

Hoijer, Harry. 1953. "The Relation of Language to Culture." In L. Kroeber (ed.), *Anthropology Today*, pp. 554–73. Chicago: University of Chicago Press.

1954. *Language in Culture: Proceedings of a Conference on the Interrelations of Language and Other Aspects of Culture*. Comparative Studies of Cultures and Civilizations, no. 3. Menasha, Wis.: American Anthropological Association.

Holmes, J., and Dorothy F. Brown. 1976. "Developing Sociolinguistic Competence in a Second Language." *TESOL Quarterly* 10(4): 423–31.

Hoopes, David S., (ed.). 1971–80. *Readings in Intercultural Communication*, vols. 1–5. Chicago: Intercultural Press.

Hoopes, David S., and Paul Ventura (eds.). 1979. *Intercultural Sourcebook; Cross-cultural Training Methodologies*. SIETAR. Chicago: Intercultural Press.

Hsu, Francis L. K. 1970. *Americans and Chinese: Purpose and Fulfillment in Great Civilizations*. New York: Natural History Press.

Hull, W. Frank IV. 1978. *Foreign Students in the United States: Coping Behavior Within the Educational Environment*. New York: Praeger.

Hymes, Dell H. 1962. "The Ethnography of Speaking." In T. Gladwin and W. C. Sturtevant (eds.), *Anthropology and Human Behavior*, pp. 13–53. Washington, D.C.: Anthropological Society of Washington.

(ed.). 1964. *Language in Culture and Society: A Reader in Linguistics and Anthropology*. New York: Harper & Row.

1967. "Models of the Interaction of Language and Social Setting." *Journal of Social Issues* 23(2): 8–28.

1972. "On Communicative Competence." In J. B. Pride and Janet Holmes (eds.), *Sociolinguistics*. Harmondsworth, England: Penguin.

1980. *Language in Education: Ethnolinguistic Essays*. Language and Ethnography Series 1. Washington, D.C.: Center for Applied Linguistics.

Ianni, F. A., and E. Story (eds.). 1973. *Cultural Relevance and Educational Issues: Readings in Anthropology and Education*. Boston: Little, Brown.

Ibrahim, Saad E. M. 1970. "Interaction, Perception and Attitudes of Arab Students Toward Americans." *Sociology and Social Research* 55(1): 29–46.

Imhoof, Maurice. 1968. "Controlling Cultural Variations in the Preparation of TESOL Materials." *TESOL Quarterly* 2(1): 39–42.

Indochinese Students in U.S. Schools: A Guide for Administrators. 1981. Washington, D.C.: Center for Applied Linguistics, Language and Orientation Resource Center.

Irvine, Judith T. 1982. "Language and Affect: Some Cross-cultural Issues." In

Heidi Byrnes (ed.), *Contemporary Perceptions of Language: Interdisciplinary Dimensions.* Georgetown University Round Table on Languages and Linguistics, 1982. Washington, D.C.: Georgetown University Press.

Jakobovits, Leon A. 1969. "The Affect of Symbols: Towards the Development of a Cross-cultural Graphic Differential." *International Journal of Symbology* 1: 28–52.

Jaramillo, Mari-Luci. 1973. "Cultural Differences in the ESOL Classroom." *TESOL Quarterly* 7(1): 51–61.

Jarvis, Donald K. 1977. "Making Crosscultural Connections." In J. K. Phillips (ed.), ACTFL *Foreign Language Education Series,* vol. 9. Skokie, Ill.: National Textbook.

Jarvis, Gilbert A. (ed.). 1974. "Responding to New Realities." ACTFL *Review of Foreign Language Education,* vol. 5. Skokie, Ill.: National Textbook.

Jedan, Dieter. 1978. "Advertisements – An Index to German Culture in the Classroom." *Die Unterrichtspraxis* 11(2): 40–7.

Jenkins, James J. 1969. "Language and Thought." In J. F. Voss (ed.), *Approaches to Thought.* Columbus, Ohio: Merrill.

Jenks, Frederick L. 1972a. "Teaching Culture Through the Use of American Newspapers." *American Foreign Language Teacher* 2(4): 28–9, 40.

1972b. "Toward the Creative Teaching of Culture." *American Foreign Language Teacher* 2(3): 12–14, 42.

1976. "Fifteen-Year-Old Students Can Do Cross-cultural Research." In Frank M. Grittner (ed.), *Careers, Communication, & Culture in Foreign Language Teaching.* Skokie, Ill.: National Textbook.

Johnson, Jerrilou. 1979. *Living Language: USA Culture Capsules for ESL Students.* Rowley, Mass.: Newbury House.

Johnston, Jean. 1983. "Being There." *On TESOL '82.* Washington, D.C.: TESOL.

Jordan, Cathie. 1983. "Cultural Differences in Communication Patterns: Classroom Adaptations and Translation Strategies." *On TESOL '82.* Washington, D.C.: TESOL.

Kabakchy, V. V. 1978. "Cultural Identity and Foreign Language Teaching." *English Language Teaching Journal* 32(4): 313–18.

Kachru, Braj. 1976. "Models of English for the Third World: White Man's Linguistic Burden or Language Pragmatics?" *TESOL Quarterly* 10(2): 221–39.

1982. *The Other Tongue: English Across Cultures.* Urbana: University of Illinois Press.

Kahne, M. J. 1976. "Cultural Differences: Whose Troubles Are We Talking About?" *International Educational and Cultural Exchange* 11(1): 36–40.

Kaplan, Bert (ed.). 1961. *Studying Personality Cross-culturally.* New York: Harper & Row.

Kaplan, Robert B. 1966. "Cultural Thought Patterns in Inter-cultural Education." *Language Learning* 16(1, 2): 1–20.

Keating, Caroline. 1976. "Nonverbal Aspects of Communication." *Topics in Culture Learning* 4: 12–13.

Key, Mary R. 1977. *Nonverbal Communication: A Research Guide and Bibliography.* Metuchen, N.J.: Scarecrow Press.

Bibliography

Kimball, Solon T. 1974. *Culture and the Educative Process: An Anthropological Perspective*. New York: Teacher's College Press, Columbia University.

Klein, Marjorie H., A. A. Alexander, Kwo-Hwa Tseng, Milton H. Miller, Eng-Kung Yeh, Hung Ming Chu, and Fikre Workreh. 1971. "The Foreign Student Adaptation Program: Social Experiences of Asian Students in the U.S." *International Educational and Cultural Exchange* 6(3): 77–90.

Klineberg, Otto. 1976. *International Educational Exchange: An Assessment of Its Nature and Its Prospects*. The Hague: Mouton.

Kluckhohn, Clyde. 1949. *Mirror for Man*. New York: McGraw-Hill.

Kluckhohn, Florence, and Fred L. Strodtbeck. 1961. *Variations in Value Orientations*. Westport, Conn.: Greenwood Press.

Kouwenhoven, John. 1961. *The Beer Can by the Highway; Essays on What's American About America*. Garden City, N.Y.: Doubleday.

Kraemer, A. J. 1973. *Development of a Cultural Self-awareness Approach to Instruction in Multicultural Education*. Alexandria, Va.: Human Resource Research Organization.

Kramsch, Claire J. 1983. "Culture and Constructs: Communicating Attitudes and Values in the Foreign Language Classroom." *Foreign Language Annals* 16(6): 437–48.

Krasnick, Harry. 1984. "From Communicative Competence to Cultural Competence." *On TESOL '83*, pp. 209–21. Washington, D.C.: TESOL.

Krathwohl, David R., Benjamin Bloom, and Bertram Masia. 1974. *Taxonomy of Educational Objectives: Handbook II, the Affective Domain*. New York: McKay.

Krout, M. H. 1942. *Introduction to Social Psychology*. New York: Harper & Row.

Kupper-Herr, Beth. 1982. "Communicative Competence in Non-native Speakers of English: Some Cross-cultural Factors." In *Working Papers*, pp. 59–71. Manoa: Department of English as a Second Language, University of Hawaii at Manoa.

LaBarre, Weston. "The Cultural Basis of Emotions and Gestures." *Journal of Personality* 16: 49–68.

Lack, Pamela B. 1978. "The Ways of Americans, Through Vietnamese Eyes." *The New York Times*, January 24.

Lado, Robert. 1957. *Linguistics Across Cultures*. Ann Arbor: University of Michigan Press.

1967. *Language Testing*. New York: McGraw-Hill.

Ladu, Tora T. 1975a. *What Makes the French French?* Detroit: Advancement Press of America.

1975b. *What Makes the Spanish Spanish?* Detroit: Advancement Press of America.

Lafayette, Robert C. (ed.). 1975. *The Cultural Revolution in Foreign Language Teaching*. Skokie, Ill.: National Textbook.

1978. *Teaching Culture: Strategies and Techniques*. Language in Education: Theory and Practice Series 13. Arlington, Va.: Center for Applied Linguistics.

Lambert, Richard, and B. Freed. 1982. *The Loss of Language Skills*. Rowley, Mass.: Newbury House.

Lambert, Wallace E. 1967. *Children's Views of Foreign Peoples.* New York: Appleton-Crofts.

1972. *Language, Psychology, and Culture.* Stanford, Cal.: Stanford University Press.

1974. "Culture and Language as Factors in Learning and Education." Paper presented at the 8th annual TESOL conference.

Lambert, Wallace E., Alison d'Anglejean, and G. Richard Tucker. 1972. "Communicating Across Cultures: An Empirical Investigation." Mimeographed. Montreal: Department of Psychology, McGill University.

Lamson, Howard. 1974. "Intensive Language and Cultural Immersion: A Cooperative Method." *Foreign Language Annals* 7(6): 668–73.

Lange, James A. 1979. "*Der Deutschlandspiegel* for Culture and Language." *Die Unterrichtspraxis* 12(2): 37–9.

Lanier, Alison R. 1973. *Living in the U.S.A..* New York: Scribner's Sons.

Larson, Donald N., and William A. Smalley. 1972. *Becoming Bilingual: A Guide to Language Learning.* New Canaan, Conn.: Practical Anthropology.

Lee, Eve. 1980. *The American in Saudi Arabia.* Chicago: Intercultural Press.

Lewis, E. Glyn. 1975. *The Teaching of English as a Foreign Language in Ten Countries.* Stockholm: Almquist & Wicksell International.

Littell, Joseph F. (ed.). 1971. *The Language of Man.* Evanston, Ill.: McDougall, Littell.

Loftus, Elizabeth F. 1976. "Language Memories in the Judicial System." Paper presented at the NWAVE Conference, Georgetown University.

Loveday, Leo. 1980. "Communicative Interference." *Cross Currents* 7(2): 17.

Lozanov, Georgi. 1978. *Suggestology and Outlines of Suggestopedy.* New York: Gordon & Breach.

Lukmani, Y. 1972. "Motivation to Learn and Language Proficiency." *Language Learning* 22(2): 261–73.

Mandelbaum, David G. (ed.). 1949. *Selected Writings of Edward Sapir in Language, Culture, and Personality.* Berkeley: University of California Press. Reprinted in 1964.

Manes, Joan, and Nessa Wolfson. 1981. "The Compliment Formula." In F. Coulmas (ed.), *Conversational Routine. Janua Linguarum.* The Hague: Mouton.

Manual for Indochinese Refugee Education. 1976. Washington, D.C.: English Language Resource Center, Center for Applied Linguistics.

Maquet, J. 1972. *Africanity.* New York: Oxford University Press.

Marckwardt, Albert. 1961. "The Cultural Preparation of the Teacher of English as a Second Language." *Language Learning* 11(3, 4): 153–6.

1978. *The Place of Literature in the Teaching of English as a Second or Foreign Language.* Hawaii: University of Hawaii Press.

Marquardt, William. 1967. "Literature and Cross-cultural Communication in the Course in English for International Students." *Florida FL Reporter* 5(2): 9.

1969. "Creating Empathy Through Literature Between the Members of the Mainstream Culture and the Disadvantaged Learners of the Minority Cultures." *Florida FL Reporter* 7(1): 133–41.

Marshall, Robert A. 1973. *Can Man Transcend His Culture? The Next Chal-*

lenge in Education for Global Understanding. Washington, D.C.: American Association of State Colleges and Universities.

Maslow, Abraham. 1954. *Motivation and Personality.* New York: Harper & Row. Reprinted in 1970.

Mathiot, Madeleine (ed.). 1979. *Ethnolinguistics: Boas, Sapir, and Whorf Revisited.* The Hague: Mouton.

McKay, Sandra. 1982. "Literature in the ESL Classroom." *TESOL Quarterly* 16(4): 529–36.

McLeod, Beverly. 1976. "The Relevance of Anthropology to Language Teaching." *TESOL Quarterly* 10(2): 211–20.

Mead, Margaret. 1948. "Some Cultural Approaches to Communication Problems." In Lyman Bryson (ed.), *The Communication of Ideas.* New York: Harper & Row. Reprinted in 1964.

———. 1971. "Cross-cultural Significances of Space." *Ekistics* 32: 271–2.

———. 1974. "How Anthropology Can Become a Component in a Liberal Arts Education." In Howard Altman and Victor Hanzeli (eds.), *Essays on the Teaching of Culture: A Festschrift to Honor Howard Lee Nostrand.* Boston: Heinle & Heinle.

Meade, Betsy, and Genelle Morain. 1973. "The Culture Cluster." *Foreign Language Annals* 6(3): 331–8.

Mehrabian, A. 1972. *Nonverbal Communication.* Chicago: Aldine-Atherton.

Mellgren, L., and M. Walker. 1973. *New Horizons in English #1.* New York: Addison-Wesley.

Merleau-Ponty, Maurice. 1962. *The Phenomenology of Perception.* Translated from the French by Colin Smith. New York: Humanities Press.

Milburn, Douglas. 1984. "The Name of This Country Is Houston: Three Years Among the Vietnamese." *Houston City Magazine,* February.

Miller, J. Dale. 1973. "Proverbs Supply Gems of Culture." *Accent on ACTFL* 3(4): 9.

Miller, J. Dale, and Russell H. Bishop. 1977. *U.S.A.–Mexico Culture Capsules.* Rowley, Mass.: Newbury House.

Miller, J. Dale, and Maurice Loisseau. 1977. *U.S.A.–France Culture Capsules.* Rowley, Mass.: Newbury House.

Miron, M. S., and S. Wolfe. 1964. "A Cross-linguistic Analysis of the Response Distributions of Restricted Word Associations." *Journal of Verbal Learning and Verbal Behavior* 3: 376–84.

Mollica, Anthony. 1975. "Cartoons in the Language Classroom." *Canadian Modern Language Review* 32(4): 424–44.

Morain, Genelle G. 1971a. "Teaching for Cross-cultural Understanding: An Annotated Bibliography." *Foreign Language Annals* 5: 82–3.

———. 1971b. "Cultural Pluralism." In Dale Lange (ed.), *Britannica Review of Foreign Language Education,* vol. 3, pp. 59–95. Chicago: Encyclopedia Britannica.

———. 1976a. "The Cultural Component of the Methods Course." In Alan Garfinkel and Stanley Hamilton (eds.), *Designs for Foreign Language Teacher Education.* Rowley, Mass.: Newbury House.

———. 1976b. "Visual Literacy: Reading Signs and Designs in the Foreign Culture." *Foreign Language Annals* 9(3): 210–16.

1978. *Kinesics and Cross-cultural Understanding.* Language in Education: Theory and Practice, No. 7. Washington, D.C.: Center for Applied Linguistics.

1979. "The Cultoon." *Canadian Modern Language Review* 35(4): 676–90.

1983. "Commitment to the Teaching of Foreign Cultures." *The Modern Language Journal* 67(4): 403–12.

Morris, Desmond, Peter Collett, Peter Marsh, and Marie O'Shaughnessy. 1979. *Gestures.* New York: Stein & Day.

Murdock, George P., Clellan S. Ford, Alfred H. Hudson, Raymond Kennedy, Lew W. Simmons, and John W. M. Whiting. 1971. *Outline of Cultural Materials,* vol. 1. New Haven: Human Relation Area Files.

Muto, Toshio. 1979. "Cultural Orientation in Teaching American Literature to Japanese Students." *Cross Currents* 11(2): 77–89.

Nababian, P. W. J. 1974. "Language, Culture, and Language Teaching." *Regional English Language Center Journal* 5(2): 18–30.

Nelson, T. M. 1978. "Further Comparisons of Cultures with Respect to Content of Recalled Dreams and Actual Events." *Canadian Modern Language Review* 34(3): 310–26.

Nguyen, Dang Liem. 1975. "Culture in South-east Asian Language Classes." *Babel* (Journal of the Australian Federation of MLT Association) 11(2): 31–4.

Niedzielski, Henri. 1975. *The Silent Language of France.* Dubuque, Iowa: Educational Research Associates.

Nilsen, Don L. F., and Alleen Pace Nilsen. 1978. *Language Play.* Rowley, Mass.: Newbury House.

Nostrand, Frances, and Howard L. Nostrand. 1970. "Testing Understanding of the Foreign Culture." In H. Ned Seelye (ed.), *Perspectives for Teachers of Latin American Culture.* Springfield, Ill.: Office of Public Instruction.

Nostrand, Howard Lee. (ed.). 1967. *Background Data for the Teaching of French.* Seattle: University of Washington.

1974. "Empathy for a Second Culture: Motivations and Techniques." In G. A. Jarvis (ed.), *Responding to New Realities.* ACTFL Foreign Language Education Series, vol. 5. Skokie, Ill.: National Textbook.

Nye, Naomi Shihab. 1985. "Bridging the Waters." *Texas Journal* 8(1): 28–33.

Oberg, K. 1960. "Culture Shock: Adjustment to New Cultural Environment." *Practical Anthropologist* 7: 177–82.

Oller, John W., Jr., Lori L. Baca, and Fred Vigil. 1977. "Attitudes and Attained Proficiency in ESL: A Sociolinguistic Study of Mexican-Americans in the Southwest." *TESOL Quarterly* 11(2): 173–83.

Oller, John W., Jr., Alan J. Hudson, and Phyllis F. Liu. 1977. "Attitudes and Attained Proficiency in ESL: A Sociolinguistic Study of Native Speakers of Chinese in the United States." *Language Learning* 27(1): 1–27.

Osgood, C. E. 1960. "The Cross-cultural Generality of Visual-Verbal Synesthetic Tendencies." *Behavioral Sciences* 5(2): 146–69.

Osterloh, Karl-Heinz. 1977. "Traditionelle Lernweisen und Europäischer Bildungstransfer: Zur Begründung einer adaptieren Pädagogik in den Entwicklungsländern." *Neue Sammlung* 17: 219–36.

1978. "Eigene Erfahrung – fremde Erfahrung. Für einen umweltorientierten Fremdsprachenunterricht in der Dritten Welt." *Unterrichtswissenschaft* 3: 189–99.

Parsons, Talcott. 1961. "Language as a Groundwork of Culture." In Talcott Parsons, Edward Shils, Kaspar D. Naegele, and Jesse R. Pitts (eds.), *Theories of Society*, 2 vols. Glencoe, Ill.: Free Press.

Patai, Rafael. 1973. *The Arab Mind.* New York: Charles Scribner.

Paulston, Christina B. 1975. *Developing Communicative Competence: Role-plays in English as a Second Language.* Pittsburgh: University Center for International Studies and the English Language Institute, University of Pittsburgh.

Perez, M. 1984. *The Relation of Social Attitudes and Language Study Motivation with English Ability Among Immigrant High School Spanish Speaking Students.* Unpublished doctoral dissertation, University of Houston – University Park.

Pfister, Guenter G., and Petra A. Borzilleri. 1977. "Surface Cultural Concepts: A Design for the Evaluation of Cultural Material in Textbooks." *Die Unterrichtspraxis* 10(2): 102–8.

Phillip, P. J. 1972. "Emerging Issues in Cultural Relations in an Interdependent World." *Topics in Culture Learning* 5: 68–78.

Phillips, J. K. (ed.). 1977. *The Language Connection: From the Classroom to the World.* Skokie, Ill.: National Textbook.

Pierce, K. E. 1964. *Life in a Turkish Village.* New York: Holt, Rinehart & Winston.

Pierson, Herbert D., Gail S. Fu, and Sik-yum Lee. 1980. "An Analysis of the Relationship Between Language Attitudes and English Attainment of Secondary Students in Hong Kong." *Language Learning* 30(2): 289–316.

Pifer, G. W., and N. W. Mutoh. 1977. *Points of View.* Rowley, Mass.: Newbury House.

Pike, Kenneth L. 1967. *Language in Relation to a Unified Theory of the Structure of Human Behavior*, 3rd rev. ed. The Hague: Mouton.

Pincas, Anita. 1963. " 'Cultural Translation' for Foreign Students of English Language and Literature." *Language Learning* 13(1): 13–25.

Politzer, Robert. 1959. "Developing Cultural Understanding Through Foreign Language Study." *Report of the Fifth Annual Round Table Meeting on Linguistics and Language Teaching*, pp. 99–105. Washington, D.C.: Georgetown University Press.

Povey, John F. 1968. "Literature in TESL Programs: The Language and the Culture." *TESOL Quarterly* 1(June): 40–6. Reprinted in Harold B. Allen and Russell Campbell (eds.), *Teaching English as a Second Language: A Book of Readings*, 2nd ed. New York: McGraw-Hill.

1984. *Literature for Discussion.* New York: Holt, Rinehart & Winston.

Price-Williams, Douglass R. 1975. *Exploration in Cross-cultural Psychology.* San Francisco: Chandler & Sharp.

Prosser, Michael H. (ed.). 1973. *Intercommunication Among Nations and Peoples.* New York: Harper & Row.,

1978. *The Cultural Dialogue.* Boston: Houghton-Mifflin.

Pruitt, France J. 1976. *The Adaptation of African Students on Ten Campuses in the U.S.* Washington, D.C.: Department of State, Bureau of African Affairs.

Pusch, Margaret (ed.). 1979. *Multicultural Education: A Cross-cultural Training Approach.* Chicago: Intercultural Press.

Putnam, Constance E. 1978. "A *Stadtplan* for Teaching Culture." *Die Unterrichtspraxis* 11(2): 26–33.

Rey, Jean-Noel, and Georges V. Santoni. 1975. *Quand les français parlent: langue en contexte, culture en contraste.* Rowley, Mass.: Newbury House.

Richards, Jack C. 1972. "Some Social Aspects of Language Learning." *TESOL Quarterly* 6(3): 243–54.

—— 1981. "Talking Across Cultures." *Canadian Modern Language Review* 37(3): 572–82.

Rivers, Wilga M. 1981. *Teaching Foreign Language Skills*, 2nd ed. Chicago: University of Chicago Press.

—— 1983a. *Speaking in Many Tongues: Essays in Foreign-language Teaching*, 3rd ed. New York: Cambridge University Press.

—— 1983b. *Communicating Naturally in a Second Language.* New York: Cambridge University Press.

Robinett, Betty W. 1978. *Teaching English to Speakers of Other Languages: Substance and Technique.* New York: McGraw-Hill.

Robinson, Gail. 1981. *Issues in Second Language and Cross-cultural Education: The Forest Through the Trees.* Boston: Heinle & Heinle.

Robinson, W. P. 1972. *Language and Social Behavior.* London: Penguin.

Romney, A. Kimball, and R. G. D'Andrade (eds.). 1964. "Transcultural Studies in Cognition." *American Anthropologist* 66(3), Part II.

Ross, Stanley R. (ed.). 1978. *Views Across the Border: The United States and Mexico.* Albuquerque: University of New Mexico Press.

Sadow, Stephen A., and Monica A. Maxwell. 1983. "The Foreign Teaching Assistant and the Culture of the American University Class." *On TESOL '82.* Washington, D.C.: TESOL.

Saitz, Robert L., and Edward J. Cervenka. 1972. *Handbook of Gestures: Colombia and the United States.* The Hague: Mouton.

Samarin, William. 1965. "The Language of Silence." *Practical Anthropology* 12: 115–19.

Samovar, Larry A., and Richard E. Porter (eds.). 1972. *Intercultural Communication: A Reader.* Belmont, Cal.: Wadsworth.

Santoni, Georges V. 1976. "Langue et culture en contexte et contraste." *French Review* 49(3): 355–65.

Santos, Percilia. 1974. "Examples of Figurative Language and Gestures Which Characterize the Brazilian People." *American Foreign Language Teacher* 4(4): 22–5.

Sapir, Edward. 1958. *Culture, Language, and Personality.* Berkeley: University of California Press. Reprinted in 1964.

Sarbaugh, L. E. 1978. *Intercultural Communication.* Rochelle Park, N.J.: Hayden Book.

Saville-Troike, Muriel. 1975. "Teaching English as a Second Culture." *On TESOL '74*, pp. 83–94. Washington, D.C.: TESOL.

Bibliography

Scheflen, Albert E., and Alice Scheflen. 1972. *Body Language and the Social Order*. Englewood Cliffs, N.J.: Prentice-Hall.

Schulz, Renate A. 1981. "Literature and Readability: Bridging the Gap in Foreign Language Reading." *Modern Language Journal* 65(1): 43–53.

Schumann, John H. 1976a. "Second Language Acquisition: The Pidginization Process." *Language Learning* 26(2): 391–408.

1976b. "Second Language Acquisition Research: Getting a More Global Look at the Learner." *Language Learning*, special issue no. 4: 15–28.

1976c. "Social Distance as a Factor in Second Language Acquisition." *Language Learning* 26: 135–43.

1978. *The Pidginization Process: A Model for Second Language Acquisition*. Rowley, Mass.: Newbury House.

Scott, Reid. 1969. *Cultural Understanding: Spanish Level I*. Hayward, Cal.: Alameda County School Department.

Seelye, H. Ned. 1966. "Field Notes on Cross-cultural Testing." *Language Learning* 16(1, 2): 77–85.

1968. "Analysis and Teaching of the Cross-cultural Context." In E. M. Birkmaier (ed.), *Foreign Language Education: An Overview*. ACTFL Foreign Language Education Series 6. Skokie, Ill.: National Textbook.

1970. "Performance Objectives for Teaching Cultural Concepts." *Foreign Language Annals* 3(4): 566–78.

1973. "Teaching the Foreign Culture: A Context for Research." In Jerald R. Green (ed.), *Foreign Language Education Research*. Chicago: Rand-McNally.

1974. *Teaching Culture: Strategies for Foreign Language Teachers*. Skokie, Ill.: National Textbook.

Selinker, Larry. 1972. "Interlanguage." *International Review of Applied Linguistics* 10(3): 209–31.

Senior, Clarence. 1967. "Their Culture – and Ours." *On Teaching English to Speakers of Other Languages*, series 3, pp. 123–127. Washington, D.C.: TESOL.

Shaftel, Fannie R., and George Shaftel. 1967. *Role-playing for Social Values: Decision-making in the Social Studies*. Englewood Cliffs, N.J.: Prentice-Hall.

Sharma, S. 1973. "A Study to Identify and Analyze Adjustment Problems Experienced by Foreign Non-European Graduate Students Enrolled in Selected Universities in the State of North Carolina." *California Journal of Educational Research*, 24(3): 135–46.

Shoaf, B. 1982. "Communicating Between Cultures: Understanding the Nature of Codes, Contexts, and Communication." *CATESOL Newsletter* 13(5).

Silberstein, Sandra. 1984. "Language in Culture: Textbuilding Conventions in Oral Narrative." *On TESOL '83*, pp. 67–80. Washington, D.C.: TESOL.

Simon, Paul. 1980. "The Tongue-tied American: Confronting the Foreign Language Crisis." New York: Continuum.

Slobin, Dan I. 1963. *A Field Manual for Cross-cultural Study of the Acquisition of Communicative Competence*. Berkeley: University of California Press.

Smith, Larry E., and Khalilullah Rafiqzad. 1979. "English for Cross-cultural Communication: The Question of Intelligibility." *TESOL Quarterly* 13(3): 371–80.

Speer, David C. (ed.). 1972. *Non-verbal Communication.* Beverly Hills, Cal.: Sage.

Spielberger, Charles D., and Rogelio Diaz-Guerrero (eds.). 1976. *Cross-cultural Anxiety.* Washington, D.C.: Hemisphere Publishing.

Spindler, George D. 1969. "The Transmission of American Culture." *Florida FL Reporter* 7: 1–9.

Spolsky, Bernard. 1969. "Attitudinal Aspects of Second Language Learning." *Language Learning* 19(3): 271–85.

Spradley, James P., and Michael A. Rynkiewich. 1975. *The Nacirema: Readings on American Culture.* Boston: Little, Brown.

Stauble, Ann-Marie E. 1978. "The Progress of Decreolization: A Model for Second Language Development." *Language Learning* 28: 29–54.

Stephens, William. 1963. *The Family in Cross-cultural Perspective.* New York: Holt, Rinehart & Winston.

Stevick, Earl. 1976. *Memory, Meaning and Method.* Rowley, Mass.: Newbury House.

Stewart, Edward C. 1966. "The Simulation of Cultural Differences." *Journal of Communication* 16: 291–304.

1972. *American Cultural Patterns: A Cross-cultural Perspective.* Chicago: Intercultural Press.

Subrahmanian, K. 1975. "The Need for a Contrastive Analysis of Cultures of the Source and Target Languages." *Regional English Language Center Journal* 6(2): 1–7.

Szanston, David. 1966. "Cultural Confrontation in the Phillipines." In Robert Textor (ed.), *Cultural Frontiers of the Peace Corps.* Boston: MIT Press.

Taylor, Barry P., and Nessa Wolfson. 1978. "Breaking Down the Free Conversation Myth." *TESOL Quarterly* 12(1): 31–9.

Taylor, Darrel H., and John L. Sorenson. 1961. "Culture Capsules." *Modern Language Journal* 45(6): 350–4.

Taylor, D. M., R. Meynard, and E. Rheault. 1977. "Threat to Ethnic Identity and Second Language Learning." In H. Giles (ed.), *Language, Ethnicity, and Intergroup Relations.* London: Academic Press; Harcourt Brace.

Taylor, Harvey M. 1975. "Training Teachers for the Role of Nonverbal Communication in the Classroom." *Papers in English as a Second Language.* Selected conference papers of ATESL. Washington, D.C.: National Association for Foreign Student Affairs.

Taylor, Imgard C. 1977. "Beware of Clichés." *Die Unterrichtspraxis* 10(2): 108–14.

Textor, Robert B. (ed.). 1967. *A Cross-cultural Summary.* New Haven: Human Relations Area Files Press.

Thomas, Jenny. 1983. "Cross-cultural Pragmatic Failure." *Applied Linguistics* 4(2): 91–112.

Trager, George L., and Edward T. Hall, Jr. 1954. "Culture and Communication: A Model and an Analysis." *Explorations* 3: 137–49.

Triandis, H. C. 1972. *The Analysis of Subjective Culture.* New York: Wiley Interscience.

1973. "Work and Nonwork: Intercultural Perspectives." In Marvin Dunnette (ed.), *Work and Nonwork in the Year 2001.* Monterey, Cal.: Brooks/Cole.

Trifanovitch, Gregory J. 1973. "On Cross-cultural Orientation Techniques." *Topics in Culture Learning* 1: 38–47.

   1978. *Culture Learning/Culture Teaching*. Honolulu: Culture Learning Institute.

Troyanovich, John. 1972. "American Meets German: Cultural Shock in the Classroom." *Die Unterrichtspraxis* 5(2): 67–79.

Tuttle, Harry G., Jorge Guitart, Anthony Papalia, and Joseph Zampogna. 1979. "Effects of Cultural Presentations on Attitudes of Foreign Language Students." *Modern Language Journal* 63(4): 177–82.

Ueda, K. 1974. "Sixteen Ways to Avoid Saying 'No' in Japan." In John C. Condon and Mitsuko Saito (eds.), *Intercultural Encounters with Japan*. Tokyo: Simul Press.

Upshur, John A. 1966. "Cross-cultural Testing: What to Test." *Language Learning* 16(3, 4): 183–96.

Valdes, Joyce Merrill. 1970. "Starting English Late." *TESOL Quarterly* 4(3): 277–82.

Valdes, Maria Elena de. 1977. "Thematic Organization of Cultural Content in Second-Language Teaching." *Canadian Modern Language Review* 33(3): 354–80.

Via, Richard A. 1976. *English in Three Acts: A Culture-learning Monograph*. Honolulu: The University Press of Hawaii.

von Raffler-Engel, Walburga. 1975. "Studies in Paralanguage and Kinesics." LASSO (Journal of the Linguistic Association of the Southwest) 1(2): 30–45.

   1980. "Kinesics and Paralinguistics: A Neglected Factor in Second-Language Research and Teaching." *Canadian Modern Language Review* 36(2): 225–37.

Wallach, Martha Kaarsberg. 1972–3. "Cross-cultural Educational and Motivational Aspects of Foreign Language Study." *Foreign Language Annals* 6(4): 465–8.

Wallwork, J. F. 1981. "Some Cultural Aspects in the Training of Language Teachers." *Récherches et échanges* 6(1): 1–11.

Walsh, John E. 1973. "Thoughts About 'Thought and Expression' in Culture Learning." *Topics in Culture Learning* 1: 3–12.

   1979. *Humanistic Culture Learning*. Honolulu: The University Press of Hawaii.

Wardhaugh, Ronald. 1976. *The Context of Language*. Rowley, Mass.: Newbury House.

Waters, Barbara (ed.). 1981. "How Teacher Aides Present Cultural Topics in the Elementary French Classrooms." *Canadian Modern Language Review* 38(1): 88–105.

Watson, O. Michael. 1970. *Proxemic Behavior: A Cross-cultural Study*. The Hague: Mouton.

Weeks, William H., P. B. Pedersen, and R. W. Brislin. 1975. *A Manual of Structured Experiences for Cross-cultural Learning*. La Grange, Ill.: Intercultural Network.

Weitz, Shirley (ed.). 1974. *Nonverbal Communication: Readings with Commentary*. New York: Oxford University Press.

West, Fred. 1975. *The Way of Language: An Introduction.* New York: Harcourt Brace Jovanovich.

Whorf, Benjamin Lee. 1956. *Language, Thought, and Reality.* Cambridge, Mass.: MIT Press.

Widdowson, Henry G. 1975. *Stylistics and the Teaching of Literature.* London: Longman.

   1982. "The Use of Literature." *On TESOL '81*, pp. 203–14. Washington, D.C.: TESOL.

Wong-Fillmore, Lily. 1983. "The Language Learner as an Individual: Implications of Research on Individual Differences for the ESL Teacher." *On TESOL '82*, pp. 157–73. Washington, D.C.: TESOL.

Wright, Albert R., and Mary Ann Hammons. 1970. *Guidelines for Peace Corps Cross-cultural Training.* Estes Park, Col.: Center for Research and Education.

Wylie, Laurence, and Rick Stafford. 1977. *Beaux Gestes: A Guide to French Body Talk.* Cambridge, Mass.: Undergraduate Press.

Yousef, Fathi S. 1968. "Cross-culture Testing: An Aspect of the Resistance Reaction." *Language Learning* 18(3, 4): 227–34.

   1974. "Cross-cultural Communication: Aspects of Contrastive Social Values between North Americans and Middle-Easterners." *Human Organization* 33(4): 383–7.

Zintz, M. V. 1963. *Education Across Cultures.* Dubuque, Iowa: Brown.

Index